A574

History, Politics, and the Novel

Emile Durkheim: Sociologist and Philosopher

A Preface to Sartre

Madame Bovary *on Trial*

Rethinking Intellectual History: Texts, Contexts, Language

History & Criticism

Modern European Intellectual History: Reappraisals and New Perspectives

History, Politics, and the Novel

Dominick LaCapra

Cornell University Press

ITHACA AND LONDON

First published 1987 by Cornell University Press.

International Standard Book Number 0-8014-2033-4
Library of Congress Catalog Card Number 87-6686
Printed in the United States of America
Librarians: Library of Congress cataloging information appears on the last page of the book.

The paper in this book is acid-free and meets the guidelines for permanence and durability of the Committee on Production Guidelines for Book Longevity of the Council on Library Resources.

For Jane, Molly, and Véronique

Contents

Acknowledgments		ix
Introduction		1
1.	Stendhal's Irony in *Red and Black*	15
2.	Notes on Dostoevsky's *Notes from Underground*	35
3.	In Quest of Casaubon: George Eliot's *Middlemarch*	56
4.	Collapsing Spheres in Flaubert's *Sentimental Education*	83
5.	Mann's *Death in Venice:* An Allegory of Reading	111
6.	History, Time, and the Novel: Reading Woolf's *To the Lighthouse*	129
7.	History and the Devil in Mann's *Doctor Faustus*	150
8.	Singed Phoenix and Gift of Tongues: William Gaddis, *The Recognitions*	175
	Epilogue	203
	Index	215

Acknowledgments

Chapter 8 first appeared in *Diacritics,* and a French version of Chapter 4 appeared in *Annales: Economies-Sociétés-Civilisations.* The Woodrow Wilson Foundation included Chapter 5 in a publication for participants in the Institute on Interpreting the Humanities held at Hobart and William Smith Colleges during the summer of 1986. The other chapters are published for the first time.

I am grateful to William Gaddis and to Candida Donadio & Associates for permission to quote from *The Recognitions,* copyright © 1955 by William Gaddis.

I also thank Jane Pedersen, Richard Terdiman, and an anonymous reader for Cornell University Press for offering many fruitful suggestions. Finally, I thank Patricia Sterling for her editorial assistance.

Dominick LaCapra

Ithaca, New York

History, Politics, and the Novel

It is not exactly a matter of free choice whether or not a cultural historian shall be a literary critic, nor is it open to him to let his virtuous political and social opinions do duty for percipience.

Lionel Trilling, *The Liberal Imagination*

This manner of portrayal is simply the artistic expression of that genuine historicism—the conception of history as the destiny of the people—which motivated the classics.

Georg Lukács, *The Historical Novel*

"Comment perdre son temps à des inepties pareilles?" disait Pécuchet.

"Mais par la suite, ce sera fort curieux, comme documents."

"Va te promener avec tes documents! Je demande quelque chose qui m'exalte, qui m'enlève aux misères de ce monde!"

Gustave Flaubert, *Bouvard et Pécuchet*

If we write novels so, how shall we write history?

Henry James, "George Eliot's *Middlemarch*"

Introduction

> Art draws its power of resistance from the fact that the real-
> ization of materialism would also be the abolition of mate-
> rialism, that is, of the domination of material interests. Weak
> as it may be, art anticipates a spirit that would step forth at
> that point. To this corresponds an objective need or, better,
> neediness of the world, which is the opposite of the subjec-
> tive-ideological needs people presently have for art. Art has
> its footing in that objective need alone.
>
> Theodor W. Adorno, *Aesthetic Theory*

I do not attempt in the following essays to provide a "total"
or even a general approach to the problem of the role of the
novel in history and criticism. My project is more modest, but I
would like to believe that it is a necessary part of any larger and
more ambitious venture. What I attempt to do is to provide a
series of readings and interpretations, all of which begin with a
problem or perspective that is either absent or underdeveloped
(to the best of my knowledge) in the existing literature. These
readings and interpretations are meant to be provocative yet
also to mediate and supplement the relation between formal
and thematic interpretation. The result is perforce a hybridized
or mixed generic performance in historical criticism.

In the course of it, I broach questions of historical context,
psychoanalytic reading, and political implication. Especially in
the last respect, my efforts are tentative, for the very texts I
discuss may at times seem more or less inhospitable to political readings or to call for them only in the most indirect of
ways. I did not choose these texts in accordance with any theoretical principle or aesthetic conviction that in literature only

the indirect relation to politics is legitimate. The direct, even the militantly didactic—what Stendhal would have termed the pistol shot at the concert—may have its place at least insofar as it does not descend to the level of manipulative propaganda. The texts I have chosen, however, at times pose difficult problems for anyone who does want to link literary and political reading. My own inclinations go in this direction, and I am willing at times to pay the price of a certain straining for connections in emphasizing political and broadly sociocultural concerns. At present it may even be instructive if the fissures and stress marks caused by this effort remain visible and are not cosmetically concealed by rhetorical or stylistic devices.

It will become evident that my effort is not directed toward furnishing as complete and well documented a picture of the past as is possible. Nor is it oriented toward the refinement or redefinition of period concepts in historical and literary research. Rather, I try to stimulate a more engaging dialogue or critical exchange between past and present in which the interpreter is implicated as historian and as critic. The approach I take may, however, test existing period concepts (realism, symbolism, modernism, postmodernism, and so forth) with the implication that more subtle concepts are needed and that the role of these concepts is not to fixate the past in positivistic amber but rather to facilitate a different understanding of our relation to it.

I would in no sense deny that the limiting ideal of research is to work out a general approach whereby specific readings and a larger critical perspective exist in an open, mutually informative, and reciprocally challenging relation. I do, however, feel that at present the best means of access to this approach is asymptotic, with different studies taking different, nonexclusive emphases. At the risk of remaining at an overly particularized level of analysis, I try to avoid the tendency to sacrifice the subtlety and insistence of specific readings to reductive larger perspectives that prefigure the material and assure the analyst that he will arrive where he wanted to go before he undertook his investigation. The great temptation in recent "political" readings has been to interpret all cultural artifacts predominantly if not exclusively as symptomatic expressions of dominant discourses and historical pressures and to mention forces that question or contest these discourses and pressures only *en passant* (if at all). Hence "realism" may be taken as symptomatic of early market capitalism, "high modernism" of imperialism, and "postmodernism" or "poststructuralism" of contemporary consumer, multinational capitalism. The problem in this kind of approach—aside from the fact that it pours seemingly new wine into decidedly old bottles—is the replication of a dominant, indeed an imperial and domesticating discourse in what may be intended to be a critique of it. To point this out is not to deny the importance of dominant discourses and hegemonic historical pressures or of the attempt to attribute to them a crucial importance and sense of urgency in historiography and literary criticism. Nor is it to assume that critical attention should be focused exclusively on great monuments or be premised on elitist assumptions, mandarin tastes, and the pathos of cultural pessimism. Furthermore, one need not believe (if anyone possibly could) that a novel or even an entire novelistic or literary tradition can, in and of itself, change the course of empire or effectively combat capitalism and the process of commodification. But one *may* insist that even losing forces in history, be they revolts in the streets or currents in texts, have as much right to close attention as do dominant forces and pressures. To think otherwise is to capitulate to the type of historicism and *Realpolitik* that typifies the object of criticism and whose replication is one element in the conversion of revolutionary movements into repressive regimes. It is also to deprive oneself of the forms of language that can be a force, however weak and anticipatory, in preventing the subversion of ends by means and the sacrifice of historical and political complexity on the altar of one-dimensional, self-defeating preconceptions.

It should be apparent that there is at work in these readings an *esprit systématique* (in contrast to an *esprit de système*), and it cohabits, in a state of more or less amiable rivalry, with an emphasis on "close-ups" and an appreciation for indirect approaches. I do not attribute to the novel a paramount or even

3

a privileged place in the attempt to relate culture or, more restrictedly, literature to society and history. But to observe that the novel is one significant artifact of modern history does not attain the level even of the banal ballast one has come to expect in intellectual history. There have of course been a series of "theories of the novel" in modern cultural and intellectual history. Rather than enter into frontal debates with their proponents, I refer to them explicitly or implicitly in the course of a discussion that questions or refines certain of their aspects.

A recurrent question nonetheless guides my approach to interpretation: how does a text relate in symptomatic, critical, and possibly transformative ways to its pertinent contexts of writing and reading? My answers to this question are perforce limited and make no pretense to being exhaustive. But my contention is that particularly significant texts, such as "classic" novels, are not only worked over symptomatically by common contextual forces (such as ideologies) but also rework and at least partially work through those forces in critical and at times potentially transformative fashion. Indeed, the novel may be especially engaging in both being worked over by and critically working through problems in a gripping and forceful way. But the novel tends to be transformative—at least with reference to social and political contexts—in general, suggestive, and long-term respects. And it may have transformative effects more through its style or mode of narration than in the concrete image or representation of any desirable alternative society or polity.

Although this feature is not prominent in the works I discuss, it is conceivable that the novel may at times contain programmatic elements in outlining desirable alternatives. Most likely, they would be embodied in the perspectives of characters. But the difficulty in specifying cogent alternatives generally induces the relativization or even the critical framing of characters' perspectives on desirable change. And even when the writer desires to be programmatic in his or her own voice, the turn to the extranovelistic essay or speech (as in the case of Dostoevsky, Eliot, or Mann) does not transcend difficulties disclosed in the novelistic discourse itself. I cannot pretend to have gone beyond my sources in programmatic cogency or specificity, particularly with respect to the crucial issue of institutions that might realize certain goals (such as a more viable interaction between work and play in modern society). But I have tried to motivate my readings and my very selection of pertinent contexts by a desire to loosen the soil of critical thought and to suggest general transformative implications relevant to the texts I discuss. At least in limited respects, reading "classic" texts with a sensitivity to the way they negotiate relations among symptomatic (or ideologically reinforcing), critical, and transformative effects may itself be one way to reopen the canon and to counteract the hegemonic functions it may serve. It may, in other words, be one approach to a more critical and self-critical appropriation of an intellectual and literary heritage.

For an approach that focuses on specific readings of texts, the most pressing issue is to bring the text out of the isolation often imposed by "close reading" and to treat it in a manner that indicates, or at least suggests, its bearing on broader interpretive and critical considerations. This is the issue I try to keep most consistently in sight without making of it an obsession. Indeed, aspects of the readings I offer, instead of merely illustrating or confirming my guiding ideas, may test the limits of an orientation employing sociocultural and political categories of interpretation (such as ideology and critique). These aspects of the novel have often been placed under the headings of "play" and "fantasy," but perhaps they should—at least vis-à-vis attempted "political," sociocultural, and historical readings—be left in heterological positions that are not subjected to preconceived labels. These forms of "otherness" or alterity may prove to have unexpected transformative implications, and I shall later suggest how they may be related to broader considerations in their very interaction with more "productive" categories of thought and activity both in the novel and in the larger society and culture.

The labels affixed to the products of the kind of interpretive and critical effort attempted in these essays (intellectual history, literary or cultural criticism, critical theory) should be of secondary importance. The principal question is whether the effort brings about fruitful work having both cognitive and practical significance and, if so, whether it deserves a place either in existing disciplines or in possible alternatives. Finding or making institutional sites for hybridized ventures is a problem with no ready-made solutions, and it is bound to generate paradoxes; it is a problem one does not solve but lives with in more or less desirable ways. One condition in this form of life is the active recognition that fruitfulness in certain areas coexists with tension and with the interaction of cooperation and controversy—controversy that may be disorienting and unassimilable to a harmonistic or organic model of disciplinary consensus.

A hybridized genre is not necessarily "blurred," however. The effect of blurring is a derivative of perception from within the confines of putatively clear positions and unproblematic boundaries. I would even argue that in culture one "begins" with the hybrid and that "pure" genres or disciplines are the result of exclusionary procedures that are suspect on both intellectual and sociopolitical grounds. In culture, moreover, the hybrid is migratory and may reproduce. Indeed, this is what makes it so threatening. In addition, the seemingly "pure" genre, which becomes established through intellectual and institutional pruning and breeding, is never quite "pure" enough, for it always includes at least a little of the other genres. The very lack of definitional purity instigates disciplinary and rhetorical intolerance. Today, for example, literary criticism seems in certain ways to be an unassimilable "other" in conventional historiography, just as historical understanding may be either limited to relatively innocuous "background information" or dismissed as unchallenging reportage in certain forms of literary criticism. This dubious division of labor is being challenged on a number of fronts in recent research, and I think that it is through the exploration of modes of hybridization that one may arrive at some notion of better ways to undertake (and perhaps to organize institutionally) research into significant problems in both the humanities and the so-called human sciences.

The notion of relating—or seeing the interactive relation between—texts and contexts in terms of a variable conjunction of symptomatic, critical, and possibly transformative tendencies is a formula for a project that cannot be reduced to formulas. It is a project, as I have intimated, that recognizes the value of problematic, hybridized genres in which one is able to follow problems where they lead, even at the risk of venturing into areas in which one has little or no professional training and expertise. The realization of the project (to the extent that realization is possible) depends upon working through existing historical research and existing critical theories in the effort not simply to apply them or to rewrite the past in their terms but to elaborate further or rearticulate them in ways that enable them better to engage one another, illuminate problems in history and criticism, and disclose their own limits or limitations. The proportions of this project may imply that any one individual can undertake it only to a limited extent and that the most fruitful form of intervention in an academic setting may be in teaching and research that address both theoretical issues and specific texts or problems in analysis. Particular studies that simultaneously provide "local knowledge" and suggest tentative generalizations on the basis of concrete cases—in contrast to massive and massively reductive surveys, as well as hermetically sealed monographs—may also furnish the best field for an exchange with the past that implicates the historian and critic in ways having both intellectual and political import for the present and future. The limited but nonetheless significant objective in this respect is to develop approaches that are historically informed and critically alert to the interpretation of specific artifacts without being either narrowly historicist (in reducing texts to mere documentary symptoms of contexts) or formalist (in isolating and remaining rigorously but ascetically—at times rather preciously—within the internal workings of texts).

The horizon of this study, which I hope to make less distant in future work, is the relation between narrative in literature and in historiography. The turn toward narrative, particularly in the work of Hayden White, has justifiably been seen as a necessary corrective to the stress in modern historiography upon modes of explanation modeled on the natural and social sciences. Yet the rather sophisticated theories of narrative developed by White and others have, for the most part, not been complemented in historiographical practice by comparably sophisticated mutations of narrative or by challenging combinations of narrative and analysis in a revised understanding of the allowable range of historical accounts. The kinds of narrative employed by historians have tended to remain rather conventional, whether the historians in question have turned from the exclusive preoccupation with social-scientific explanation or continued to tell old stories in spite of calls for more explanatory and intellectually demanding procedures.

Here one may observe an oft-noted phenomenon, upon which I commented in my earlier book *History & Criticism.* Until the professionalization of history in the late nineteenth century, there were strongly interactive relations between novelistic and historical narratives, indeed at times an almost agonistic rivalry. With the widespread professionalization of history and the importance of a scientific self-understanding in the historical profession came a significant parting of the ways. Narrative in historiography either continued largely along its preprofessionalized, nineteenth-century tracks (the path of much popular history), or was at times complemented, at times displaced, by more scientific ambitions and the demand for rigorous explanatory procedures. By contrast, in the novel we have had a proliferation of experimental interventions in narration as well as in the combination of narration with self-reflexive theory, displaced religious quest, direct or indirect social criticism, grotesque realism, montage, interior monologue, disrupted or syncopated dialogue, and so forth. We have also witnessed at least the beginnings of a better understanding of how so-called traditional novels may have involved tendencies brought into greater prominence or at least visibility in the more recent past. Especially noteworthy in the mutations of

narrative has been a complex and varied exploration of repetitive temporality (often interpreted reductively as "spatial
form"). Indeed, the modern novel has brought to a high point—
perhaps to a breaking point—the heterogeneous, polyphonous,
and "carnivalized" interaction of voices that Mikhail Bakhtin
considered the criterion of the entire tradition of the novel as a
self-contestatory and self-renewing genre.

It is only quite recently that professional historians have
become more attentive to the implications of mutations in
novelistic narrative for the theoretical understanding and practice of their discipline. One issue with far-ranging implications
is that of the historian's "voice" or "voices" in narration and
analysis—an issue that may cast the debate over objectivity
and subjectivity in a different light and bring out the limitations of an assumed unity between authorial and narratorial
voice in historiography (not to mention the illusionistic disap-
pearing act this voice performs in much historical narrative).
The general questions, however, are whether one needs a significantly different idea of the relation of the historian both to
the past and to his or her own society, and whether the novel,
as well as its critical interpretation, may have provocative implications for historical discourse—a discourse that has often
been taken by both historians and critics as the relatively unproblematic provider of factual information or contextual
grounding in interpretation. A prerequisite in addressing these
questions is to arrive at a better understanding of the nature of
narrative in the novel itself—and here a series of sufficiently
diverse "case studies" may bring out features that are necessarily submerged in macroscopic surveys of the rise of the
novel or its relation to other genres. What is nonetheless evident in my own approach is a conception of historical discourse which is neither presentist nor "passéist": I try neither
to projectively reprocess the past in the terms of the present
through an ahistorical reading technology nor to see the past
exclusively in its own putative terms through some kind of
total empathetic "teletransportation." The "voice" or perspective that informs these essays is one that attempts to work out
"dialogical" connections between past and present through

which historical understanding becomes linked to ethicopolitical concerns. These connections may at times disclose the possibly transformative implications of aspects of the past that help provide critical distance on the present, especially insofar as aspects of the past sedimented by intervening historical developments (including interpretations) emerge in more or less contestatory moments of "profane illumination."

My basic premise is that the past is not an "it" in the sense of an objectified entity that may either be neutrally represented in and for itself or projectively reprocessed in terms of our own narrowly "presentist" interests. Still, to employ the notion of "dialogue" to designate one's relation to the past (including its texts) is obviously to employ a metaphor. A text cannot literally answer one back in an "I-thou" relation in the manner in which a face-to-face conversation presumably allows. But the metaphor, in its power of catachresis, may open up relations and possibilities that literal-mindedness conceals. The more basic sense of dialogue is conveyed by *dia-logos*—a divergence or dehiscence in the logos that itself enables anything like an "I-thou" rapport to emerge in a face-to-face encounter. Literal conversations or dialogues may at times approximate a more or less reduced ritual in the exchange of clichés. The contestatory and potentially transformative power of a divergence, if not an agon, in the logos may be more in evidence in the workings of certain texts that engage us and with which we enter into an exchange. It should be abundantly clear from everything I have indicated that I do not hypostatize or idealize this "exchange" or "dialogue" with texts but rather see it as one element in the cultivation of a general critical sensibility in society and culture. In its social implications, a critical sensibility does not exclude the possibility of commitments able to withstand or even (at least in intimate relations) to obviate the need for explicit criticism, just as a "dialogical" relation may eventuate in a variable concatenation of solidarity or mutual recognition—at least amiable rivalry—and dissension or conflict. In these respects the specific sociocultural and political contexts of exchange are crucial.

I have quite deliberately taken a more or less theoretically informed "dialogical" approach to the reading of specific texts which is situationally prompted by my understanding of the existing critical literature and which at best will stimulate further responses, both to the texts and to suggested interpretations of them, in those who read this study. (Hence I have omitted much of the "filler" material often expected in this kind of study.) This approach is in keeping with the "model" of thought in society to which I am very much committed. Here it may be useful to sketch, in however condensed, inadequate, and even tendentious a manner, the larger historical and ethicopolitical perspective that guides without entirely predetermining—my specific readings. One specific aspect of such a "model" of social and intellectual activity is a normative in contrast to a status-quo pluralism—that is, a pluralism based not upon the validation of existing groups and structures with their vastly different power and possibly wayward imperatives but upon a notion of legitimate structures articulating relations among roughly equal groups and solidaristic but also resistant social individuals. And the primary sense of "transformative" in my usage of the term is social and political. The implications of texts such as novels are of course problematic, but I have tried to suggest ways in which they may be seen as having sociopolitical import. A crucial principle in this respect is that a certain approach to reading texts may help to create a viable interaction between structure and play in modern society—or, more specifically, between productive work and carnivalesque forces.

Carnivalesque institutions and practices underwent a process of suppression and repression in modern history under the pressure of political, economic, religious, moral, and cognitive change. An increasingly centralized state subjected numerous sectors of social life to surveillance and control, and dimensions of popular culture—prominently including carnival itself—were suspect as sources of subversion, rebellion, and general unruliness. The bureaucratic organization of large groups performing functionally rational tasks was of course common to the state and to other large institutions: factories, prisons, schools, hospitals, asylums. Groups organized on bureaucratic lines were quite compatible with the serialization of atomized, putatively autonomous individuals and with the confinement of intimacy and solidarity to the emotionally overcharged family unit. Work in general tended to become functionally rational and was inserted into a commodity system. Play too—alienated from the productive cycle and "recuperated" on the level of consumption—was largely adjusted to the commodity form and, as "leisure time," serviced by "culture industries." Reformed religion, which in its extreme forms was hostile to ritual, stressed the transcendence of the sacred and an ethic of seriousness, sobriety, and hard labor. Analytic rationality rigorously defined conceptually pure binary opposites that were adjusted to the control of human or natural objects and to the separation of spheres of thought and action (sacred and profane, high and low, private and public, work and play, and so forth). The maxims stating that "business is business" and that "one should not mix business with pleasure" were proverbial attestations to the hostility aroused by ambivalence, hybridization, and contestatory interaction. Modes associated with the carnivalesque—such as laughter, irony, parody, role reversal, the "lower body stratum," and the interactive rhythm of work and play in the organization of time—underwent repression and displacement to reappear as reduced, hierarchically managed, and often distortedly dissociated forms. In this respect, one may simply mention parades and pageants sponsored or authorized by the state; national, military, and imperial celebration; technological boosterism; the tendency of fairs and expositions to subordinate festivity to trade; commercial and advertising instrumentalization of humor and ironic self-reflexivity; and pathological dramatizations of privatized ritual (hysterical symptoms, obsessive fixations, somatic mimicry). Art and literature themselves became restricted repositories of socially and politically displaced carnivalesque forms, and the question in part answered by our reading and use of them is whether—or to what extent—their "transgressive" initiatives were compensatory bromides or contestatory forces in reinscribing the carnivalesque. In addressing this question, however, one must engage each text (or tradition) and work carefully through the problem of its specific relation to broader issues such as the actual and desirable relation of "high," "low," and "commodified" culture in the modern period.[1]

I would add that, despite my respect for his work and my agreement with certain of its aspects, I have not tried to emulate the recent initiative of Paul Ricoeur, which I think at times bespeaks more of an *esprit de système* than a self-critical *esprit systématique*.[2] The massive theoretical machine he pieces together—what might be called his *Schein und Zeit*—seems to me often to produce rather conventional readings of specific texts and even to serve as a justification for such conventionality. I do not think that historical or "real" events are subjected to a process of purely imaginative suspension or phenomenological bracketing in fiction or that the apparent contrast between history and fiction is then recuperated on a higher level by phenomenological philosophy itself in the role of magisterial mediator and source of more or less abstract aporia. Nor do I think that one may rely on the prevalent binary opposition between the "real world" and narrative wherein contingency or dissonance is placed on the side of reality and narrative is conceived in terms of the conventional, well-made plot that transcendently "refigures" reality in terms of an "unreal," purely imaginative beginning-middle-end structure. This entire frame of reference may ideologically "fit" certain artifacts insofar as both it and they are symptomatic of modern divisions and disarray. But it curtails the critical potential of

[1]For a remarkable discussion of some of these problems, which tends, however, to devote little attention to the impact of "commodification" upon both "high" and "low" culture and to stress the symptomatic more than the critical and possibly transformative dimensions of "high" culture itself, see Peter Stallybrass and Allon White, *The Politics & Poetics of Transgression* (Ithaca, 1986). See also Richard Terdiman's excellent study, *Discourse/Counter-Discourse: The Theory and Practice of Symbolic Resistance in Nineteenth-Century France* (Ithaca, 1985). Both these books make selective use of the work of Mikhail Bakhtin. For a less abbreviated treatment of problems evoked in the preceding paragraph, see my *Emile Durkheim: Sociologist and Philosopher* (Ithaca, 1972; Chicago, 1985), *Rethinking Intellectual History: Texts, Contexts, Language* (Ithaca, 1983), and *History & Criticism* (Ithaca, 1985).
[2]See his *Temps et récit*, 3 vols. (Paris, 1983–85).

literature and oversimplifies its more intricate and subtle relations with historiography and philosophy, on the one hand, and "reality" (or "experience"), on the other.

One basic point is that the relation between order and disorder, plot and contingency, consonance and dissonance, and so forth, is not coterminous with the relation between narrative and reality, for narratives complicate plot with contingency (in a particularly intriguing way when they explore repetitive temporality) and "reality" is at least partially structured (most obviously in terms of the plotlike, means-end schema of projects or quests but also in terms of its own intricate variants of repetitive temporality). Indeed, a narrative may radically question dubious relations between structure and its "others" in "reality" and at least suggest the possibility of alternative articulations, in part through its own textual operations in "working through" the problems it explores. In contrast to what may be termed the meaning-mongering of much recent theory, a recurrent motif in the following essays is that one way a novel makes challenging contact with "reality" and "history" is precisely by resisting fully concordant narrative closure (prominently including that provided by the conventional well-made plot), for this mode of resistance inhibits compensatory catharsis and satisfying "meaning" on the level of the imagination and throws the reader back upon the need to come to terms with the unresolved problems the novel helps to disclose. A related motif is that one chance of arriving at better, more challenging theoretical formulations of the complex nature of narrative (including the way it inscribes "reality" or "experience") lies in elaborating better, more challenging readings of specific, complex texts—readings that are not predetermined by overly reductive categories but exist in mutually testing and modifying relations with general theoretical assumptions and conclusions. Hence in this study an *esprit de géométrie* tends to be inflected in the direction of an *esprit de finesse*—which, however, in no sense implies an end to theory or a shortsighted, "activist" disdain for reflection about the past.

I

Stendhal's Irony in

Red and Black

> C'est l'esprit de parti, reprit Altamira. Il n'y a plus de pas sions véritables au XIXe siècle: c'est pour cela que l'on s'en nuie tant en France. On fait les plus grandes cruautés, mais sans cruauté...
>
> Julien était au comble de bonheur... Quel beau bal, dit-il au comte, rien n'y manque.
>
> Il y manque la pensée, répondit Altamira...
>
> Vous y êtes, monsieur le comte. N'est-ce pas, la pensée est conspirante encore?
>
> Je suis ici à cause de mon nom. Mais on hait la pensée dans vos salons.
>
> Stendhal, *Le Rouge et le noir*

In the foregoing passage from *Red and Black* (1829–30), Stendhal's famous irony appears in an especially subtle and disconcerting way. The Count Altamira seems to be the very image of authenticity—the *grand seigneur sans culotte* whose commitment to popular revolution has condemned him to death in his own country and made his life in France subject to the threat of extradition. In Mathilde de la Mole he inspires the baroque thought that only condemnation to death distinguishes a man. In Julien he revives and intensifies the heroic ardour and Napoleonic ambition that have been suppressed during his service with the Marquis de la Mole. Altamira's aristocratic yet liberal distance from his age seems to reflect that of Stendhal himself; it is epitomized in the magnificently penetrating statement that in the modern period the greatest cruelties are perpetrated without cruelty—a condition later termed the banality of evil. Yet soon after this statement, the count, in an exchange with Julien, unintentionally undercuts another profound observation about the absence of thought at the ball that Julien found so captivating. In response to the count's deflationary observation, Julien remarks, "Vous y êtes, monsieur le comte. N'est-ce pas, la pensée est conspirante encore?" Julien's statement is quite ambiguous. It could be read in this way: "You're right on target, Count. Isn't it the case that thought is still considered conspiratorial [under this oppressive regime]?" The Count, however, interprets it thus: "But you are here, Count. And thought is still conspiratorial, isn't it [because of your presence as a thinker]?" Instead of taking the more self-effacing route, as one might expect from his commitment to revolution and larger causes, the count unselfconsciously reveals, in the very midst of his high-mindedness, his own egotism, and he does so with no hesitation or afterthought. Egotism comes naturally to him, just as hypocrisy—along with boredom, the bane of existence in nineteenth-century France for Julien—will return to Julien himself even in his seemingly purified state in a cell when he too is condemned to death.

This scene involving Julien and Count Altamira might be taken as emblematic of the pervasive nature—and the difficulty of interpreting the role—of irony in Stendhal. It also highlights the conundrum of how to classify or, more generally, of what to do with Stendhal in the history of the novel. His "genius" and psychological acuity are readily acknowledged, but how to fit him into a pattern of development poses a problem even for theorists committed to historicist schemes. Erich Auerbach spends most of his analysis in *Mimesis* discussing Stendhal's attitudes rather than his texts, and his attempt to place Stendhal as a founding father of modern tragic realism is a bit strained. Dissonant notes—at times of a gratuitous tenor—appear in his appreciation of Stendhal's contribution to modern tragic realism, based on the concrete apprehension of contemporary life.

Beyle-Stendhal was a man of keen intelligence, quick and alive, mentally independent and courageous, but not quite a great figure. His ideas are often forceful and inspired, but they are erratic, arbitrarily advanced, and, despite all their show of boldness, lacking in inward certainty and continuity. There is something unsettled about his whole nature: his fluctuation between realistic candor in general and silly mystification in particulars, between cold self-control, rapturous abandonment to sensual pleasures, and insecure and sometimes sentimental vaingloriousness, is not always easy to put up with; his literary style is very impressive and unmistakably original, but it is short-winded, not uniformly successful, and only seldom wholly takes possession of and fixes the subject. But, such as he was, he offered himself to the moment; circumstances seized him, tossed him about, and laid upon him a unique and unexpected destiny; they formed him so that he was compelled to come to terms with reality in a way which no one had done before him.[1]

This account almost sounds like a segment from a funeral oration for a deceased husband delivered by a not altogether satisfied wife. One could, of course, turn defects into virtues by stressing the uses of uncertainty in Stendhal and pointing to his liminal position between classicism and romanticism—a position suggested by his own notions of (classical) *logique* and (romantic) *espagnolisme.* And one could stress Stendhal's "outsider" status in the history of the novel and have it resonate with his own fascination with outsiders in general. Especially at present, this strategy has an undeniable appeal. What I would like to stress, however, is the importance of a critical exchange with Stendhal in which problems of classification and periodization do not assume a paramount role.

One could take my analysis as a chapter in a critical history of irony. But could one hope to arrive at cogent periods in such a history? Indeed, how should this history itself be written? Straight or ironically? One may at least begin with a sensitivity to one's own implication in the problem under investigation.

---

[1] *Mimesis* (1946; Princeton, N.J., 1953), p. 459.

And one might submit that its elaboration beyond the text in question would require an attempt to trace modulations of a repetitive temporality in specific contexts. Such modulations might at times suggest traumatic ruptures or breaks. But it is difficult to envision them as total or absolutely decisive. Stendhal's irony is not Flaubert's or Beckett's. But is that to say that irony akin to Stendhal's is limited to his period and that nothing like it appears before or after? Stendhal himself looked back to the sixteenth century, and to the Old Regime during its twilight years as well, in seeking analogues for his own sense of grace, wit, elegance, sensuality, and sophistication. We might in part look to Nietzsche and in part to Thomas Mann for later mutations of Stendhal's outlook. But any more extensive and cogent account of the permutations of irony, even if restricted to "literary" figures alone, would pose enormous problems. Thus the relation of this chapter to any larger survey must remain somewhat indeterminate.

On an initial approach to the text, one might argue that *Red and Black* involves an interaction between two related movements or levels—one a more logical, classical, thematically ordered, and symbolically satisfying "traditional" level and the other a more intricate, open, *espagnoliste* level. A unifying structure is challenged by complex forces that reopen the reading of the novel and the problem of its relation to the issues it explores. Prominent here as well are two interacting modes of irony—one a rather stable or "monological" form in which the narrator masters or dominates the story and the other involving the narrator in "dialogically" participatory and self-questioning movements that contest the status of novelistic narration itself as an adequate answer to the problems it treats. The second, more self-questioning tendency becomes, I think, increasingly pronounced and insistent in the concluding chapters. The first is more in evidence in the story before the point at which the epigraphs disappear. But the two tendencies interanimate each other in a kind of agonistic contest throughout the novel, and one function of the concluding chapters may be to invite the reader to go back and reread the text in terms of the interplay between its tendencies. The concluding chapters also raise forceful questions about the limits of the novel as an adequate symbolic response to the problems raised in the novel itself. I shall begin with the first movement or tendency and then try to indicate how the two movements interact and generate certain questions.

On one level, *Red and Black,* read as a relatively traditional novel, has a beginning-middle-end plot structure that organizes the story in an oriented way. And the viewpoint of the narrator is informed by stable irony that places him above the story with superior insight and a secure grasp of the problems agitating the characters, notably Julien Sorel. The beginning of the story, moreover, seems to resonate with its anticipated ending. In the opening lines there is a brief, evanescent image of rural calm—a seeming image of happiness as utopian reconciliation and peace in the country: "The little town of Verrières must be one of the prettiest in the Franche-Comté. Its white houses with their steep, red tile roofs spread across a hillside, the folds of which are outlined by clumps of thrifty chestnut trees. The Doubs flows a couple of hundred feet below the town's fortifications, built long ago by the Spaniards and now fallen into ruins."[2] This might be seen as a subdued, understated, fairytale opening based upon the fiction of a traveler coming into town from a distance. It presents the small town, seen from afar, in the light of a peaceful rural idyll; the town is a silent, homelike womb.

But the peaceful idyll is almost immediately disrupted and the privileged moment of rural calm broken as the narrative camera moves in for a closer look. "As soon as one enters the town, one is deafened by the uproar of a noisy machine of terrifying appearance"—the mayor's nail factory. Here is the first instance of the way the town converts its natural beauty into a commodity and the pretext for making money. Everything in this world is either seen in terms of yielding a return or threatened with commodification. And this is a crucial source of the double binds with which Julien Sorel as prob-

---

[2]*Red and Black,* trans. and ed. Robert M. Adams (New York: Norton, 1969), p. 1. Page numbers are cited in the text.

lematic hero (in Georg Lukács's phrase) is repeatedly confronted. The ruined fortifications in the initial passage also announce the motif of walls that spring up everywhere in the opening pages to block harmony with nature and to herald the theme of imprisonment.

Near the beginning of the novel, one has another blatant annunciation of the future course of events. In church, Julien mistakes holy water on the floor for blood. This may be read both as heralding the shooting of Madame de Rênal in church and as anticipating the scene during the funeral procession in which Mathilde has the severed head of Julien on her lap. Julien also notices a scrap of paper on the lectern "set there as if for him to read." Looking at it, he sees, "Details of the execution of Louis Jenrel, executed in Besançon on the . . ." The next paragraph begins: "The paper was torn. On the other side were the first words of a line: 'The first step' " (p. 20). The name Louis Jenrel is of course an anagram of Julien Sorel, and the annunciation of the end is a bit too melodramatic and contrived to be taken at face value. In the very last paragraph, one returns to the understated idyll and to the womb in a fleeting hint of utopian reconciliation—the reunion beyond the grave of Julien and Madame de Rênal, who appropriately does not survive the hero's death.

On this first level, Stendhal narrates the story in a way that seems omniscient. The basis of the stable ironic distance between narrator and characters is the fact that the narrator knows what characters do not know—notably, in this case, that Julien is a divided self immersed in self-deception and bent on a suicidal destiny. From his superior vantage point, the Stendhal-narrator can be what he has always been seen as being—a master psychologist and witty kibitzer. In terms of social psychology, he provides insight into the emulation, rivalry, and tension of social relations in a context that lacks stable norms and internalized limits to assertion and ambition. In this context, status is in doubt; people are on the make; and a sense of justification has to be achieved. Older forms of nobility by birth are to some extent anachronistic, although they still have value as tokens of prestige. They are stronger in the

Restoration period in which the novel is set than they will be later in the century, and their nuances are more pronounced in Paris than in the provinces. But they are not as secure as they once were, and Stendhal senses their precariousness. Moreover, from his perspective the only true nobility in postrevolutionary France is nobility of the spirit. Yet the general image of society is one of rampant factionalism, intrigue, and individualistic self-interest—a general image the novel shares with a work such as Alexis de Tocqueville's *Old Regime* (1856).

In terms of individual psychology, the narrator's superior knowledge and insight provide him with the basis for a gentle but penetrating and at times critical perspective on Julien, his problem child. Irony on this first level marks the paternal and tender but patronizing superiority of the narrator, whose interest is most captivated by his male offspring. The role the narrator assumes is close to that of a novelistic *haut bourgeois* or even *grand seigneur sans culotte* who somehow manages to retain the secure position that threatens to elude characters in the story. I think that a function of the chapter headings and chapter epigraphs is, on this level, to mark the relatively stable ironic perspective of the narrator and to underwrite the firmness and security of his privileged voice. They are, in a sense, narrative analogues of the *prénoms et qualités* of an older social world. The titles and epigraphs betoken a seemingly superior knowledge of what will occur in the chapters and thus give the reader a sense of what to expect.

The ironic distance between the narrator and Julien is related to the character structure of Julien himself. Julien is a divided self in that he combines an inner or spiritual nobility with a self-interested desire to gain social acceptance and to succeed in the established ways of an alienated world. He embodies a divisive inner-outer, private-public split. His inner, private self is elevated, poetic, spontaneous, passionate, idealistic, even exuberant. But his mind is calculating, and it operates shrewdly to achieve worldly success and public acclaim. His *logique* is the means-end rationality of a man on the make. Julien does have the only kind of nobility that still makes sense in the modern world—inner nobility of soul and character; he is an aristocrat of the spirit in contrast to the ludicrously affected and ineffective comportment of many of the novel's aristocrats by birth. But Julien also wants to make it big in a world he knows is unjust and distorted. To succeed, he must compromise his inner self in ways to which he would prefer to remain blind. With some misgiving, Julien can be a real operator who does not want to sell himself short. He continually feels constrained to act against his better self and to do things that go against the grain. But he would like to believe that his essential inner self remains undefiled.

Julien is thus a problematic hero who does not appear to see how and why he is problematic. Until a certain point in the novel he seems blind to the way in which he is a hypocritical, self-deceived idealist—someone who would like to keep his inner self and his ideal model of himself pure of contamination but who defines himself by external acts that threaten to reduce his noble self-image to a hollow fiction. Stendhal as narrator sees and takes an ironic view of this self-deception. The moment of tragic insight in Julien seems to come when he too sees his impossible situation, lucidly assumes his identity as a stranger or outsider, and flouts society (especially in his courtroom speech). He then withdraws into himself and seems heroically to seek death. (The ending of Albert Camus's *The Stranger* appears terribly derivative in this light.) I shall return to this recognition scene shortly, for here one has the seeming climax of the story.

On this first level, the setting of the story is quite realistic. One has a pointed portrait of the social and political life of Restoration France—a chronicle of 1830, as the subtitle tells us. Immediately after the subtitle, however, a fictitious editor's note puts the reader on guard by providing a false date for the novel's composition. This dissonant note indicates that the realism of the story is not simply photographic or positivistic. The novel offers a reading of the times, but it is a highly critical reading—a portrait of an alienated society and of self-deceived individuals.

On the level of a realistic but critical representation of society and politics, the celebrated temporal perspective of Stendhal seems to have a largely contemplative function. Continual contrasts of past and present serve to cast the present in a nonessentialized, contingent mold, and there is a constant undercutting of ideological attempts to legitimate the status quo. But for the narrator there seems to be no issue from the existing state of affairs; within the narrated story, nothing can be done to change society—a point that may be read either as a sign of political defeatism and the flight into symptomatic transcendental egotism on the level of narrative irony or as a sign of the refusal to offer purely symbolic, novelistic solutions to real social and political problems. In any event, society as represented seems to be an endless round of political intrigue, petty bickering, struggle for advantage, and rabid infighting— *plus ça change, plus c'est la même chose.* While the social scene is not legitimized, there is no indication of viable social groups or forces that might decisively change it. In Julien, the image of Napoleon is the object of a cult that has not yet declined into a legend, but it functions in a largely privatistic manner as a basis of nostalgia and of inner exultation. Julien's only directly political role as secretary of the Marquis de la Mole is to act as go-between for a royalist conspiracy that fizzles. The more popular revolutionary conspiracy of Count Altamira remains somewhat vague; it serves largely as a background for his mordant comments on the times and his personally charismatic appeal for Julien and Mathilde. The two principal women in the novel can hardly be interpreted as models of feminist protest, for the one is an idealized mother image and the other the narcissistic mirror-image of Julien himself. In short, there seem to be no effective protest movements in the world of the novel: the peasantry is represented by Julien's scheming, much hated father; the working class is notorious by its absence; and the prototypical intellectual is a hopelessly divided self.

Development does seem to occur on the individual and psychological level, however, especially with respect to Julien. In terms of plot rather than description, society is almost reduced to a backdrop for individual activity. Julien at least appears to progress to the point of tragic insight into both himself and society. And the reader is induced to identify with his progress and achieve cathartic purgation through tragic insight. In this movement, the novel might be argued to provide a purely individual, tragic response to social and political problems. It is noteworthy that the woman characters do not undergo comparable development. Madame de Rênal remains the alluring yet naive mother figure for Julien, and at the end the grave becomes their shared womb. Mathilde by and large remains a role-playing alter ego for the male lead.

Yet Julien's own seeming progress is paradoxically set in a larger pattern of hollow, deadly repetition. Liberation coincides with further confinement in society and the self. One has what might be called an aborted or stalled dialectic of seeming escape or liberation leading to further imprisonment. In the course of the novel, Julien moves from the small town of Verrières to the middle-sized provincial town of Besançon and finally to the urban center and national capital, Paris. Geographically and culturally, his movement is from the periphery to the center. Verrières in the Franche Comté is on the outskirts of France—the remote margins of the nation. Besançon is closer to the heart of things. Paris is the center in every respect, the center of the nation and the center of Julien's (somewhat Bovaresque) dreams. Socially, Julien moves up the ladder, but he goes down it existentially, and external victory coincides with inner defeat. His seeming liberation itself comes with further imprisonment until he is literally in prison and locked into his own abstracted, withdrawn self, awaiting death. His existential space is smaller in his cell in Besançon than it was in the countryside of Verrières, and in Paris he spends most of his time in three confined rooms—the drawing room, the library, and the bedroom.

In Paris, Julien seems to be on the verge of total worldly success. He is about to marry Mathilde de la Mole, the most Olympian aristocrat of them all; his acceptance into aristocratic society could not be more complete. He is even to be provided with a myth of aristocratic origins that will abolish his peasant past and reveal that his "real" father was a noble. (The petty origin of the myth is a story circulated to cover the embarrassment of a noble who has dueled with Julien but fears ridicule when he discovers that Julien is merely the secretary of the Marquis de la Mole.) But at the very *point culminant* of his social ascent Julien does something bizarre; in response to a letter from Madame de Rênal that describes him as a schemer and an opportunist, he behaves in just the opposite way by rashly and unopportunistically rushing off to shoot her in church. The reception of the letter and Julien's reaction to it seem to constitute a turning point and a scene of self-recognition that preface his journey into the interior of his imprisoned self. But the interpretation of these obviously decisive events has justifiably puzzled commentators.

One curious point is that Julien himself almost forces the letter to be sent by urging the Marquis de la Mole to write for information about his intended son-in-law. In effect, he tells the father of his new lover to get a letter of recommendation from his old lover—a dangerous practice at best—and thus seems to court his own undoing, to play out Freud's death drive. But is this really an *explanation* for his behavior or another name for what is puzzling and bizarre about it? Instead of stopping at this point, one should perhaps be induced to look again at the text.

Madame de Rênal, Julien's first lover, herself writes the letter under the dictation of a pious priest. It is therefore almost an anonymous, poison-pen letter with no specific author. Yet what it says, although distorted by venom and blurred by tears, is partially true: Julien *is* a schemer who manipulates women to get his own way. Julien later offers stereotyped explanations of why he reacted to the letter as he did: he says he felt it was his duty to do something. The text also refers to his self-esteem and revenge as motives; the note of revenge is struck in the epigraph right after the shooting. Yet Julien's revenge, like Madame de Rênal's writing of the letter, is deeply ambivalent, and it suddenly turns to joy and love when he discovers that she is still alive. What is perhaps especially significant is that these explanations are explicitly situated in the text after the fact of the shooting. They do not precede or accompany it. Their position would almost seem to signal their status as ex post facto rationalizations or secondary revisions.

Commentators, sensing the need for a plausible, realistic psychological explanation of the shooting, have offered various interpretations. The Frenchman Henri Martineau refers to Julien's morbid psychology to explain his rash behavior. The Englishman F. W. J. Hemmings argues that Julien is trying to erase a smear on his character.[3] These explanations are interesting, since they rely on little textual evidence and seem to confirm the most banal stereotypes of national character: the "kinky" but dashing Frenchman is concerned about morbid psychology and rashness, while the properly phlegmatic Englishman is preoccupied with defamation of character. In the absence of textual evidence about its putative meaning, the shooting functions as a kind of Rorschach test that may elicit the most conventional responses.

I offer a basically psychological interpretation, in keeping with the reading I have attempted thus far, and then raise certain questions about this interpretation. These questions indicate that the alluring, even gripping, first-level reading is only partially valid and that other features of the text contest it and call for a somewhat different reading.

The letter Julien receives is from someone who may well be the most significant other in his life. Note that we know about Julien's real father and his brothers but absolutely nothing about his mother. The literal mother is a marked absence in the text. Madame de Rênal is both lover and mother for Julien, the only mother he or we know. The letter from an other who is so close to Julien presents him not as he would like to see himself ("inwardly") but as others see him. It presents him—almost through his own eyes—not in terms of his noble, sensitive, inner self but in terms of his opportunistic and scheming outer self, as a paltry logician of self-interest. In short, the other who is mother and lover sees him just as *any* other might see him, and this turns Julien inside out. Her letter reveals that

---

[3]See their essays in *Red and Black*, pp. 446–63, and 521–38.

he is compromised; his noble purity is an illusion; his equivocal, divided self is untenable. To use Sartrean language (which seems almost natural here), Julien's acts have defined him. His inner, noble self is disclosed as empty, and he has become what he appears to be. His outside is his essence—an unacceptable essence.

With the letter, Julien seems to acquire tragic insight. The scales of self-deception drop from his eyes, and he is no longer blind to his predicament. His act of shooting Madame de Rênal seems to be his first truly spontaneous act—an *acte gratuit:* that is, premeditated but unmotivated, an act of the head, not of the heart. Before this act his behavior is always contrived and imitative, the behavior of a performing monkey, epitomized in the feats of memorization that astonish provincial boors. The shooting is also like the act of a being fully divided between an inner and an outer self. Julien shoots Madame de Rênal in a hypnotic or somnambulistic state of reverie, and it is physically difficult for him to pull the trigger. He acts like a ghost in a machine—in a fully abstracted, schizoid way.

With the shooting, the traditional structure of the novel also seems shot—wounded but—like Madame de Rênal herself—perhaps not fatally. The position of the narrator is jeopardized in important respects; his own transferential relation to Julien becomes more insistent and active as any status approximating that of a detached, transcendental ego is undermined. Something similar may perhaps be said for my reading thus far: it too is wounded but perhaps not fatally. The first-level reading I have suggested remains legible, intelligible, and significant. One might perhaps say that it is correct or valid within limits. But it is questioned and contested by other elements and forces in the novel.

Note again the position of the shooting in the text. What is notable is that Stendhal, the acknowledged master of psychological analysis, does not offer a psychological explanation. This fact marks or accentuates the shooting in a special manner. In a sense, there is an obvious and a somewhat less obvious relation between the shooting and the mother in the text: Julien shoots his mother surrogate, and both the shooting and the mother are surrounded by significant silences. The shooting itself invites a plethora of psychological interpretations but is not exhausted by them. A lack in the narration prompts an excess of interpretations that fail to fill it, and the reader is tempted to reveal himself or herself in the very explanation or interpretation offered. The reader's own transferential relation to the text is thus drawn out and made explicit.

After the shooting Julien sees into himself and approaches a lucidity approximating the narrator's own. This lucidity seems to reach its climactic point in Julien's speech before the court during his trial for attempted murder. Here Julien clearly sees himself as a divided self, alienated from society. He speaks in what may be anachronistically called Marxian terms in his appearance before the court. The jury is bought and perhaps even softened by pity and sentiment. They are ready to acquit Julien, and the audience is clearly on his side; all he has to do is to play up to them. But Julien's speech is an accusatory confession that shocks the jury and brings it to its senses. His speech makes the jury class-conscious. Yet afterward Julien leads no troops, real or imaginary, into battle; he leaves society and withdraws into himself to face death. Still, at least on a private level, his seemingly heroic self-constitution as scapegoat appears to provide the plot element and the object of reader identification that function to assure meaningful narrative closure.

The final four chapters of the novel, following the speech in court, have no titles and no epigraphs; these are also silenced. In a sense, the chapters become headless as Julien himself is soon to become headless. The shooting and its aftermath undercut the distance between Stendhal as narrator and Julien as character. With Julien's courtroom confession, he and the narrator are on the same level of "insight," and there is no basis for a privileged, stable ironic distance between them. The grounds of stable irony are undercut; the narrator with his secure vantage point is also faced with decapitation; and the titles and epigraphs that seem to mark stable irony are lopped off. The problem child has grown up, and problems are generalized.

With tragic insight into his suicidal destiny, Julien now sees what Stendhal as narrator sees, and the narrator is drawn into the story, his secure position questioned. The ironic narrator becomes at least in part a participant, and the mode of irony shifts: it is no longer stable, invidious, tender yet patronizing, monologically firm, and caringly patriarchal. The final chapters generate more subtle and challenging ironies. Irony now seems to designate an interaction of forces in which the narrator is also at stake, for he is transferred into the events being recounted. And as Julien attains the same level of tragic insight as the narrator, the insufficiencies of that insight also threaten to be disclosed. Insight does not amount to saving grace; it is not a basis for a position of superiority. Indeed, as the narrator is drawn into the story, questions are generated about the temptation—including the reader's temptation—simply to settle within the story, its ironies and tragic insights. The more complex variations in the final chapters set up a multiple movement. They invite the reader to go back into the novel and notice the forces that complicate a unified, thematic reading of it that provides satisfying symbolic sense; they pose problems that withhold the kind of meaning the traditional or conventional reader expects from the narrative contract. Things that happen in the last few chapters reopen the question of how to read (and to use) the text.

At the end of the novel Julien has attained a certain nobility. But this nobility is not the simple product of a tragic and heroic affirmation of his true inner identity as a stranger understandably condemned by the ignoble crowd outside. The very image of Julien as a purified, alienated individual—one who has joined the narrator in puncturing romantic illusion to attain superior novelistic truth and who becomes thereby a scapegoat or martyr eliciting the cathartic identification of the individual reader—is too simple. Why?

The famous speech at the trial in which Julien lectures the court on class conflict is itself not unproblematic. Its status as a dramatic climax is challenged by the fact that it is somewhat histrionic and self-involved. In the speech Julien still romantically courts suicide and glorifies his own ego. He plays to the crowd even when he offends it—especially, the text tells us, with respect to the pretty women in the audience. And the narrator impatiently cuts his speech short by abruptly commenting, "For twenty minutes Julien talked in this vein" (p. 388). Stendhal as narrator is in certain ways closer to Julien than he is earlier in the text, but he will still take an ironic distance at certain points—which may also indicate a distance from his privileged narrative self.

In addition, Julien's tragic insight—to the extent that it exists—is impotent. It confirms his withdrawal into himself, and it has no relation to effective action in society. It is purely symbolic—something which without further ado might become a fetish. Julien's seeming liberation comes with imprisonment and death. And even in prison, stoical withdrawal into the self is not perfect. Julien is still besieged by the inner and outer forces he wants to escape: hypocrisy, his father, a priest, Mathilde. All the old problems recur; hence Julien is not quite the purified victim he seems to be. He even behaves like a petulant adolescent toward Mathilde when she comes to see him. He does not see or want to see any change in his relation to her.. And he himself reflects that even in his prison cell awaiting death, he remains a hypocritical child of the times. He does not find the spiritual consolation that should come as symbolic recompense to the lucid scapegoat and martyr.

The final scene in the last paragraph of the novel poses significant problems as well: "Mme. de Rênal was true to her word. She never tried in any way to take her own life; but three days after Julien, she died in the act of embracing her children. The End" (p. 408). This is highly contrived, minimally romantic, extremely elliptical, and laconically utopian. These characteristics cast doubt upon any intimation of a possible reunion of starcrossed lovers beyond the grave. Indeed, they almost make the paragraph a parody of the romantic ending. And the paragraph is followed by an ironic and anticlimactic epilogue—or perhaps epitaph—that suspiciously stresses the role of fiction in the novel in the manner of an "any reference to persons living or dead is purely coincidental" proviso.

How do these observations about the final chapter flow back

on one's reading of the novel and help one to notice less obvious traits of earlier chapters one might otherwise have missed? What do they imply for the status of the last few chapters and of the novel as a whole?

An initial point is that Stendhal's earlier perspective as narrator is not entirely based on purely stable irony. There are subdued and subtle movements of another sort. Even in the earlier chapters, Stendhal is at times close to Julien. He even threatens to "lose his ironic cool" in being either for or against his protagonist in ways that show his emotional investment in the story. And the titles and epigraphs do not serve only to mark stable irony. The play of title, epigraph, and principal text is at times multivalent. An epigraph's relation to what occurs in a chapter may be open to question and difficult to decipher; it may call for interpretation and argument. And epigraphs may play off against one another or against aspects of chapters they do not preface. One example is Stendhal's famous reference to the novel as a mirror, which prefaces Book 1, chapter 13, and is picked up and elaborated in the principal text of Book 2, chapter 19. The epigraph reads, "A novel: it's a mirror being carried along a highway—Saint-Réal" (p. 60). The later textual reference reads: "Look here, sir, a novel is a mirror moving along a highway. One minute you see it reflect the azure skies, next minute the mud and puddles of the road. And the man who carries the mirror in his pack will be accused by you of immorality! His mirror shows the mud and you accuse the mirror! Rather you should accuse the road in which the puddle lies, or, even better, the inspector of roads who lets the water collect and the puddle form" (p. 289).

The attribution of the epigraph, like that of a number of others, is probably false. Its putative author, Saint-Réal (whose name itself is oxymoronic), published a work in 1672, *Conspiracy in Venice*. This fiction was for a long while mistakenly taken as a factual contribution to history. Far from being a simple attestation to Stendhal's realism, the mirror image in the epigraph is thus caught up in a complex play of reality and illusion—a play intensified by the passage in the principal text that takes up the mirror image. The direct address to the reader ("Look here, sir") paradoxically reveals the manipulating hand of the narrator in the very reference to the novel as a mirror—an interpellation of the interlocutor that functions as an alienation effect. And the mirror that reflects sky and road is curiously described as carried in a pack—a location that would seem to obscure all vision. The final exclamations indicate at the very least that, to the extent that the novel is a mirror, it is a critical one and not an innocent reflector.

In the earlier chapters, moreover, Julien's personality structure is not simply that of a divided self. It is somewhat more complicated. There is a sense in which, at the end of the novel, he cannot find his identity as a stranger because his is already a strange identity. His personality has aspects that cut across the inner-outer dichotomy of nobility and self-interest. Take his ambivalent sense of duty—something offered as a reason for his shooting Madame de Rênal *and* something that straddles the opposition between his inner noble self and his outer scheming self. At times his sense of duty makes him behave in an icy, formal, external, false way with an almost bureaucratic or perhaps military sense of rigid obligation. Thus he loses all pleasure when Madame de Rênal first surrenders her hand to him after his constrained stratagem in taking it succeeds. But his sense of duty also gives him a critical sense of distance on events, and it is part of his inner nobility and spiritually aristocratic bearing. It marks him with an elevated spiritual reserve and, in counteracting his natural timidity, even gives him a superior sense of shyness—the only things that make heroism and seduction a challenge and save them from boorishness in the world of Stendhal.

Like his sense of duty, Julien's attachment to books is also ambivalent. It makes him artificial and derivative, and it can exacerbate his hypocrisy. But it also cultivates his ideal model of himself. Books lie to hand everywhere in Julien's world, notably his three favorites: Rousseau's *Confessions*, a collection of bulletins from the Grande Armée, and the *Mémorial de Sainte-Hélène*. Even his most spontaneous acts are implicated in his reading of books or destined to become "literary" models.

A final point about the text is the difficulty in interpreting Julien's decapitation. I have said that it is in one sense an analogue in the novel of the stylistic fact that the last few chapters have lost their headings. (A formalistic interpretation, which had lost its head, could even engender the idea that his beheading is merely a device to motivate the absence of headings in the last few chapters.) Decapitation is an obvious sign of loss, often seen in Freudian terms as castration or impotence. But it is also possibly a sign of renewal, an uncrowning or bringing low of the head and a fecundation of the earth with the blood of what is the seat of the human's highest powers— thought and spirituality. In a sense, it might also be taken as a novelistic regicide—the beheading of the king in narration: that is, of the stable and secure narrator, who graciously provides full and satisfying symbolic sense for the reader in a kind of private contract.

In a similar vein, one might suggest that the last few chapters enact a reversal and displacement of the preceding text without marking a total break. The tendencies that were uppermost in the earlier chapters are brought low, and the tendencies that were more submerged in them are raised up. Becoming especially explicit are the facts that the narrator has no unquestioned right to a privileged position above the story and that the reader cannot simply use the novel, in a rapport with the narrator and an identification with the hero, as a symbolic resolution to the problems disclosed in the novel. The parodic-romantic ending itself—as opposed to a conventional, resonant ending—functions as might a tip of the hat that is so rapid and perfunctory that it registers at best on a subliminal level; one is left not with a feeling of reconciliation but with doubt about whether a hat has been tipped at all. The reader's desire to identify with the seemingly central character and to find cathartic release or surrogate "meaning" through the reading of fiction is also challenged and displaced, for the reader and the narrator confront comparable issues; indeed, the reader is placed in the position of the narrator when he or she must interpret the novel and draw implications concerning its ideological, social, and political significance. In this sense, the last few chapters make explicit the question of taking a novel as a symbolic and individual or private solution to problems explored thematically and formally in the novel itself.

2

Notes on Dostoevsky's
Notes from Underground

> If anyone proved to me that Christ was outside the truth, and
> it *really* was so that the truth was outside Christ, then I
> should prefer to remain with Christ than with the truth.
>
> Fyodor Dostoevsky

If one were to inquire into the question of the relationship
between Dostoevsky's context and his texts, one could do
worse than to begin with the commonplace idea of the breakdown of tradition. The crucial form this breakdown took for
Dostoevsky was, of course, religious crisis. The Westernized
intellectual had a privileged relation to the crisis as one who
both aggravated it and came to an acute critical consciousness
of it. For Dostoevsky, the West itself embodied an ideology of
free, critical inquiry and secular rationalism that endangered
traditional religious faith.

The Underground Man is in one sense the limiting case or
extreme representative of the Westernized intellectual. And
there was a sense in which Dostoevsky could never fully eliminate from himself what he saw as the Western influence—the
nexus between freedom and critical questioning that contested
or even endangered faith. His inner division might itself be
taken as indicative of the dubiousness of the very binary opposition between West and East, for it bears witness to the
problematic insertion of the West in the East (and vice versa).

In his life, Dostoevsky at first subscribed to what he later
saw as a Westernized position and placed secular faith in radi-

cal politics, and his later reaction against radical politics coincided with his movement toward Russian Orthodox religion. As a young man he sympathized with radical groups that opposed the role in Russia of a despotic political regime, a reactionary church, and a secret police and spy system. Their criticism was fed by a familiarity with Western thinkers such as Saint-Simon and Fourier. In the late 1840s, Dostoevsky was a member of the Durov circle within the larger Petrashevsky circle, a group of reformers who met to read and discuss socialist and liberal literature. Perhaps unrealistically, Dostoevsky believed that had this circle not been liquidated, it would have gone on to take revolutionary action and would have had large-scale popular support. The Durov circle was the most activist group within the Petrashevsky circle. Its members believed that violence might be necessary and took a terroristic oath of revolutionary solidarity to kill any member who betrayed the group. (There is similar group in *The Possessed*, and one of the more probing aspects of this novel is its disclosure of the way privileged groups might themselves be permeated with revolutionary ideas.)

The 1848 Revolution in France led to a crackdown in Russia, and in 1849 Dostoevsky was slated for execution. In melodramatic fashion, a courier from the Czar arrived at the eleventh hour with a commuted sentence. This gesture, confirming the divine-right status of the ruler in his command over life and death, had a telling effect upon the prisoners. One of the condemned went mad. Dostoevsky himself apparently was filled with mystical awe.[1]

Dostoevsky subsequently spent four years in Siberia under extremely harsh conditions and dated his epileptic seizures from this period in his life. He explicitly looked upon his imprisonment as a merited punishment that enabled him to atone for the errors of his corrupt youth. And he sought solace and salvation in religion. The only book he had in prison was

---

[1]A useful source of information on Dostoevsky's life and writing is E. J. Simmons, *Dostoevsky: The Making of a Novelist* (London, 1950). See also Joseph Frank, *Dostoevsky*, 3 vols. (Princeton, 1976, 1983, 1986).

the New Testament. It was shortly after his release from prison that he wrote to his brother the words that serve as my epigraph. Yet whether or not these words are accurate with respect to Dostoevsky's lived relation to religion, they do not serve to characterize the treatment of religion in his novels. For in them there is no simple alternative between belief and disbelief, revealed religion and secular "truth." Rather, religious belief is powerfully contested even when it is powerfully affirmed, and the most extreme atheist exists on the margin of possible belief. It is the abiding value of Mikhail Bakhtin's analysis to have brought out the internally "dialogized" nature of all ideologies in Dostoevsky's literary texts.[2]

Still, upon leaving prison, Dostoevsky saw political radicalism as both wrongheaded and sinful. In the 1860s he condemned the new generation of radicals whose most prominent exponent was Chernyshevsky. One explicit object of caricature, parody, and polemical attack in *Notes from Underground* is of course Chernyshevsky's *What Is to Be Done?* with its faith in rationalism and progress. Dostoevsky himself seemed increasingly to tend toward a conservative but populistically based Slavism. He openly affirmed the value of Russian Orthodox religion, mother Russia, and the simple, pious Russian people.

In 1862 a trip to western Europe (discussed in *Winter Notes on Summer Impressions*) confirmed Dostoevsky in his convictions. He saw capitals such as Paris and London as the scene of egotism, materialism, and hypocrisy. The West was decadent. By contrast, Dostoevsky affirmed the need for self-sacrifice, compassion, and brotherly love.

Certain things, however, remained relatively constant or changed only in degree in Dostoevsky's outlook over time. He was always opposed to what he saw as the total Westernization of Russia. He rejected extreme liberalism and believed that it could only encourage a flight from freedom. He also attacked capitalism from the beginning to the end of his life. He opposed

---

[2]See *Problems of Dostoevsky's Poetics*, trans. Caryl Emerson (Minneapolis, Minn., 1984).

the introduction of capitalism in Russia because he thought it would upset the old order and give rise to divisive class conflict. He also always believed in the special mission of Russia and her people. From his perspective, the most Russia should do with the Western tradition was to overcome it in a higher synthesis. Indeed, he saw Russia in an idealized light as a synthesizing force with a capacity for universal reconcilability, universal humanity. And he always believed that intellectuals in Russia should avoid the twin dangers of extreme Westernization and uprooted detachment from the people. The uprooted Westernized intellectual was the stereotypical "superfluous man"—and *Notes from Underground* contains this prevalent theme of Russian literature. Dostoevsky thought Russian intellectuals should not emulate Westerners but see in the people the salvation of Russia. In his idealized view of Russia, her faith, and her people, Dostoevsky seemed to find the saving grace of suffering and compassion.

What Dostoevsky came to see more forcefully in time—and to oppose vehemently—was the possibility that Russia faced its greatest threat of disruption from its Westernized intellectuals. Here, from the opposite end of the ideological spectrum, one seems to have a remarkable convergence with the thought of Lenin. But Russia in Dostoevsky's time, in contrast to Lenin's, had as yet no significant capitalistic bourgeoisie or proletariat. And Dostoevsky opposed the large-scale introduction of capitalism precisely because it would create conditions incompatible with his values. Yet even without these conditions, a Westernized intelligentsia was an active force that might upset the status quo. The apparent and apparently decisive difference between the young and the later Dostoevsky was the difference between support of, and opposition to, this possibility. But in his novels and perhaps in his life—certainly in the relation between the two—the will to believe does not simply and complacently culminate in belief, and the "Westernized" other is within as well as without. One name for this "Westernized" other is the Underground Man.

In *Notes from Underground* (1864), one finds at least two modes of "dialogue" (in the Bakhtinian sense) that are not simple opposites. First and most obvious is the broken but often terribly funny dialogue of an evasive voice internally divided against itself. "Dialogue" here takes the form of split monologue. This internally dialogized, sidesplitting monologist is always on the lookout for loopholes. He can level existing structures, and he generates paradoxes that are explosive, often hilariously so. But these paradoxes seem to lead nowhere. In a sense, one has here the voice of the self-conscious and explicitly self-parodic superfluous man or Westernized intellectual.

The second dialogue or aspect of dialogue is the hint or hope of a transformative relationship where an interanimation of voices may have a regenerative function. The Underground Man both evades and seeks this transformation. This second and more submerged possibility of dialogue is indicated at two important places in the text (which are discussed below). On another level, it may be implied in the relation between the writer and the reader of the text.

These two dialogues and the voices related to them are mutually implicated in a kind of life and death struggle. And the relations among author, narrator, and reader are also complex and multivoiced.

Dostoevsky as author seems to take his distance from the Underground Man at one very strategic place—at the very beginning of the text. But he does so in an imperious and perhaps suspect way. In an introductory note to the title, which is actually signed by Dostoevsky, he seems to reduce the text to a mere document, a detached case history of a representative character of modern times.

> The author of these notes and the "Notes" themselves are, of course, imaginary. Nevertheless, such persons as the writer of these notes, not only may, but positively must, exist in our society, considering those circumstances under which our society was in general formed. I wanted to expose to the public more clearly than it is done usually, one of the characters of the recent past. He is one of the representatives of the current generation. In this excerpt, entitled "Underground," this person introduces himself, his views, and, as it were, tries to explain the reasons

why he appeared and was bound to appear in our midst. In the following excerpt, the actual notes of this person about several events in his life will appear. *Fyodor Dostoevsky.*

In his own name and with the authority of his signature, Dostoevsky thus seems to position himself securely above the mouse-man of the text, the Westernized intellectual caught in traps of his social conditioning and his own morbid making. But the obvious question is whether this note totally masters the work and play of the text by providing an exclusive or privileged way of reading it. For one thing, the note itself may not entirely escape the self-contestatory movements generated by the text, for it may be read as a parodic echo of the beginning of Mikhail Lermontov's *Hero of Our Time* and thus not be taken entirely "straight." One danger of simply taking the note at face value is that this interpretive gesture would deprive the text of much of its force, disimplicate both writer and reader from its challenge, and render nugatory many of its most gripping movements.

At the end of the text, in another complex gesture to which I shall return, distance is again put between the author and the Underground Man in a manner not quite identical to that of the initial note. For the rest of the text, the Underground Man is himself the narrator, speaking in the first person. Yet he does not have a proper name that would clearly attach his "I" to someone whose identity could be underwritten with a signature. This fact adds to the indeterminate status of the narrator-protagonist and furthers his complicity with both the author and the reader. The interactions among Dostoevsky as author, the Underground Man as narrator, and the reader form an intricate network of relations of proximity and distance—even of love and hate.

The narrative is divided into two parts: "The Underground" and "Apropos of Wet Snow."[3] Part One is chiefly a conceptual or theoretical form of discourse in which the Underground

[3]I am using Ralph E. Matlaw's translation of *Notes from Underground* (New York: Dutton, 1960); page numbers are cited in the text.

Man in the present tense reflects or theorizes about consciousness and its (sometimes hilarious) paradoxes. It is like a self-parodic preface to a phenomenology of alienation and resentment. The Underground Man is introduced as a retired civil servant who has, at the age of forty, settled into a rut in life. He has decided, at the threshold of middle age, to reflect on existence, and he gives us his parodic credo. Part Two is largely a narrative of previous events, a story that involves a remembrance of things past, occurrences at the age of twenty-four. It can also be funny, but it is at times serious and searing, especially at the end. Twenty-four is of course another liminal age—the threshold of adult maturity.

The relation between the two parts is an offset superimposition of threshold on threshold. In significant ways the parts seem paradoxically to undercut each other and to exist in a bewildering form of counterpoint, for each part is a suspicious alibi or pretext for the existence of the other. And neither part has a fully cogent *raison d'être*. "Alibi" literally means "in another place," and each part of the *Notes* displaces (or disorients and de-Westernizes) the other and is partially inside its counterpart: there are events in Part One and theorizing in Part Two.

The Underground Man writes Part One to introduce Part Two and Part Two to illustrate Part One. This is the simplest and most commonsensical relation between the parts. Yet the relations between the parts are complex, involving displacement, repression, and even distortion. The text enacts dreamwork, and scenes are often dreamlike. One sign of displacement and distortion is the fact that the servant who appears as an unnamed woman in Part One becomes a man—Apollon—in Part Two. The sex of the servant is reversed as one moves from part to part, and as a male he acquires a name—a name that recalls Apollo.

The problem of displacement and distortion cuts across many levels—that of the relation of consciousness to life, of theory to events, of Part One to Part Two. Hyperconsciousness distorts and displaces life, excessive theory distorts and displaces events, Part One distorts and displaces Part Two, and vice versa. In addition, the excessive theorizing of Part One can be seen as a way of repressing or delaying as well as illuminating—at times artificially or even falsely—the narration of events in Part Two. It is a way of beating about the bush and not getting to the point. But one cannot take the first part as a simple theoretical statement or even as diversionary intellectual free (or fore) play. It is not entirely serious in tenor; it carnivalizes theory, (proleptically) including psychoanalytic theory, which one might be tempted to use uncritically in interpreting the text. And in Part One there is explicit criticism of a fully coherent and comprehensive theory of human behavior.

As for the chronology of the text, Part One is something that occurs after the fact of the events of Part Two. Yet it is placed first in the text; the relation between the time of narration and the time of the narrated phenomena is reversed. And once in each part the broken dialogue that evades issues intimates the possibility of a transformation, though the possibility is quickly sidestepped by the Underground Man: the "Damn Underground" passage and its sequel in the first part (pp. 33ff.); in the second part the suggestion of love with Liza, which is followed by a departure from the narrative past tense and a return to the present tense and the accusatory tone of Part One (pp. 111ff.).

Let us look at these two parts and their relationship more closely. Part One leads to Part Two through the image of wet snow. The condensed and largely theoretical first part thus culminates in an image which, by an apparent process of free association in the remembrance of things past, triggers in the second part a process of recollection of seemingly repressed or avoided events. The image of wet snow is paradoxical, for it joins the two parts with a bond that is as elusive and insubstantial as wet snow itself. Yet the snow fills a gap between the parts and invites us to interpret it. I offer three more or less plausible interpretations suggested by the text—but they do not entirely account for this seemingly aleatory yet necessary image that has the important function of enabling the transition from Part One to Part Two.

First, the wet, yellow, dingy snow is an obvious symbol of

lost purity. Wet snow exists in contrast to a utopia or at least a livable life (what Dostoevsky sometimes refers to as "living life"), a life not distorted by hyperconsciousness, perhaps a life of faith, perhaps something else (a life of both heart and mind?). In the text as we have it, the alternative to wet snow remains as elusive and insubstantial as wet snow itself.

Second, the image of wet snow is related to the writing process. Writing tries to do something with wet snow, to give an account of it: "Today, for instance, I am particularly oppressed by a certain memory from the distant past. It came back to my mind vividly a few days ago, and since then, has remained with me like an annoying tune that one cannot get rid of. And yet I must get rid of it. I have hundreds of such memories, but at times some single one stands out from the hundreds and oppresses me. For some reason I believe that if I write it down I will get rid of it. Why not try?" (p. 36). Writing is thus to exorcize an obsessive image. Yet Part Two begins with a poem by Nicolai Nekrasov that is blatantly an object of parody. Writing thus does not seem to serve the purpose of working through and exorcizing compulsive or obsessive memories related to the events of the second part.

A third thing recalled or brought to mind by wet snow is the polluting potential of the city where falling snow quickly turns to dirt and mud. The urban environment of the Underground Man is the city of Petersburg, and there is an obvious elective affinity between the man and his city. "To be hyperconscious is a disease, a real positive disease. Ordinary human consciousness would be too much for man's everyday needs, that is, half or a quarter of the amount which falls to the lot of a cultivated man of our unfortunate nineteenth century, especially one who has the particular misfortune to inhabit Petersburg, the most abstract and intentional city in the whole world" (p. 6).

Petersburg was literally an abstract and premeditated or intentional city. It was a masterpiece of rationalized urban planning that had no natural foundation: it was built on a bog. And it was illuminated by the northern lights, white lights that Dostoevsky saw as unnatural, demonic. With the white lights, there was no natural rhythm between darkness and light but only continual, eerie illumination. Like his city, the Underground Man is an artificial construct, built on a bog and illuminated by the white lights of a hyperconscious, dissociated lucidity.

The increasing obviousness of these interpretations should serve as a signal that they are not altogether acceptable. The Underground Man seems clearly to be the product of a distorted form of civilization. But in this text the alternative to him is neither a naive utopia of natural simplicity nor a life of unquestioned faith. Nor is the Underground Man a purely negative figure. He is a bewilderingly paradoxical combination of the lowest and the highest in humanity. He is both below and above the statistical norm. The reader is tempted to follow the lead of the introductory authorial note and to see him simply as a case history if not as a convenient scapegoat, but the text brings out his ambivalence in ways that contest giving in to this temptation.

Especially in his weak and evasive side, the Underground Man seems below the common level of humanity. In a more literal translation of the title, he is the man from under the floorboards—a mouse-man. He would, it seems, love to have a fixed identity, even to be known definitively as a lazy person. But he has no clear-cut identity, no "I", and hence his use of the "I" in narration must be paradoxical. His seeming confession avoids the full revelation of himself, which is the ostensible object of the confessional mode. He cannot bare all because he has no "all" to bare. His self or character is split, a fractured nonentity of many contradictory levels and voices. The narrative he employs explores his double or multiple binds. In his ordinary reality, he is abject and desperate, a hole-and-corner man with a perpetual yellow stain on his pants. In his dreams, he is titanic—an overman. Yet his imagination, which fabricates these dreams, is oppressive. It tyrannizes over him. He is perpetually looking at himself as he does something and is petrified by his own look, which internalizes the oppressive look of others. Embittered, frustrated, and resentful in his alienation from society, he tries to make his presence felt and to act by forcing himself on or bumping into others in boorish, ridiculous, or brutal ways. He is forever rattling a non-existent sword. In his inverted existence, suffering and degradation become both masochistic sources of pleasure and sadistic bases for attacks upon others. He is like a stand-up comic of the morbid psyche. At times he is close to being an antiintellectual intellectual who uses logic to destroy logic and who delights in sophistic, self-indulgent, evasive rhetoric.

Yet at least two further points may be made about him. First, his use of irony, parody, and self-parody is in part effective. He does demolish the grounds for narrow, one-sided rationality, closed systems, and simplistic solutions to life's problems. He defends from underground the partially creative force of radical criticism and even of chaos and destruction. He is the bearer of negative capability in a postromantic age, and he insists upon the power of ambivalence and mystery in life's economy. Here his forceful and near hysterical sense of humor plays a crucial role: he laughs and ridicules things into a state that reveals their questionableness. In performing this feat, he is not invidious. He also dismembers, anatomizes, and carnivalizes his own hyperconscious self in a grotesque and convulsive way. He is a lucid juggler, a fool who is diabolical and perhaps a bit holy. At the very least he is unsettling, and he may unsettle the reader. The text can be effective only if the reader *is* unsettled and does not simply look down upon the narrator and his antics.

A second related point is that he may be superior to the unselfconscious reader who relies on simplistic solutions and safe, invidious irony to feel superior to the Underground Man. Baited and berated by his wily adversary, this reader is inclined to carry superficiality to new heights and to rely on ideological complacency to put the Underground Man securely in his place. Yet the Underground Man is already inside this reader in a way that the reader may repress or deny in order to retain a sense of normality and superiority. But the text insistently challenges strategies of avoidance and denial. Not only is the reader actually someone who is reading this book to acquire insight into himself or herself; the reader is made part of the text by the narrative technique itself. The Underground Man addresses the reader as if the reader were a part of himself and of the text. The reader is thus internalized by the Underground Man and may at times be internally persuaded by him. Indeed, the Underground Man and the reader are reciprocally inside one another in an agonistic relation that both courts and evades reciprocity. The force of the text depends upon this mutual internalization and uncanny (non)recognition. If what seems terribly unfamiliar and disconcerting does not register as strangely familiar or at least as inhospitably within the threatened self, the text remains powerless: it makes no claim upon the reader and becomes an inert case history.

In Part One the reader is offered a number of other personae or roles to try on for size—roles even less tenable than that of the Underground Man. These roles or personae are often related to the views of other writers; they are ways the text internalizes other texts or existential options as masks or stylized caricatures. These seeming alternatives to the underground are objects of devastating criticism and uproarious parody: for example, there is the stupid and limited man of action with his relation to the wall; the advocate of the sublime and the beautiful—a parodic version of the romantic beautiful soul; *l'homme de la nature et de la vérité*—a caricature of Rousseau. The obvious question not directly addressed but at least intimated is whether there are other options not so easily reduced to comic-book versions and able to pose more potent challenges to the hyperbolic onslaughts of the Underground Man.

One especially important persona or role model for the reader in Part One is the ideologist who affirms pure, one-sided rationality that eliminates everything questionable in life and reduces all problems to puzzles. As I indicated earlier, a literary and political source for this model is Chernyshevsky in *What Is to Be Done?*—perhaps too easy an adversary for the Underground Man's polemical verve. The images related to this model are those of the organ stop, the piano key, the chicken coop, the crystal palace, the "two plus two" approach to life. The less caricatural and quite "realistic" object of attack here is the tendency toward an exclusive technological rationality that in its very occlusion of any broader and more internally contested version of reason invites seemingly irrational outbursts and self-indulgent yet self-lacerating refusals.

In one sense, the Underground Man lies by saying that he writes only for himself. All his words are uttered with an almost paranoid sideward glance at the reader. Yet in another sense, his statement is true, for he has already taken the reader into his own split self as an alter ego. His very narrative technique is to anticipate what the reader will say; to undercut, frustrate, or provocatively play with the reader's expectation; to put words into the reader's mouth, refuse to let the reader put words into his mouth, and try to end up thumbing his nose, sticking out his tongue, or perhaps even baring his narrative behind at the reader. Often the Underground Man makes the reader play the role of straight man in burlesque and comic scenes—intellectual analogues of a Punch-and-Judy show. But the Underground Man not only intimidates but also fears the reader, for he both dreads and desperately desires the type of understanding or insight into himself that would enable something approximating communication. This very strong form of ambivalence in him prevents his relation to the reader from being reduced to a classical master-slave dialectic. One cannot sketch out stages of inferiority and superiority or clear-cut procedures of domination and subordination in the life-and-death struggle between the Underground Man and his internalized other. Nor is their labile and mutually implicated agon resolvable in some future totality. Whatever is beyond underground that the Underground Man hopes for yet cannot reach would seem to be different both from his way and from a speculatively "dialectical" *Aufhebung* of it.

In the story itself, the highly complex figure of Apollon is like the reader in certain ways. In a sense he is another persona or mask—an alter ego—internalized by the Underground Man as a fluid projection of himself. Apollon is a servant who is his master's master, yet he has at best a paradoxical, inconclusive master-slave relation to the Underground Man. He is a retainer who should serve the master but who judges him and is tyrannical instead. He is like the Apollonian in relation to the Dionysian, or the superego in relation to the id. He is, however, also part of the Underground Man's fragmented self. At times he even seems like a hallucination or at least a very shadowy figure in a dreamlike world. He is related to the question of distortion, but he is also a belated carnivalesque figure and a mask—a servant who at times behaves like a master in a topsy-turvy world that is devoid of any regulated collective rhythm of social life wherein institutionalized carnival might alternate with work and ordinary life. The Underground Man and Apollon must play it by ear, and their almost Beckettian vis-à-vis, in its shifting, surly, and pathetic interdependence, threatens to be emblematic of relations in general.

The critique of a total system, particularly one of utility or advantage, receives an intriguing (and shockingly contemporary) textual development in section 7 of Part One. "Oh, tell me, who first declared, who first proclaimed, that man only does nasty things because he does not know his own real interests; and that if he were enlightened, if his eyes were opened to his real normal interests, man would at once cease to do nasty things, would at once become good and noble because, being enlightened and understanding his real advantage, he would see his own advantage in the good and nothing else, and we all know that not a single man can knowingly act to his own disadvantage" (p. 18). Whoever the first proclaimer of these enlightened tidings may have been, they bring the name of Socrates immediately to mind. "Oh, the babe! Oh, the pure, innocent child!" exclaims the Underground Man, and he is off on his histrionic yet impassioned dismemberment of the "advantage" theory of systematic closure:

> Why, in the first place, when in all these thousands of years has there ever been a time when man has acted only for his own advantage? What is to be done with the millions of facts that bear witness that men, *knowingly*, that is, fully understanding their real advantages, have left them in the background and have rushed headlong on another path, to risk, to chance, compelled to this course by nobody and by nothing, but, as it were, precisely because they did not want the beaten track, and stubbornly, wilfully, went off on another difficult, absurd way seeking it almost in the darkness. [Pp. 18–19]

After this pathos-charged invocation of the empirical resistance to closure (which is not fixated as a uniquely modern
or modernist phenomenon), the Underground Man raises more
conceptual and definitional questions: "Advantage! What is
advantage? And will you take it upon yourself to define with
perfect accuracy in exactly what the advantage of man consists
of? And what if it so happens that a man's advantage *sometimes* not only may, but even must, consist exactly in his
desiring under certain conditions what is harmful to himself
and not what is advantageous" (p. 19). This quasi-philosophical
outburst recalls the earlier invocation of masochistic pleasure
in pain, "enjoyment [. . .] in the hyperconsciousness of one's
own degradation," with no possibility of escape or change for
the better (p. 7). In the face of anticipated laughter as the
ridiculing response of his interlocutor, the narrator plays his
trump card: "Why does it happen that all these statisticians,
sages and lovers of humanity, when they calculate human advantages invariably leave one out? They don't even take it into
their calculation in the form in which it should be taken, and
the whole reckoning depends upon that. There would be no
great harm to take it, this advantage, and to add it to the list.
But the trouble is, that this strange advantage does not fall
under any classification and does not figure in any list" (p. 19).

The supplementary advantage that gives the slip to any system of classification paradoxically leads the narrator to the
question of the "one most advantageous advantage (the very
one omitted of which we spoke just now) which is more important and more advantageous than all other advantages" (p. 20).
The paradox here is that to name this advantage would bring it
under the very system that it presumably eludes—a quasi-the-
ological situation. Faced with this double bind, the narrator
defers mentioning the "most advantageous advantage" and
teases the reader with its delayed disclosure. Then, at the end
of section 7, he apparently does name it:

One's own free unfettered choice, one's own fancy, however wild
it may be, one's own fancy worked up at times to frenzy—why
that is the "most advantageous advantage" which we have overlooked, which comes under no classification and through which

all systems and theories are continually thrown to the devil. And
how do these sages know that man must necessarily need a ra-
tionally advantageous choice? What man needs is simply *independent* choice, whatever that independence may cost and wher-
ever it may lead. Well, choice after all, the devil only knows. . .
[P. 23]

Reducing radical desire to need and naming the "most advantageous advantage" would seem to encompass the supplementary play of excess and lack within the system it de-
constructs and displaces. Yet the manner in which the
"advantage" is named keeps both its contestatory force and its
dubiousness in play. Choice itself is taken to the extreme point
of wildness and frenzy, thus transgressing the boundaries implied by choice and naming. Independence itself is stressed
with a simplicity that would seem indistinguishable from intransigently obdurate irresponsibility. The section ends with a
seemingly aimless ellipsis and a deferment of knowledge to the
proverbial devil. Yet in this movement, "choice" has been returned to "chance," which is where the section began before
the invocation of the "most advantageous advantage." Thus
the revelation is itself *trompe-l'oeil*, and what narrative expectation led one to believe would be an ultimate disclosure or a
fully convincing argument becomes caught up in repetition.
What is notoriously absent between "chance" and "choice," as
both mediation and supplement, is precisely a flexible yet
binding structure of relationships or an institutional network
of norms and roles that might enable social life to achieve a
"livable" rhythm countering both abstract, totalizing systems
and the appeal of absolute risk or chance/choice. Given this
significant absence, a restless critical animus agitates thought
and destroys false "utopian" solutions, but nothing construc-
tive may arise as an alternative to the given, however limited
in effect, self-critical in nature, and open to contestatory forces
such an alternative must remain. To offer the "filling in" of
this absence as a "total solution" to the problems explored in
the text would be to encase it in precisely the kind of utilitarian or sociologistic armature that it effectively dismantles.
To avoid posing the institutional and social problem as related

to a significant modification of the terms explored in the text would be to remain unquestioningly within its limits, turns, and aporetic impasses.

Yet I have already intimated that, especially at two points, the broken but at times critical and funny dialogue activated in the text seems on the verge of exploding, and the momentary hope of a more regenerative dialogue is hinted at, only to be avoided by the Underground Man. Toward the end of Part One, before the appearance of the image of wet snow, the Underground Man seems close to self-insight but immediately resorts to defensiveness, shying away from reciprocity with the reader. "I know myself as surely as two times two makes four, that it is not at all underground that is better, but something different, quite different, for which I long but which I cannot find! Damn underground!" (p. 33). The intrusion of a self-parodic reference to the "two times two" philosophy of life introduces a dissonant note, but the exclamatory force of this statement is still insistent.

In Part Two, in a somewhat analogous place in the text, one has Liza, who also seems to damn the underground and to represent a genuine possibility of communication and self-insight through love. Her potential as a saving grace is enhanced by the fact that it comes after the hysterically ridiculous failure of human contact in the *pas de deux* with the boorish officer on the Nevsky prospect and the abortive scene of renewed friendship with Zverkov and company. Liza, genuinely taken in by the bookish words and fictitious poses of the Underground Man, suffers in a self-sacrificing way that promises hope. She is of course the pure prostitute, and the unavoidable question is whether she is too stereotyped to be altogether credible as the carrier of redemption. Indeed, she too may be read as a parody of a character in Chernyshevsky's *What Is to Be Done?* And the Nekrasov poem that introduces Part Two announces the love scene in an extremely deflationary fashion. Yet, in her love, Liza does seem to have gone beyond the man of resentment, and the Underground Man resents this very fact. Liza makes him feel like a fool because she seems willing to accept him with all his foolishness.

In a gratuitous act that is premeditated but unmotivated, the

Underground Man refuses her offer of a seemingly saving love: he places money in her hand and reduces her act to the gesture of a prostitute. As the Underground Man himself puts it, "I can say this for certain: though I did that cruel thing purposely, it was not an impulse from the heart, but came from my evil brain. This cruelty was so affected, so purposely made up, so completely a product of the brain, of *books*, that I could not keep it up for a minute—first I rushed to the corner to avoid seeing her, and then in shame and despair rushed after Liza" (p. 112). Of course, it is too late for the Underground Man. But it is noteworthy that his most vile act is not a product of pure unreason or excess. Rather it has a false model and amounts to a resentful literary gesture—an act of cruelty committed without cruelty.

In a letter to his brother, Dostoevsky intimates that the censors deleted a passage in which he gave his own religious idea of an alternative to the underground. In Part One, section 10 there had been a passage stating that the Underground Man could have been saved by faith and Christ.[4] The obvious question is whether this solution would have seemed highly out of place in the context of the *Notes*, especially if it were not developed in a compelling way, as it is to some extent in *The Brothers Karamazov*. The censors may unknowingly have acted like good literary critics here, although they were probably concerned with eliminating what might have seemed contaminated by blasphemy in such a text. In any case, it is significant that Dostoevsky did not reinsert the deleted passages in subsequent editions of the *Notes*. In the text we have, the path not taken comes in the form of human love and compassion without religious sanction—the offer of love by Liza, an offer warped by its stereotypical frame and outrageously implausible in nature but moving nonetheless.

With Liza gone, the style of the Underground Man toward

---

[4] "Those swinish censors left in the passages where I railed at everything and *pretended* to blaspheme; but they deleted passages where I deduced from all this the *necessity of faith and Christ*. What are they doing, those censors? Are they in league against the government, or something?" (quoted in Matlaw's translation, p. 195).

the end of Part Two reverts to the style of Part One. He writes in the present tense and becomes direct, didactic, and accusatory in addressing or even indicting the reader. He seems to be forcing on the reader the realization that he or she too carries around an encrypted Underground Man.

> Even now, many years later, I somehow remember all this as very bad. I have many bad memories now, but—hadn't I better end my "Notes" here? I believe I made a mistake in beginning to write this *story;* so it's hardly literature so much as corrective punishment. After all, to tell long stories, for example, showing how I have ruined my life by morally rotting in my corner, through lack of fitting environment, through divorce from reality, and vainglorious spite in my underground, would certainly not be interesting; a novel needs a hero, and all the traits of an anti-hero are *expressly* gathered together here, and what matters most, it all produces an unpleasant impression, for we are all divorced from life, we are all cripples, every one of us, more or less. We are all so far divorced from it that we immediately feel a sort of loathing for actual "real life," and so cannot even stand to be reminded of it. After all, we have reached the point of almost looking at actual "real life" as an effort, almost as hard work, and we are all privately agreed that it is better in books. And why do we sometimes fret, why are we perverse and ask for something else? We don't know why ourselves. It would be worse for us if our capricious requests were granted. [P. 114.]

The wary reader might well ask what "actual 'real life'" (or "living life") means, especially in the mouth of the Underground Man, and whether it transcends all the problems explored by him in this far-from-bookish text. It would be easy to agree that "it would be worse for us if our capricious requests were granted." But the statement that we are all crippled, more or less, has a strong impact even if the reader might object to being called a cripple by a cripple who may still be projecting and trying to engender complicity with the reader. Still, these penultimate statements seem forceful because they are the only instances where the dark prince of obliqueness and indirection drops his ironic pose and makes direct and rather pathetic statements. Indeed, these are statements that might open him up to ironic counterattack by a reader whom he, in accordance with his own skewed pedagogical imperative, has helped to educate. For here he seems to expose his face and not simply his behind. To the last, however, the Underground Man anticipates the response of the reader and, unable to shut up, continues:

> "Speak for yourself," you will say, "and for your miseries in your underground holes, but don't dare to say 'all of us.'" Excuse me, gentlemen, after all I do not mean to justify myself with that "all of us." As for what concerns me in particular I have only, after all, in my life carried to an extreme what you have not dared to carry halfway, and what's more, you have taken your cowardice for good sense, and have found comfort in deceiving yourselves. So that perhaps, after all, there is more "life" in me than in you. [P. 115]

In this rather didactic rejoinder, the Underground Man invokes Dostoevsky's highest value—living life. And in rather biblical tones, he seems to appeal to the story of the Good Samaritan, the story of an alien who is closer to virtue than the upright religious officials who pass by a person in need. In any event, toward the end of the text, Dostoevsky seems close to the Underground Man, seems to side with him in the accusations he hurls at the complacent reader enjoying feelings of superiority. But "life" in the passage I just quoted is itself in quotes, as is "real life" (or "living life") in the earlier passage—indicating that Dostoevsky is not willing to place his values in the Underground Man's mouth in an unqualified way. And after this passage, distance is taken from the Underground Man in a manner different from but reminiscent of the author's gesture in the note to the title of the text. The question is whether in these gestures Dostoevsky opens the possibility for a "dialogue" or exchange with the reader who does not feel securely superior to the Underground Man but who does agree that something different is desirable.

The last words of the text follow a break (indicated by a line in the Matlaw translation): "The 'notes' of this paradoxicalist do not end here, however. He could not resist and continued them. But it also seems to me that we may stop here" (p. 115). There is no ending to the notes of the Underground Man. After evading the possibility (however problematic) of a certain kind of "ending" in love, there is no ending to the infinite series of paradoxes and vicious circles he can generate. The Underground Man may go on cutting capers until he kicks off. The text has no satisfying ending, and so it is arbitrarily terminated. Yet an arbitrary termination may paradoxically be the only plausible ending to this kind of text—one that, like the image of wet snow, is both aleatory and necessary.

This terminal passage has a clear shift in voice, but the direction of the shift is not clear. Unlike the introductory note, the final passage bears no signature. Who terminates the text as the great liquidator? Who are the "me" and the "we" referred to in the seeming *hors-texte?* Who contractually agrees to stop here? One can give no self-certain and definite answer to these questions. In a sense, language has come to its limits, at least in this discursive context. One might, however, suggest that this "ending" that is not an ending terminates the complicity between the author and the Underground Man and opens up the possibility of a relationship between the (reversible roles of) writer and reader in the context of a more general "textuality." (Indeed, it is dubious to continue, as I have done, to follow the established convention of employing the name, "the Underground Man," to designate the narrator, for it gives him a nominal consistency and a semblance of a unified self that the text itself questions and that the concluding passage obliterates.)

The text of the *Notes* provides no answers to the questions it raises; it restricts itself to intimations of the need for another way. Marking its own limits, it thus refuses any purely symbolic or cathartic solution to the problems it has explored with hyperbolic insistence and intensity. But in shifting grounds and opening the text to a problematic writer-reader relation that is emblematic of relations "outside" this text (in its delimited and conventional specificity), this parodic, paradoxical, and extremely "modern" text may come close to older forms of parable from which it differs markedly—notably in its self-conscious difficulty in coming to an end.

3

In Quest of Casaubon:

George Eliot's *Middlemarch*

Curious to turn from Shakespeare to Isaac Casaubon, his contemporary.

George Eliot, *"Middlemarch" Notebooks*

Richard Ellmann, whose psychological and biographical approach to the figure of Edward Casaubon can hardly be said to be on the cutting edge of contemporary critical thought, justifies his analysis in these terms: "George Eliot, contrary to T. S. Eliot, made no claims for the impersonality of the artist. She confided that her first work of fiction, *Scenes of Clerical Life*, drew upon family reminiscences, and many characters from her books have been pursued to prototypes in her experience, often with her help. She worked from models then, probably habitually."[1]

Ellmann proposes a series of biographical models for Casaubon. These figures share some significant traits with the fictional character, although they differ from him in other ways. Ellmann notes that the man most often mentioned as prototype for Casaubon is Mark Pattison, rector of Lincoln College, Oxford. Pattison was unhappily married to a younger woman, and he wrote "a life of the Swiss scholar (of the sixteenth century) Isaac Casaubon." Ellmann adds that "George

[1]Richard Ellmann, "Dorothea's Husbands," in George Eliot, *Middlemarch* (1872–73; New York: Norton, 1977), p. 751. Further references to Ellmann's discussion as well as to Eliot's novel will be to this edition, hereafter cited in the text as *MM*.

Eliot obviously borrowed from him the name of his subject" (p. 751). Other contenders for the role of prototype include Herbert Spencer, whom Ellmann thinks an unlikely model, given both his eminent reputation at the time and his regard for George Eliot as "the greatest woman who ever lived" (p. 752); Dr. R. H. Brabant, who intended to eliminate the supernatural from religion in an epochmaking study that he was unable to bring to fruition; Robert William Mackay, whose *Progress of the Intellect as Exemplified in the Religious Development of the Greeks and Hebrews* (1850) was reviewed by Eliot in terms that anticipate both Casaubon's search for a "Key to all Mythologies" and criticisms of that project, such as Will Ladislaw's comment that "he [Casaubon] is not an Orientalist, you know" (quoted, p. 754). The last candidate for the role of Casaubon's model is George Eliot herself, for she harbored a Casaubon within her as did Flaubert his Madame Bovary. Ellmann sees Eliot as trying in particular to exorcise the Casaubon who in his "sexual insufficiency" stands for the "fruitless fantasies" of an erotic sort that had been stimulated in the young evangelical Eliot herself by the reading of novels (p. 757). This "psychoanalytic" (if somewhat Bovaresque) interpretation of Casaubon as a fictional whipping boy for novelistically induced girlish desire is, however, left on a rather vague and suggestive level: Ellmann supports it only through an analogy between the "images of darkness" in Eliot's early accounts of her childhood erotic fantasies and the imagery used to characterize Casaubon in the novel.

In contrast to Ellmann's approach, Neil Hertz's "Recognizing Casaubon" may seem to be not only at but perhaps beyond the cutting edge of contemporary criticism.[2] For while Ellmann's assertions threaten to be crudely reductive and are formulated with almost schematic boldness, Hertz's analyses are so subtle and suggestive that they become sources of continually renewed reflection. Thus any attempt to "summarize" Hertz's account would itself be an inducement to fruit-

[2]In *The End of the Line* (New York, 1985), pp. 75–96 (hereafter cited in the text as Hertz).

less fantasy. One way to approach it, however, is in terms of the seemingly similar operations it performs on two rather different appreciations of *Middlemarch:* J. Hillis Miller's "deconstructive" analyses, particularly in his essays "Narrative and History" and "Optic and Semiotic in *Middlemarch,"* and Richard Ellmann's psychobiographical approach to which I have referred above.

Of Miller's readings, Hertz writes:

> Casaubon, he notes, "is a text, a collection of signs which Dorothea misreads, according to that universal propensity for misinterpretation which infects all the characters in *Middlemarch."* Miller is right about Casaubon, but the point he would make is still more inclusive: he is arguing for a reading of the novel that would see every character as simultaneously an interpreter (the word is a recurrent one in *Middlemarch*) and a text available for the interpretations (plural, always partial, and often in conflict) of others. [. . .] Miller's argument is persuasive, and the reading of the novel he sketches is a bold and attractive one: he takes *Middlemarch* to be simultaneously affirming the values of Victorian humanism which it has been traditionally held to affirm— for example, a belief in the consistence of the self as a moral agent—and systematically undercutting those values, offering in place of an ethically stable notion of the self the somewhat less reassuring figure of a focus of semiotic energy, receiving and interpreting signs, itself a "cluster of signs" more or less legible. Miller's movement towards this poised, deconstructive formulation, however, is condensed and rapid, and may still leave one wondering how those two notions of the self are held in suspension in the novel, and what the commerce is between them. [Hertz, pp. 77–78]

Hertz attempts to slow down and expand Miller's reading, and while his account may serve to intensify one's wonder over the relation between the "ethically stable self" and the "less reassuring figure of a focus of semiotic energy," he intends to dwell on the figure of Casaubon and to ask "what it might mean, if *all* the characters of *Middlemarch* may be thought of as texts or as clusters of signs, for the signs of textuality to cluster so thickly around one particular name"—a name that seems to mark "a quasi-allegorical figure, the personification of the dead letter, the written word" (Hertz, p. 78). He immediately digresses, however, to turn to passages in which Eliot herself is the figure "around which are clustered the signs of egotism and writing," and his inquiry into Eliot's own anxiety about the egotistical messiness and "hieroglyphic indecipherability" (Hertz, p. 79) of her handwriting leads him to a consideration of Ellmann's interpretation:

> Richard Ellmann, for example, has found in the language associated with Casaubon echoes of images linked, in an early letter, with the novelist's fears of her own erotic fantasizing. "The severity with which Casaubon is treated," Ellman [sic] speculates, "would then derive from her need to exorcise this part of her experience. [. . .] To berate Casaubon, and to bury him, was to overcome in transformed state the narcissistic sensuality of her adolescence." To seek an author's personal allegory behind the realistic surface she has woven is often as unrewarding as it is methodologically dubious, but in the case of George Eliot's works, because they are explicitly about the imagining of others—about the status of the image of one person in the imagining mind of another—the play between the imaginer and the imagined, between author and character, and the possibility of narcissistic confusion developing between the one and the other, has already been thematized and made available for interpretations such as Ellmann's. If anything, his claims are too modest; what he presents as a contingent psychobiographical detail—an author's uneasiness about her own "narcissism"—may be read as neither contingent nor primarily biographical, but as part of a sustained and impersonal questioning of the grounds of fiction. [Hertz, p. 82]

Hertz thus suggests a radicalization of Ellmann's approach that would have it converge with a rendition of Miller's deconstructive reading. The point of convergence would be pursued through an inquiry into the imagination as the uncanny force relating the author and fictional objects. Hertz focuses upon the threat of narcissism as hermetic enclosure in projective images of the self—something Eliot fears in herself and thematizes in the novel, in good part through the figure of Casaubon. Yet he seems to assume that Dorothea is able to overcome her own "narcissism" and to "recognize" Casaubon, although such (ethically stabilizing) "recognition" may come at the cost of domesticating the disorienting yet "sublime" cascade of images that threaten to overwhelm her during her wedding trip to Rome. The very passage Hertz quotes on the way to this gloss (a passage to which I shall recur) seems to leave in doubt whether Dorothea ever quite manages to take this step beyond herself and whether Casaubon is ever "recognized" at all:

> Today she has begun to see that she had been under a wild illusion in expecting a response to her feeling from Mr. Casaubon, and she had felt the waking of a presentiment that there might be a sad consciousness in his life which made as great a need on his side as on her own.
>   We are all of us born in moral stupidity, taking the world as an udder to feed our supreme selves: Dorothea had early begun to emerge from that stupidity, but yet it had been easier for her to imagine how she would devote herself to Mr. Casaubon, and become wise and strong in his strength and wisdom, than to conceive with that distinctness which is no longer reflection but feeling—an idea wrought back to the directness of sense, like the solidity of objects—that he had an equivalent centre of self, whence the lights and shadows must always fall with a certain difference. [Quoted in Hertz, p. 83]

Recognition would seem to depend upon a tenuous and endangered ability (perhaps a stabilizing "stupidity") that enables one to mediate two complementary pathologies of the imagination: narcissistic self-enclosure *and* total empathetic expenditure of the self. Without discussing whether the relation between the pathologies of narcissism and total empathy might bear upon the interplay between the ethically stable and the "semiotically" shifty self, toward the end of his analysis Hertz does touch upon the threat and temptation of total empathy, but he does so without recognizing it as such. Rather, the reference is made in his treatment of a seemingly feverish crescendo of "sublime" moments in chapters 20 and 21 of the novel; he includes this famous passage: "If we had a keen vision and a feeling for all ordinary human life, it would be like hearing the grass grow and the squirrel's heart beat, and we should die of that roar on the other side of silence. As it is the quickest of us walk about well wadded in stupidity" (quoted in Hertz, p. 92).

Hertz contends that "the sublimity of the image of the roar on the other side of silence emerges from the thoroughly negative insight" into the "fictitiousness and willfulness of such identifications" between author and character (p. 95). This image of the sublime rising projectively from the abysmal depths of narcissism indicates how Hertz's essay itself may be read as a provocative attempt to combine the decorum and poise of more traditionally elegant style, characteristic of a critic such as Miller, with the reading strategies of Paul de Man—no mean feat of critical transfusion. Referring to his earlier discussion of the novel's grammatological depiction of Casaubon's own circulatory system, Hertz concludes: "If, for example, one were to bring a drop of Casaubon's blood into focus, one might see nothing but semicolons and parentheses. That is the possibility that is written into *Middlemarch* in the idiom of the sublime; it is clearly not a possibility to be steadily contemplated by a working novelist—it must be repressed if books like *Middlemarch* are to be written at all. One sign of that repression is the recognition and exorcism of Casaubon" (Hertz, pp. 95–96). Here Casaubon seems to become the very materiality of the signifier, which prompts strangely disconcerting doubt about whether the sign is a sign and signifies anything at all or whether, suspended between narcissistic self-enclosure and empathetic self-evacuation, it is rather an uncanny stimulus to the madness of empty repetition and to life in a "quite different world from other people" (in Locke's phrase, which Hertz quotes).

I think that the danger in Hertz's fascinating analysis is that it threatens to take what is indeed a recurrent possibility and to fixate it in an ahistorical, essentializing manner, thus giving it an ideological status. I would like to try to situate the threats of empty repetition and "sublime" disorientation in a textual and contextual manner that—without simply domesticating such threats (and temptations)—does imply the historical possibility of significant variations in the sociocultural and political interaction of meaning and its contestatory "others." In the process, I would like both to arrive at a somewhat different general apprehension of the figure of Casaubon and to trace more closely what might be called the narration of this figure, including the specific modulations of the "sublime," in the text of *Middlemarch*.

I would like to begin at a place that to my knowledge has received no critical attention: the historical figure of Isaac Casaubon and what he has been argued to represent, for this figure is a significant point of comparison and partial contrast with the fictional Casaubon—a point that provides some insight into the larger historical situation of the latter. Mark Pattison's own *Isaac Casaubon 1559–1614*[3] was first published in 1875, a few years after *Middlemarch*, so there is no question of its having been a "source book" for the novel. But aside from the possibility that Pattison discussed his views with Eliot, his treatment of Isaac Casaubon provides what may still be the standard view of the latter's historical role and significance; in any case, it may be used for one set of "intertextual" comparisons.

Pattison's biography presents the life of Casaubon largely as a heroic, stoical struggle toward impressive erudition and scholarly acclaim. Isaac was the son of a Huguenot pastor who had to "fly to the hills in the Reign of Terror" in France (Pattison p. 49). He was born in Geneva and in time taught at the university there. "It was its moral intensity, more than its pure orthodoxy, which gave Geneva the lead of the calvinistic churches and caused its schools to be sought from all parts. [. . .] Vice and luxury here were criminal offenses. Casaubon's lectures are coloured, without being corrupted, by the same tone" (Pattison, p. 46). Casaubon did not disdain professorial

[3]Oxford, 1892, hereafter cited in the text as Pattison.

teaching in the manner of his friend and fellow *érudit* Joseph Scaliger, but his heart, like Scaliger's, was in research. Of special note among the long series of editions and other publications he put forth was his *De rebus sacris et ecclesiasticis exercitationis XVI*, a close examination and critique of the first half of the first volume of Cesare Baronius's twelve-volume *Annales Ecclesiastici*. (He had intended to extend his parasitic critique to all twelve volumes of the work of the Catholic Counter-Reformation scholar, but he was mercifully interrupted by death.)

Pattison situates Casaubon's critique of Baronius in this way:

> At the opening of the seventeenth century the relative position of the two religious parties was reversed. The catholic party had recovered, and more than recovered, their ascendency in the west of Europe. It was a moral ascendency over opinion of which they now found themselves possessed, an ascendency founded on superiority of numbers and wealth, but intensified by religious zeal. They were in fact making way to intellectual preponderance. At this moment appeared Baronius' "Annals." A work of such vast compass, dealing with an important theme [ecclesiastical history] would have been, at any time, a considerable phenomenon in the literary world. Appearing at the moment it did, it had the significance not of a mere literary publication, but of a political event. The [Protestant] "Centuries" had shown the history of the church as the growth of the spirit of evil waxing through successive ages, till it was consummated in the reign of anti-Christ. Baronius exhibited the visible unity and impeccable purity of the church founded upon Peter, and handed down inviolate, such at this day as it had ever been. The whole case of the romanists, and especially the supremacy of the see of Rome, was here set out, under the form of authentic annals, with an imposing array of pièces justificatives, of original documents which were inaccessible to the protestant centuriators, and extinguished their meagre citations from familiar and printed books. The unsupported theory of the protestant history is refuted by the mere weight of facts. [. . .] The "Annals" transferred to the catholic party the preponderance in the field of learning, which ever since Erasmus had been on the side of the innovators. It was the turn of the protes-

tants to feel the urgent need of an antidote to Baronius. [Pattison, pp. 325–26]

Baronius's undertaking had the full support of the Catholic Church, and the Protestant cause, "exterminated in southern Europe, ground to dust in France, threatened with violence in Germany," had need of a defender. That figure did not emerge in either Holland or Britain. "There was only one man who possessed the knowledge requisite; he was some way past fifty, and exhausted by a life of desk-work. Yet Casaubon resolutely girded himself for the fray" (Pattison, p. 326).

Baronius had answered the popular demand, after a period of destructive criticism, for a renewed "desire to believe, this pious wish to have the legend authenticated"—a wish serving the interests of the Catholic church. Casaubon did not provide a counterhistory but turned to the only tools available to him, those of historical criticism, leaving room for a faith in a hidden, transcendental divinity: "A protestant history, which had no saints, no miracles, could have no success. History cannot be negative, it must have something to narrate. All that was possible therefore for Casaubon was criticism" (Pattison, p. 328). This he accomplished in an incisive if not completely convincing manner, for Baronius was indeed open to critical historical attack. His errors were not local mistakes but deep-seated faults of scholarship: he "was not in possession of the elements of learning. He knew no hebrew, no greek. He was totally destitute of the critical skill which is implied in dealing with ancient authors, so as to elicit their meaning. In fact this vast historical edifice, with its grand front and stately chambers, was a house of cards, which a breath of criticism would demolish in a moment" (Pattison, p. 329).

Casaubon readily disclosed Baronius's deficiencies in classical learning and his propensity to use apocryphal literature and fabulous history as if it were factual. But Casaubon's own efforts had major defects. Pattison saw the form of the work as especially responsible for the fact that "it was not a decisive triumph. The 'Exercitations' are a collection of detached notes on the 'Annals.' They follow the order of the 'Annals,' but have no other connection than the chronological sequence. There is no common thread of argument to give unity to the composition" (Pattison, p. 331). There was also a fault of execution: Casaubon went from critical scholarship, where he was on firm ground, to "theological controversy, thus forsaking the vantage ground of learning, and letting himself down on that of mere opinion" (Pattison, p. 333). In contrasting Casaubon with his English contemporary Lancelot Andrewes, Pattison also comments on the former's "dull matter-of-fact style," but he adds that "from a single one of the 'Exercitations' there is more to be learned than from the whole volume of [Andrewes's witty] 'Tortura Torti'" (Pattison, p. 334).

Pattison does not remain only on his own somewhat anachronistic nineteenth-century positivistic ground in criticizing Casaubon; he also notes contemporary criticisms and Casaubon's own sense of unfulfilled promise: "No one was less satisfied with his work than the author himself. . . . The single volume of the 'Exercitations' is all that was ever realized of the vast schemes of ecclesiastical history which had been conceived in the Genevan period, and which had been postponed, but never given up. [. . .] How sad must have appeared to himself the contrast between the promise and the performance eighteen years later" (p. 340).

Frances Yates, from her own perspective, adds another dimension to Casaubon's work, which Pattison only touches upon and clearly subordinates to the struggle of Catholics and Protestants and the emergence of "scientific" scholarship. For Pattison,

[Casaubon] constantly notices Baronius' recourse to apochryphal authorities, but it was not in him to take his stand on the broad principle of historical investigation, and to require that church history should be subjected to the same rigid scrutiny as all history. If he expresses a doubt of Hydaspes, Hermes, and the Sybilline oracles, it is not on critical grounds, but on the a priori improbability that God would have allowed the Gentiles to have a fuller prevision of the gospel revelation than was granted to the Jews. [Pattison, p. 335]

For Yates, however, Casaubon's work was also epochmaking in its debunking of the Hermetic and alchemical traditions—itself a significant factor in the rise of "positive" science. What was a subordinate reference, illustrating another point in Pattison, becomes a focus of attention in Yates:

> Some discoveries of basic importance for the history of thought seem to pass relatively unnoticed. No one speaks of the "pre-Casaubon era" or of the "post-Casaubon era" and yet the dating by Isaac Casaubon in 1614 of the Hermetic writings as not the work of a very ancient Egyptian priest but written in post-Christian times, is a watershed separating the Renaissance world from the modern world. It shattered at one blow the build-up of Renaissance Neoplatonism with its basis in the *prisci theologici* of whom Hermes Trismegistus was the chief. It shattered the whole position of the Renaissance Magus and Renaissance magic with its Hermetic-Cabalist foundation, based on the ancient "Egyptian" philosophy and Cabalism. It shattered even the non-magical Christian Hermetic movement of the sixteenth century. It shattered the position of an extremist Hermetist, such as Giordano Bruno had been, whose whole platform of a return to a better "Egyptian" pre-Judaic and pre-Christian philosophy and magical religion was exploded by the discovery that the writings of the holy ancient Egyptian must be dated, not only long after Moses but also long after Christ. It shattered, too, the basis of all attempts to build a natural theology on Hermetism, such as that to which [Tommaso] Campanella had pinned his hopes.
>
> Casaubon's bomb-shell did not immediately take effect and there were many who ignored it, or refused to believe it, and clung obstinately to the old obsessions. Nevertheless, though other factors were working strongly against the Renaissance traditions in the seventeenth century, Casaubon's discovery must, I think, be reckoned as one of the factors, and an important one, in releasing seventeenth-century thinkers from magic.[4]

The initial tones of Yates's defense of the importance of the obscure and overlooked are reminiscent of Eliot's own apologies for close scrutiny of the less visible and canonical aspects

[4]Frances A. Yates, *Giordano Bruno and the Hermetic Tradition* (Chicago, 1964), pp. 398–99.

of life. Of course, it is doubtful that Eliot could have arrived at such a far-ranging, well-nigh apocalyptic appreciation of the significance of Casaubon's work, although the contrast in her notebooks between Isaac Casaubon and Shakespeare is at least suggestive in this respect.[5] The textual point I would make, however, is that the fictional figure of Casaubon in *Middlemarch* is a complex composite type combining (whether or not intentionally on the part of George Eliot) features of the putative historical Casaubon and of his adversaries such as Baronius, on the one hand, and of Hermetic-alchemical figures, on the other. In all respects, however, he is an epigone—a late, reduced model and a "decadent" form symptomatic of larger historical transformations. He faces Isaac Casaubon's problem of fragmentation and predominantly critical, indeed parasitic, knowledge in an even more marked manner. Unlike his namesake, he no longer experiences the bond linking religious motivation, sociopolitical implication, and scholarly research; his knowledge has become purely intellectual and critical, and it lacks any larger rationale—social, political, or religious. It is a small, autonomized, clockwork mechanism accompanied by anxiety about its meaning and value.

It is, moreover, dissociated from his position as a cleric. Indeed, the specifically religious part of Edward Casaubon's ministry receives little attention in the novel, and the nature of his knowledge is implicitly compared in a disparaging way to the medical vocation of Lydgate or even to the witty practicality of Farebrother. He is also unlike Isaac Casaubon—the individual whom Joseph Scaliger believed to be the most learned man in Europe—in that he is an amateur without even the necessary training and skills to pursue his scholarly avocation successfully. Like Baronius, he lacks sufficient learning (in his case knowledge of German scholarship and "Orientalist" research),

---

[5]The epigraph to this essay may be found in *George Eliot's "Middlemarch" Notebooks*, ed. John Clark Pratt and Victor A. Neufeldt (Berkeley, Calif., 1979), p. 160. The fact that the Hermetic treatises were products of the Western, Christianized, neo-Platonic tradition and not of a discrete, totally alien tradition antedating it may be read as a sign of adversarial "others" or contestatory "voices" *within* this complex tradition—not simply outside it.

and he is prone to mingle fact and fiction, thus having his study of mythology become mythomorphic. He even, as we shall see, reveals traits of the degraded alchemist blindly seeking the philosopher's stone. Indeed these dangers to "positive" scholarship would seem endemic in his very quest for a unified key to all mythologies demonstrating "that all the mythical fragments in the world were corruptions of a tradition originally revealed" (p. 14)—a quest more metaphysical than scientific.

The very untimeliness and impossibility of Casaubon's quest, however, also give it the potential for sublimity and tragic grandeur. Because of both his historical situation and his personal limitations, he is able to produce only pamphlets, "small monumental records of his march"—or 'Parerga' as he called them"—not the magisterial treatise he dimly envisions (p. 193). His one source of potentially traumatizing anxiety— the one narrow font of passion that takes him outside himself and threatens to overwhelm his aloofness, distance, and self-contained rigidity—is his "writer's block," his self-doubting inability to produce the work that might, on however dissociated a formal basis, provide a measure of justification for his existence. This anxiety, with the historical and personal freight it bears, is the more specific vehicle for any undecidability or even emptiness of signification he may represent. Yet his quest takes him beyond the realm of the narrow specialist who works only on problems that may be solved, and it casts another light on the very fragmentariness and incompletion that plague his project. His intellectual timidity and spiritual dwarfishness resonate with the times in curtailing the sublimity of what might conceivably be a *beau désastre*. In his first long speech Casaubon himself admits, "I live too much with the dead. My mind is something like the ghost of an ancient, wandering about the world and trying mentally to construct it as it used to be in spite of ruin and confusing changes. But I find it necessary to use the utmost caution about my eyesight" (*MM*, p. 9).

Still, one crucial question in the way the figure of Casaubon is narrated—indeed in the very relation to it of the narrator and, by problematic extension, the author—concerns the manner in which this diminished potential for the sublime and the tragic is textually inscribed.[6] The relation of the narrator to Casaubon is, I think, the most problematic, tangled, and tension-filled one in the novel: Eliot is caught, in unresolved ways, between a tragic sense of the Casaubon figure (including the contradiction between his intellectual quest and any possibility of love with Dorothea) and a tendency to stress the petty and vindictive sides of the man, which takes her own moral concern in somewhat petty and vindictive moralizing directions.

The question of the Casaubon within George Eliot is thus quite a complicated one, for it raises the entire issue of her own highly ambivalent relationship to herself. Here one not only touches upon the hesitant movement—always interrupted by indecision between tradition and critique—that took her from evangelical belief through doubt to secular humanism, realism, and a commitment to scientific knowledge (including putatively scientific ideas of evolutionary social development); one also comes upon her very work habits as a writer and novelist. If one somewhat simplistically takes Shakespeare as a metaphor for the creative imagination of the artist and Casaubon as a figure for the critical, ascetic, fact-grubbing, and perhaps deadly intellect of the scholar, George Eliot was not unambiguously of the party of Shakespeare. Her "veracious imagination" had its own way of threatening to become voracious. She tended to work on a novel as an assiduous scholar would research a treatise. She was of course largely an autodidact without professional training in her various areas of interest, but she was possessed by a documentary mania and a desire for archival authenticity partly incumbent upon her project (so close to that of contemporary social historians) of accurately and empathetically representing the life of all segments

---

[6]The metaphysical pathos of Casaubon's quest for origins and for a unified key to all mythologies is entirely missed in W. J. Harvey's discussion of the "anachronistic" nature of his research; see "The Intellectual Background of the Novel" in *Middlemarch: Critical Approaches to the Novel*, ed. Barbara Hardy (London, 1967), pp. 33–35.

of society, especially that of the obscure and unnoticed. So great was the documentary and archival imperative in her that G. H. Lewes considered it detrimental at times to her novelistic imagination. The vast quantity of material contained in her notebooks and in the so-called *Quarry for Middlemarch*[7] gives some idea of the research that went into the making of the book. The threat of an excessive critical intellect, a scholarly approach that smelled of the lamp, the constrained distance from less controlled *sprezzatura,* and the sense of panic before an empty sheet of paper not surrounded by little mountains of notes—these were at least some of the things Eliot might have been inclined to "exorcise" through the figure of Casaubon. But exorcism would have required the kind of "working through" that the figure of Casaubon does not quite receive.

The contrast between the narrator's treatment of Dorothea Brooke and Will Ladislaw, on the one hand, and of Mr. Casaubon, on the other, is quite telling. Dorothea is a misplaced Saint Theresa, "a foundress of nothing": the times provide no objective correlative for her epic-like quest for "some illimitable satisfaction" (*MM,* p. xiii). She sees Casaubon as the embodiment of her own image of the great man and marries him through a misrecognition that traumatically emerges but does not turn into any substantive recognition. Their relationship is one of the greateast mismatches in a novel punctuated by mismatches. Will Ladislaw is the seeming opposite of Casaubon—young, enthusiastic, handsome, seductive. Yet it is obvious that both Dorothea and Will share significant traits with Casaubon. Dorothea's quest is untimely, like Casaubon's; she too is naive in love, has a strong ascetic inclination to devote herself to self-sacrificing ideals, and tends to leave her grandiose projects uncompleted. One crucial question is the relation between Dorothea's idealism and her self-involvement, for her devotion to ideals has its strongly imaginary side, which at times approximates that of an Emma Bovary. Here she is both like and unlike Casaubon in that his self-involvement is ego-

[7]Ed. Anna Theresa Kitchel (Berkeley, Calif., 1950).

tistic without being narcissistic. Narcissism requires a lively imagination, and this Casaubon lacks. His egotism stems from need, including the chauvinistic need to have a traditional, self-sacrificing wife to "round and complete" his own reduced existence (*MM*, p. 32). Dorothea's later marriage to Will repeats in another register her life with Casaubon; with Will she also assumes a traditional, subordinate role.

Will himself is an amateur but one on the hyperbolic side; he can never recognize his affinity with Casaubon. Indeed, he is the source of the criticisms of Casaubon's scholarship that come to haunt Dorothea—the idea that Casaubon's quest must fail because he is ignorant of German scholarship and is not an "Orientalist." Given Will's own amateurish status, one may perhaps have some doubt about the validity of his criticism. (Casaubon might after all be seen as a somewhat mystified, early archetypal critic working on a different level from narrowly empirical scholarship, and his distance from "Orientalism" might today be considered a virtue.) Without either waxing Borgesian or belaboring the obvious, I would simply note that there are bases for more insistently critical or at least more problematic narratorial relations to Dorothea and Will. Yet Dorothea tends to be an object of identification, and Will one of infatuation, modulated only by relatively mild tones of irony befitting a superior, omniscient narratorial consciousness.

The case of Casaubon, as I have intimated, is quite different. A relatively early narratorial intrusion is intriguing in this respect. What seems to be a protesting reminder to the reader is also one to the narrator, for Casaubon is almost never seen "from the inside" (as is Dorothea, for example). He is typically presented through the narrator's eyes, the perception of other characters, or his own rather constipated words and constrained actions. The intrusion is, moreover, extremely quixotic, for it too keeps its distance from Casaubon and offers some strange speculations on the sources of "pity."

If to Dorothea Mr Casaubon had been the mere occasion which had set alight the fine inflammable material of her youthful illusions, does it follow that he was fairly represented in the minds of those less impassioned personages who have hitherto delivered their judgments concerning him? I protest against any absolute conclusion. [. . .] Suppose we turn from outside estimates of a man, to wonder, with keener interest, what is the report of his consciousness about his doings or capacity: with what hindrances he is carrying on his daily labours; what fading hopes, or what deeper fixity of self-delusion the years are marking off within him; and with what spirit he wrestles against universal pressure, which will one day be too heavy for him, and bring his heart to its final pause. Doubtless his lot is important in his own eyes; and the chief reason that we think he asks too large a place in our consideration must be our want of room for him, since we refer him to the Divine regard with perfect confidence; nay, it is even held sublime for our neighbour to expect the utmost there, however little he may have got from us. Mr Casaubon, too, was the centre of his own world; if he was liable to think that others were providentially made for him, and especially to consider them in the light of their fitness for the author of a 'Key to all Mythologies,' this trait is not quite alien to us, and, like the other mendicant hopes of mortals, claims some of our pity. [*MM*, p. 56–57]

Here indeed is the sublime presumably arising from the depths of narcissism (or at least egotism), but it is difficult to know whether the sublime collapses into the ludicrous. For we are told (ironically?) that "it is held sublime for our neighbor to expect the utmost" at least from the "Divine regard" in the very light of his egotism and, furthermore, that "some of our pity" may be elicited by the recognition that "we" are as egotistical as Mr. Casaubon. These alienated if not self-nugatory grounds for pity—which, even when treated as a bizarre partitive, is itself a rather condescending response—seem neither to bespeak much of a protest on behalf of Mr. Casaubon nor to constitute a general basis for fellow feeling of any sort.

One may acquire a fuller appreciation of the intense and intricate narratorial investment in the figure of Casaubon by inquiring more closely into movements in chapters 20 and 21 and, later, especially in chapters 42 and 48.

Chapter 20 begins with Dorothea in an apartment during her wedding trip to Rome; she is sobbing. The narrative flows backward in an attempt to account for this seemingly cathartic reaction. We are told that Dorothea "had no distinctly shapen grievance that she could state even to herself" (*MM*, p. 133). Then there is a narrative excursus on Rome itself which in its "stupendous fragmentariness heightened the dream-like strangeness of her bridal life" (*MM*, p. 134). Dorothea's "sublime" disorientation brought about by a rush of images in Rome is explicitly linked to historical and cultural dissonances, and here it is heightened rather than assuaged by her dawning but never accomplished "recognition" of Casaubon.

> To those who have looked at Rome with the quickening power of a knowledge which breathes a growing soul into all historical shapes, and traces out the suppressed transitions which unite all contrasts, Rome may still be the spiritual centre and interpreter of the world. But let them conceive one more historical contrast; the gigantic broken revelations of that Imperial and Papal city thrust abruptly on the notions of a girl who had been brought up in English and Swiss Puritanism, fed on meagre Protestant histories and an art chiefly of the handscreen sort; a girl whose ardent nature turned all her small allowance of knowledge into principles, fusing her actions into their mould, and whose quick emotions gave the most abstract things the quality of a pleasure or a pain; a girl who had lately become a wife, and from the enthusiastic acceptance of untried duty found herself plunged in tumultuous preoccupation with her personal lot. The weight of unintelligible Rome might lie easily on bright nymphs to whom it formed a background for the brilliant picnic of Anglo-foreign society; but Dorothea had no such defence against deep impression. [*MM*, p. 134]

Indeed, the impression made upon the young wife in Rome is so deep and jarring that it is traumatic: "Forms both pale and glowing took possession of her young sense, and fixed themselves in her memory even when she was not thinking of them, preparing strange associations which remained through her after-years." One has a first seeming domestication of this traumatic experience in the appeal, so common in Eliot, to common experience at least among the young and inexperienced, but this effect is immediately displaced by a resurgence of the "sublime" in the very heart of seeming domesticity and ordinariness through a self-referential appeal to the revelatory effect of Eliot's own tragic realism and its empathetic yet perhaps unlivable potential fully to transvalue the values of a reader with classical expectations. This movement is the setting for the famous passage on the "roar . . . on the other side of silence."

> Not that this inward amazement of Dorothea's was anything very exceptional: many souls in their young nudity are tumbled out among incongruities and left to "find their feet" among them, while their elders go about their business. Nor can I suppose that when Mrs Casaubon is discovered in a fit of weeping six weeks after her wedding, the situation will be regarded as tragic. Some discouragement, some faintness of the heart at the new real future which replaces the imaginary, is not unusual, and we do not expect people to be deeply moved by what is not unusual. That element of tragedy which lies in the very fact of frequency, has not yet wrought itself into the coarse emotion of mankind; and perhaps our frames could hardly bear much of it. If we had a keen vision and feeling of all ordinary human life, it would be like hearing the grass grow and the squirrel's heart beat, and we should die of that roar which lies on the other side of silence. As it is, the quickest of us walk about well wadded in stupidity.
> [*MM*, p. 135]

This climactic point in the narrative is immediately brought down to earth by a reversion to the image of the bewildered Dorothea crying, and we are told that her "new real future which was replacing the imaginary drew its material from the endless minutiae by which her view of Mr Casaubon and her wifely relation, now that she was married to him, was gradually changing with the secret motion of a watch-hand from what it had been in her maiden dream." Here the figure of Casaubon does seem to shift toward domestication of the sublime for Dorothea; still, "it was too early yet for her to fully recognize or at least admit the change" from "the imaginary" to her "new real future." Then the narrative shifts from Dorothea to Mr. Casaubon himself, but again the narrator treats him in terms of her own descriptions, Dorothea's reactions, and a series of exchanges between husband and wife (pp. 136–40). Domestication and the possibility of "recognition" are, however, once more upset by mutual blindness and Dorothea's seemingly self-sacrificing but cutting ability to provoke in Casaubon the one form of anxiety (and of imaginative activity) of which he seems capable—that concerning the futility and emptiness of his life's work (what I earlier referred to in more domesticated terms as his "writer's block"). One also finds a veiled hint, of course, that for Dorothea this reference to Casaubon's impotence in writing is a displacement of the missing erotic component of their "honeymoon" in Rome.

> "All those rows of volumes—will you not now do what you used to speak of?—will you not make up your mind what part of them you will use, and begin to write the book which will make your vast knowledge useful to the world? I will write to your dictation, or I will copy and extract what you tell me: I can be of no other use." Dorothea, in a most unaccountable, darkly-feminine manner, ended with a slight sob and eyes full of tears.
>
> The excessive feeling manifested would alone have been highly disturbing to Mr Casaubon, but there were other reasons why Dorothea's words were among the most cutting and irritating to him that she could have been impelled to use. She was as blind to his inward troubles as he to hers: she had not yet learned those hidden conflicts in her husband which claim our pity. She had not yet listened to his heart-beats, but only felt that her own was beating violently. In Mr Casaubon's ear, Dorothea's voice gave loud emphatic iteration to those muffled suggestions of consciousness which it was possible to explain as mere fancy, the illusion of exaggerated sensitiveness: always when such suggestions are unmistakably repeated from without, they are resisted as cruel and unjust. We are angered even by the full acceptance of our humiliating confessions—how much more by hearing in hard distinct syllables of a near observer, those confused murmurs which we try to call morbid, and strive against as

if they were the oncoming of numbness! [. . .] Here, towards this
particular point of the compass, Mr Casaubon had a sensitiveness
to match Dorothea's, and an equal quickness to imagine more
than the fact. [*MM*, p. 139]

Chapter 21 begins in the same place as chapter 20, with
Dorothea sobbing, but now the narrative flows forward from
this scene. Dorothea's sobbing is interrupted by a knock at the
door announcing the visit of Will Ladislaw—a visit she (via the
narrator) interprets in a disarmingly self-deceived way: "It
seemed as if the visit had come to shake her out of her self-
absorbed discontent—to remind her of her husband's good-
ness, and make her feel that she had now the right to be his
helpmate in all kind deeds" (*MM*, p. 141). Will in fact is re-
volted at the "idea of this dried-up pedant" (*MM*, p. 142) taking
the place he would like to have in Dorothea's life, and he
plants in Dorothea the seeds of doubt concerning Casaubon's
ability to accomplish his life's work. Dorothea feels "a pang at
the thought that the labour of her husband's life might be
void"—a pang that recurs in intensified form in chapter 22
when Will adds Casaubon's lack of "Orientalism" to his igno-
rance of German scholarship as a barrier to success. With Casaubon's return to the apartment, one has the setting for the
couple's joint recognition of the traumatic nature of the day
and the need for its suppression—a recognition which, if anything, inhibits their recognition of each other's needs and
lacks. This is the context in which the mere "waking of a
presentiment" in Dorothea must be read—a presentiment that
does not here (or elsewhere) culminate in the recognition of
Casaubon's "equivalent centre of self" with its shaded "difference." Indeed, the passage suggests the confluence of Dorothea's selfless devotion and self-centeredness, which join to
run against any "recognition" of the other and which make
her, in her own way, as self-enclosed as Casaubon.

There was never any further allusion between them to what had
passed this day. But Dorothea remembered it to the last with the
vividness with which we remember epochs in our experience

when some dear expectation dies, or some new motive is born. Today she had begun to see that she had been under a wild illusion in expecting a response to her feeling from Mr Casaubon, and she had felt the waking of a presentiment that there might be a sad consciousness in his life which made as great a need on his side as on her own.

We are all of us born in moral stupidity, taking the world as an udder to feed our supreme selves: Dorothea had early begun to emerge from that stupidity, but yet it had been easier to her to imagine how she would devote herself to Mr Casaubon, and become wise and strong in his strength and wisdom, than to conceive with that distinctness which is no longer reflection but feeling an idea wrought back to the directness of sense, like the solidity of objects—that he had an equivalent centre of self, whence the lights and shadows must always fall with a certain difference. [*MM*, p. 146]

In my own reading, I have been insisting that the most charged relation to Casaubon is not Dorothea's, however, but the narrator's—with the narrator serving as perhaps too direct a conduit for the author's preoccupations. In chapters 20 and 21 (with chapter 22 as a somewhat anticlimactic epilogue) there is a tense narrative balance between the metaphysical pathos and the moral idiocy of a man who can spend each day of his wedding journey in Rome squirreled away in the archives of the Vatican library while his wife sobs alone in their hotel. Once Dorothea and Casaubon are back home in Lowick, the balance tends to become undone, and the narrative oscillates rather wildly between the potential sublimity of a hopeless, selfless, yet self-centered quest and the moral deficiencies of a faulted man. In fact, the man seems at times to appear so faulted and petty that any sense of the tragic, even of pity, is overwhelmed by moral repulsion and reprobation, with the narrator's appeal to the need to see Casaubon "from the inside" becoming little more than a rhetorical topos. The narrator, while never reducing the figure of Casaubon to mere caricature, does face the danger of giving vent to uncontrolled, self-indulgent, moralizing sentiments. If Casaubon may be seen as an "encysted" character containing repressed authorial elements, one might suggest that pitiless, unmediated moralism becomes a force with which to burst the cyst but not to heal it. It also threatens to obscure or even obliterate larger cultural and historical articulations between the individual and society, necessary for both the understanding and the possible transformation of tangled, egotistical lives.

In chapter 42 pettier motives in Casaubon the man are stressed; his work is almost submerged yet resurfaces briefly at times. In chapter 48 the work becomes prominent again but is severely compromised by the all-too-human motives of jealousy, possessiveness, and vindictiveness. Indeed, it is almost given the *coup de grâce* by a narrative stratagem that approaches the level of soap opera: the *deus ex machina* of a codicil to Casaubon's will.

It is in chapter 42 that Casaubon learns of the illness from which he will die—what is diagnosed by Lydgate as "fatty degeneration of the heart" (*MM*, p. 292). In responding to his illness, Casaubon shows every sign of hardening of the heart and withdrawal into the self. He shrinks from pity (*MM*, p. 288), and he is shown none. The initial words of the following passage (perhaps the entire passage) could apply equally to Casaubon and to the narrator.

> Will not a tiny speck very close to our vision blot out the glory of the world, and leave only a margin by which we see the blot? I know no speck so troublesome as self. And who, if Mr Casaubon had chosen to expound his discontents—his suspicions that he was not any longer adored without criticism—could have denied that they were founded on good reasons? On the contrary, there was a strong reason to be added, which he had not himself taken explicitly into account—namely, that he was not unmixedly adorable. [*MM*, p. 289]

The narrator is very close to joining the others whose self-serving *Schadenfreude* is based on a limited vision of Casaubon, even when she gestures rhetorically toward a "sublimely tragic" struggle—which is here equated, in rather reductive fashion, with "passionate egotism."

Nay, are there many situations more sublimely tragic than the struggle of the soul with the demand to renounce a work which has been all the significance of its life—a significance which is to vanish as the waters which come and go where no man has need of them? But there was nothing to strike others as sublime about Mr Casaubon, and Lydgate, who had some contempt at hand for futile scholarship, felt a little amusement mingling with his pity. He was at present too ill acquainted with disaster to enter into the pathos of a lot where everything is below the level of tragedy except the passionate egotism of the sufferer. [*MM*, p. 292]

Thinking of death after her own exchange with Lydgate, Dorothea enters the scene almost as an apparition. The narratorial contrast between what she "might have represented" (a possibility so implausible at this point that it shatters any pretension to realism) and Casaubon's unresponsive rigidity is presented with a sentimentalizing yet hardhearted tendentiousness equal to that imputed to the dying scholar, and a generalizing moral sententiousness that may surpass anything attributable to Casaubon.

Then she went towards him, and might have represented a heaven-sent angel coming with a promise that the short hours remaining should yet be filled with that faithful love which clings the closer to a comprehended grief. His glance in reply to hers was so chill that she felt her timidity increased; yet she turned and passed her hand through his arm.

Mr Casaubon kept his hands behind him and allowed her pliant arm to cling with difficulty against his rigid arm.

There was something horrible to Dorothea in the sensation which this unresponsive hardness inflicted on her. That is a strong word, but not too strong: it is in these acts called trivialities that the seeds of joy are for ever wasted, until man and woman look round with haggard faces at the devastation their own waste has made, and say, the earth bears no harvest of sweetness—calling their denial knowledge. You may ask why, in the name of manliness, Mr Casaubon should have behaved that way. Consider that his was a mind which shrank from pity. [*MM*, p. 294]

The ending of chapter 42 is genuinely moving; as the narrator seems to relent, one witnesses a resurgence of the tense balance of forces in the narrative, anticipating features of chapter 48. Dorothea in her room resolves to see Casaubon again before he goes to sleep, and she goes to meet him when she hears the library door opening.

"Dorothea!" he said, with a gentle surprise in his tone. "Were you waiting for me?"

"Yes, I did not like to disturb you."

"Come, my dear, come. You are young and need not to extend your life by watching."

When the kind quiet melancholy of that speech fell on Dorothea's ears, she felt something like the thankfulness that might well up in us if we had narrowly escaped hurting a lamed creature. She put her hand into her husband's, and they went along the broad corridor together. [*MM*, pp. 295–96]

In chapter 48 Casaubon attempts to take his wife more fully into his project so that she may continue it after his death. After an evening of joint work in the library, Dorothea wakes to find Casaubon sitting by the fire. Calling him by his first name for the first time in the novel (p. 330), she asks if he is ill. (It is noteworthy that the narrator has used "Edward" instead of the typical "Mr Casaubon" only twice before, and Dorothea will use it only once again, at the moment of Casaubon's death.)[8] Casaubon takes the occasion to try to extort from his

---

[8]Here I would mention a possibility that may give more substance or at least specificity to the approach of a critic such as Ellmann. It is significant that readers probably forget that Casaubon even has a first name; in any event, he is always referred to in critical literature by his last, and his identification in the novel as Mr. Casaubon creates a narratorial distance readily accepted by the reader. "Edward" is not fully suppressed, but it is used only a handful of times. The first name that may undergo suppression or even repression, however, is "Isaac"—the name of the historical Casaubon and also the name of George Eliot's estranged brother, Isaac Evans. Brother and sister were extremely close as children (their relation may have served as a model for that between Maggie and Tom in *The Mill on the Floss*). Yet when she told Isaac of her illegitimate relation with G. H. Lewes (about three years after it had begun), his solicitor answered on his behalf because he felt he could not respond to her in a "Brotherly Spirit." Isaac did not speak to his sister from 1857 to 1880, the year of her

wife a pledge whose terms he refuses to specify. Dorothea is upset enough at the thought that he may ask her to devote her remaining days to his fruitless scholarly project, and this idea continues to preoccupy her until she seems on the point of acceding to his wish—only to realize that Casaubon is dead. As she tries to make up her mind, however, she touches upon the strangely composite nature of Casaubon's undertaking, which involves even the scarcely comprehensible remnants of alchemical and astrological traditions:

> The poor child had become altogether unbelieving as to the trustworthiness of that Key which had made the ambition and the labour of her husband's life. It was not wonderful that, in spite of her small instruction, her judgment in this matter was truer than his: for she looked with unbiassed comparison and healthy sense at probabilities on which he had risked all his egoism. And now she pictured to herself the days, and months, and years which she must spend in sorting what might be called shattered mummies, and fragments of a tradition which was itself a mosaic wrought from crushed ruins—sorting them as food for a theory which was already withered in the birth like an elfin child. Doubtless a vigorous error vigorously pursued has kept the embryos of truth a-breathing: the quest of gold being at the same time a questioning of substance, the body of chemistry is prepared for its soul, and Lavoisier is born. But Mr Casaubon's theory of the elements which made the seed of all traditions was not likely to bruise itself unawares against discoveries: it floated among etymologies which seemed strong because of likeness in sound, until it was shown that likeness in sound made them impossible: it was a

---

second (legitimate) marriage and also the year of her death. (It is, moreover, noteworthy that in her second marriage George Eliot assumed the position of Casaubon by wedding a much younger man—one whom Ellmann and others see as a model for Will Ladislaw.) Rosemary Ashton writes in *George Eliot* (Oxford, 1983), p. 95, that on the occasion of her marriage in 1880, Isaac sent her "a stiff bitter letter of 'sincere congratulations' which brought from her a disproportionate expression of gratitude: 'it was a great joy to me to have your kind words of sympathy, for our long silence has never broken that affection for you which began when we were little ones.'" It would not be implausible to see the "eroticism" presumably exorcised in Casaubon, as well as one source of her cutting severity toward him, in George Eliot's feelings toward her estranged brother during the time she was writing the novel.

method of interpretation which was not tested by the necessity of forming anything which had sharper collisions than an elaborate notion of Gog and Magog: it was as free from interruption as a plan for threading the stars together. [*MM*, pp. 331–32]

The finely threaded weave of chapter 48 comes apart when we learn in the next chapter of the codicil to Casaubon's will: it enjoins that his wife will lose all his property if she marries Will Ladislaw. This news throws Dorothea into a traumatic state reminiscent of her condition in Rome. More significantly, perhaps, it also threatens to derail the narrative by tending to eliminate any concern for Casaubon's quest and to focus on his moral pettiness and jealous vindictiveness. In any event, it shifts the reader's attention to the personal madness of a gesture that is calculated to produce what it attempts to avoid. Its effect on the narrative is to introduce into the plot a weak stratagem that both sacrifices the complexity of the Casaubon figure and fails to provide a sufficient basis for the reader's interest. It would perhaps be inexact to say that the novel approximates popular romances in placing in the foreground the question whether Dorothea will follow her heart and marry Will even if it costs much of her fortune. The problem is more complex in that the codicil exerts an influence over Dorothea because it renders explicit the feelings toward Will that she has refused to acknowledge to herself. But the reader must nonetheless resist the temptation of allowing a simplistic resolution to eclipse the earlier intricacies in the treatment of Casaubon and in the narrator's relation to him; the final "recognition" of Casaubon is hardly worth the price it would cost. It would also divert attention from the larger question of the relation between the private and the public, the individual and society, that the novel signals in its more historically and politically alert moments. For a moralizing solution, like any essentializing gesture, serves the ideological function of masking the more difficult cultural and ethicopolitical issues that the figure of Casaubon may at least help to raise.

4

Collapsing Spheres in Flaubert's
Sentimental Education

> Les affaires publiques le laissèrent indifférent,
> tant il était préoccupé des siennes. [Politics left him indiffer-
> ent, he was so preoccupied with his own affairs.]
> Said of Frédéric Moreau in Gustave Flaubert,
> > *The Sentimental Education*

The question I want to explore with respect to Flaubert's
Sentimental Education is that of the interaction among documentary, ideological, and critical levels or dimensions in the
novel's relation to society and history. This question (or set of
questions) does not, of course, exhaust the interpretation of the
novel, but it does enable one to investigate a significant
number of issues relevant to the problem of political and historical reading. I propose, moreover, to begin not with a hierarchy among these dimensions but rather with an interest in
inquiring into their interplay—an interest that is often undercut or disavowed when the interpreter presumes the existence
of a hierarchy of levels or even the more or less exclusive
primacy of one level over others. I also propose to take formal
issues in the working of the text not as being autonomous ends
in themselves but as having implications (however problematic) for political and historical interpretation.

On a documentary level one might turn to the analysis provided by Maurice Agulhon, perhaps the premier historian of
the *Annales* school who focuses on the nineteenth century;

Agulhon's analysis brings out both the possibilities and the limits of a documentary reading of the novel, particularly when it is set within the framework of a certain historiographical metaphysic and ontology. In his article "Peut-on lire en historien *L'Education sentimentale*,"[1] Agulhon assumes the validity of the familiar *annaliste* three-tiered conception of historical reality in terms of an economic foundation, a second social "series," and an upper cultural level. Fiction, in this conception, is itself the most peripheral aspect of the cultural level and thus furthest from the interests of the historian; it becomes a legitimate object of historical interest only in a parasitic, documentary manner with Flaubert in the reduced role of witness (*témoin*) of his age. Thus Agulhon can make the following statement as if it were altogether self-evident and unproblematic: "For those historians in the narrow sense of the word, historians of social and political 'realities' (fiction being excluded on principle), who are interested in the history of France between 1840 and 1851, one may ask whether *The Sentimental Education* is a useful contribution to the knowledge and understanding of the time." Agulhon goes on to answer his question in the affirmative, although he notes that Flaubert is not Homer and that "for the nineteenth century in France we have many, and many other, texts than literary ones" (p. 36). Flaubert's novel nonetheless provides useful information concerning "material realities," "mentalities," and "problems and debates" of the time. Agulhon relegates to "literary and aesthetic criticism" the problem of "commenting on the art with which Flaubert interlaces the double intrigue of Frédéric, Madame Arnoux and the Marshall [Rosanette Bron] with the peripeties of the history of the time" (p. 40). But he does try to draw a rather anti-Marxist lesson from the novel for the problem of "periods and breaks" by indicating that in *The Sentimental Education*, December 1851 (the Eighteenth Brumaire or *coup d'état* of Louis Napoleon) is more important as a period break than are the June Days of 1848 (the uprising of

[1]In Maurice Agulhon et al., *Histoire et langage dans "L'Education sentimentale"* (Paris, 1981), pp. 35–41. Page numbers are cited in the text, and the translations are my own.

workers following the abolition of the National Workshops). For such reasons, he concludes, "a historian of '48 may put the *Education* in his pedagogical arsenal" (p. 41).

In the course of his analysis, Agulhon makes a number of useful and informative points. But from the perspective I am taking, even his question is misguided and the premises on which it rests extremely doubtful. Indeed, Agulhon's approach is based upon binary oppositions of the sort that are radically questioned in *The Sentimental Education* itself. Thus his reading of it must be blind to certain of its more challenging effects and their import for one's own protocols of interpretation. The very opposition between levels of "reality" that allows an a priori exclusion of fiction obscures the role of fiction in everyday "reality" as well as its role in the organization of historical research. This exclusion functions to convert hypotheses into dogmatic assumptions about the nature of objects of interest to the historian, and it implies a division of labor between the historian of economic and social "realities" and the "literary or aesthetic critic," a division that obviates inquiry into the interaction between documentary and other dimensions of the text—as well as between the private or "sentimental" and the public or political in the novel's functioning. The latter issues cannot be confined (rather dismissively) to Flaubert's "art," if only because they bear upon the relation of art to other aspects of "reality." Agulhon's approach assumes an unbreachable barrier between historical and aesthetic interests that precludes both an understanding of the breakdown of the opposition between them and the possibility of different articulations of their relations as well as of the relations between the historian and the literary or aesthetic critic (functions or roles that may be taken up by the same social individual).

The precise manner in which so-called documentary material, which may be authenticated (within limits) through historiographical examination of "nonfictional" records, is itself "interlaced" with fictional material in a larger reading or rendition of the times is itself a crucial question from a perspective that departs from Agulhon's premises. And this question is linked to that of the relation of the novel to the differential ideological and critical reworking of the material it treats. The ideological implication of the novel is its more or less blind affirmation or even reinforcement of prevalent if not dominant discourses, stereotypes, prejudices, and clichés; the critical dimension is the degree of its ability to work through its ideological implications to achieve both a measure of distance on them and the possibility of revealing their nature and effects on social individuals and groups. It may even help disclose implications of the "interlacing" of fact and fiction for political and social transformation, not only in the novel's delimited time but also for its contemporary readers who themselves may still to some extent be beset with problems analogous to the ones the novel explores.

Two major and seemingly opposed ideologies, as we shall see, undergo in their own manner a process to which binaries in general are subjected in the novel: the "private" ideology of art for art's sake and the "public" ideology of antidemocratic political liberalism. One can find evidence in his correspondence that the biographical Flaubert affirmed both these ideologies, although even his letters introduce complications that prevent one from reading them as expressing simple beliefs or unproblematic positions. But especially around the time he was composing *The Sentimental Education*, Flaubert seemed to overlay an escapist dedication to art with a bitter critique of universal suffrage and a defense of a cultural and political elite. His turn toward antidemocratic, elitist liberalism was more pronounced after the Paris Commune of 1871, and one may even wonder whether it became the support of the aesthetic enterprise itself once withdrawal from active life and the existence of a *rentier* were jeopardized by the course of events. In a period of extreme crisis, the "private" ideology of *l'art pour l'art* and the public pose of the cultural and political mandarin may meet and, in view of their equally problematic status, may even threaten to collapse into one another like two exhausted Flaubertian figures falling into each other's arms.

In his *L'Idiot de la famille*,[2] Jean-Paul Sartre has offered the

[2]Paris, 1971–72.

most extensive analysis and critique of Flaubert as a pseudore-
alistic, aesthetic nihilist and ideologist of bourgeois rage and
impotence. Recently, Antoine Compagnon has complemented
Sartre's analysis with a detailed investigation of Flaubert's self-
contradictory position as antidemocratic, upper-bourgeois liberal at bay.[3] His thesis also seems like a displacement of Lucien Goldmann's argument about Pascal in *Le Dieu caché*,[4] for
Compagnon sees Flaubert as a representative exponent of an
ideology caught precariously if not tragically between the extremes of conservative royalism and democratic re-
publicanism. In his rejection of both universal suffrage and the
divine right of kings, Flaubert, for Compagnon, put forth arguments that converged with those of his friends Hippolyte Taine and Ernest Renan. Although the particular object of Compagnon's comments is *Bouvard and Pécuchet*, he develops his
argument on a level of generality that might easily apply to
The Sentimental Education:

> The last chapter of *Bouvard and Pécuchet*, dealing with the
> failed education which leads to the final catastrophe and prepares
> the "copy" [the resolution of Bouvard and Pécuchet at the end of
> the novel to return to their profession as copyists], represents,
> beyond the circularity of the novelistic form, the necessary
> culmination of [Taine's] *France contemporaine* in its entirety.
> The fatal failure of popular instruction, in the face of race and
> blood, verifies the impenitent malfeasance of universal suffrage,
> the illegitimacy of democracy. It is like an ass's kick against the
> right of education, the duty of instruction, contained in the rights
> of man and the dogma of the Revolution; it is like the renewed

---

[3] *La Troisième République des lettres, de Flaubert à Proust* (Paris, 1983).
Page numbers are cited in the text, and translations are my own. Compagnon
also makes an important general argument about literary criticism in France.
He argues that a nineteenth-century combination of subjective impressionism
and dogmatism in critics such as Hippolyte Taine, Emile Faguet, and Ferdinand Brunetière was displaced by a positivistic literary history in such figures
as Gustave Lanson. Contemporary critics such as Roland Barthes, who for
Compagnon are blind both to the specific history of literary criticism in France
and at times even to historical problems in general, in their understandable
reaction against positivism threaten to repeat (with variations) the features
marking nineteenth-century criticism.

[4] Paris, 1955.

proof of the moral commonplace, the geometric space of the novel, not so much a critical encyclopedia as a political sociology. [P. 304]

One need not look far in Flaubert's correspondence to find comments to support even this extremely one-sided interpretation. Here, for example, is an extract of a letter to George Sand written at the end of June or the beginning of July 1869 (that is, shortly after the completion of *The Sentimental Education* at 4:56 A.M. on May 16—as Flaubert noted with masochistic precision):

> Experience proves (so it seems to me) that no form contains the good in itself; Orleanism, the republic, the empire no longer mean anything, since the most contradictory ideas may enter into each of these boxes. All flags have been so stained with blood and sh— that the time has come to dispense with them completely. Down with words! No more symbols or fetishes! The high morality of that reign will prove that universal suffrage is as stupid as divine right, although it may be a little less odious.
>
> The question is thus displaced. It is no longer a question of dreaming up the best form of government, since they all amount to the same thing. It is rather to make Science prevail. That is the most urgent demand. The rest will follow of necessity. Purely intellectual men have rendered more services to the human species than all the Saint Vincent de Paul's in the world! And politics will be an eternal silliness as long as it is not a dependency of Science. The government of a country should be a section of the Institute and the last of all of them.[5]

In this letter, the possibly cogent critique of any form of sovereignty, be it divine or popular, merges with a peremptory dismissal of universal suffrage and the illegitimate inference that political forms in general are of little consequence. Flaubert even turns to positivism, to Science with a capital "S," in a declamatory gesture worthy of Homais. But here it may be noted that the difficulty in Compagnon's analysis is its narrowly documentary conception of ideological reading,

[5]*Correspondance*, vol. 6 (Paris, 1930), pp. 32–33 (my translation).

which simply amalgamates letters and literary texts in a synoptic, homogenized manner putatively illustrative of prevalent collective discourses and oblivious to critical forces in both collective discourses and specific texts. The question Compagnon does not elucidate is that of the precise place of ideologies in texts, including the way texts and discourses may contain currents that counter the ideologies they render or reinforce.

We shall see that Flaubert engages in an obvious self-parody concerning the cult of pure art in his treatment of Pellerin in *The Sentimental Education*. But the status of antidemocratic, elitist liberalism is more difficult to determine. For there is no strong representative of this ideological position in the novel—no one comparable to, say, Tocqueville, whose thinking went in this direction after 1848. Indeed, anything approximating an elite of intellect or merit, even on the level of isolated individuals, whether pro- or antirevolutionary, is notorious precisely through its absence in the novel. This absence of antidemocratic liberalism as well as of an elite that might serve as its bearer is equivocal. In one sense it protects the ideology from the critique and ironic deflation that other ideologies, positions, and groups undergo in the novel; but it also intimates that even in its strongest form this ideology is too self-contradictory and insubstantial to serve as a solution to the crisis disclosed, or to stand up to the ironic and parodic forces unleashed.

Weaker expressions of the ideology are either objects of withering scorn or items of ephemeral interest and insignificant weight. The figure who is closest to a liberal of at least the Orleanist stripe is Monsieur Dambreuse, the noble who drops his particle to assume an upper bourgeois status and who goes with the flow of changing political currents. He is at best a farcically reduced Tocqueville with diminished intelligence and a lack of character. (It might be noted in passing that Flaubert himself accepted the Second Empire although he disliked it, while Tocqueville, more consistent and courageous, strongly opposed it.) Dambreuse emerges as little better than a political prostitute, someone who "had acclaimed Napoleon, the Cossacks, Louis XVIII, 1830, the workers, truckling to every government, worshipping Authority so fervently that he would have paid for the privilege of selling himself."⁶ When Frédéric Moreau, "the weakest of men" (l'homme de toutes les faiblesses; p. 298) and the least consistent ideologically, himself makes a "liberal" pronouncement, he does so merely in passing, and it has as little resonance as other fleeting remarks inserted in heterogeneous series of observations. In addition, it concludes a comment in which Frédéric actually defends the workers, against the soured reaction of his friend Deslauriers, in a manner that at least mitigates the harsh treatment that socialism and the workers receive elsewhere in the novel:

> "The spark [of genuine revolution] was missing. You were just a lot of little shopkeepers at heart, and the best of you were doctrinaires. As for the workers, they've got every reason to complain; for apart from a million taken from the Civil List, which you granted them with the vilest flattery, you've given them nothing but fine phrases. The wages book remains in the employer's hands, and the employee, even before the law, is still inferior to his master, because nobody takes his word. Altogether, the Republic strikes me as out of date. Who knows? Perhaps progress can only be achieved through an aristocracy or a single man. The initiative always comes from above. The people are still immature, whatever you may say."
> "You may be right," said Deslauriers. [P. 365]

Aside from noting Deslaurier's rather noncommittal, unargued, and brief rejoinder, which retroactively increases the weightlessness of Frédéric's assertions, one may observe that Frédéric indifferently mentions an aristocracy or a single man—hardly equivalents politically. Even for liberals who defended an aristocracy of birth or merit, the rule of one man—including the man named Louis Napoleon—might be anathema. The leveling equalization of aristocratic rule and dictatorship is itself a symptomatic indication of the dubiousness and instability of antidemocratic, elitist "liberalism."

⁶*The Sentimental Education*, trans. Robert Baldick (New York: Penguin, 1964), p. 373. Subsequent quotations are from this edition, and page numbers are cited in the text.

The novel may nonetheless be seen to reinforce this ideology at least indirectly in that its most unsympathetic and one-dimensional portrayals are indeed reserved for socialism and socialist feminism. But in this respect the novel is no more on the side of liberalism than on that of the Empire or of conservative monarchism. In any event, it is often decidedly anti-socialist to the extent of presenting socialism only in its blindly messianic and authoritarian guises to the exclusion of any liberal, democratic form. (This restricted and self-justifying understanding of socialism was shared even by Tocqueville.) The narrator's attitude toward socialism seems dismissive: it is an old idea that has repeatedly failed, and its attraction derives from the dearth of ideas in modern society at large (see p. 295). Sénécal, perhaps the most unsympathetic character in the book, is the primary exponent of socialism. He is a petty, dogmatic authoritarian—a bad imitation of Blanqui, who himself imitated Robespierre (p. 301)—a derivative terrorist who becomes a policeman and kills the sympathetic Dussardier on the Eighteenth Brumaire. It should further be noted that Dussardier himself is not specifically a socialist but someone who, naively and goodheartedly, wants the reconciliation of all classes and—with retrospective misgiving—even fights against the workers in the bourgeois National Guards during the June Days of 1848. He, like Deslauriers, finally confesses his loss of faith in the workers ("the workers are no better than the middle classes"; pp. 392–93) as well as his disillusionment with revolution in general.

Dussardier's consort, la Vatnaz, is second only to Sénécal as a negative character, and she is the representative of feminist socialism. Her political role is even more compromised than Sénécal's by personal pettiness and a desire for revenge.

Like many others, she had greeted the Revolution as the harbinger of revenge; she was devoting herself passionately to Socialist propaganda. According to Mademoiselle Vatnaz, the emancipation of the proletariat was possible only through the emancipation of women. She wanted the admission of women to all types of employment, investigation into the paternity of illegitimate children, a new legal code, and either the abolition of marriage or at the very least "a more intelligent regulation of the institution." In her opinion, every Frenchwoman should be obliged to marry a Frenchman or to adopt an old man. Wet-nurses and midwives should become civil servants; and there should be a jury to examine books by women, special publishers for women, a polytechnic school for women, a National Guard for women, everything for women! And seeing that the Government did not recognize their rights, they would have to conquer force by force. Ten thousand citizenesses, armed with good muskets, would make the Hôtel de Ville tremble. [Pp. 297–98]

This is the narrator's ironic *reductio ad absurdum* of feminist socialism.

The treatment of socialism and feminism is, however, the most extreme and one-sided instance of a more general feature of *The Sentimental Education* that in other respects has a certain critical potential. What is critically disclosed is the tendency of seeming opposites to be disjoined yet also evacuated and hence to collapse into each other. This tendency is particularly marked with respect to the private and public spheres most prominent in the novel—the "sentimental" life of individuals and the political life of society. For the sentimental and private infiltrate the political and public, often in the form of the compensatory motive of revenge, while the political subsides into the sentimental as politics becomes an escape from private frustrations as well as the locus of quasi-religious romanticism and the hope of personal redemption. Yet the tendency of putative spheres of life to merge or to collapse pervades all relations in the novel, and it signals the potentially catastrophic absence of viable articulations that would allow for both limited mediation and engaging supplementary interaction between distinguishable entities or activities. Here there is no mutually challenging relation between involvement and criticism, structure and play, obedience and transgression, the expected and the aleatory. Religion is devoid of devotion, politics of commitment, and work of vocation. Sentimentality itself is to sentiment as fashion is to norm and tradition, and it pervades life in a manner that converts projects into passing fancies, reverie into evanescent daydreams, and time into hollowed-out repetition. One seems suspended between an unavailable absolute and random occurrences, with no prospect of livable modes of activity between these extremes.

The novel's treatment of institutions that might theoretically provide needed articulations for the characters is striking in the foregoing respects. Religion shades into a diffuse religiosity that colors all "spheres" in rank confusion. In any distinctive sense religion is absent, but both love and politics become the intermingled repositories of its displaced and attenuated aura in a process of generalized profanation. Madame Arnoux is for Frédéric the romantic incarnation of an ideal archetype. But not only is the incarnation suspect (as we shall see); the archetype itself is degraded into the object of a vague, quotidian Platonism indistinguishable from fetishism or obsessive fixation. In a context of generalized profanation or prostitution, moreover, it is difficult if not impossible to distinguish marriage from adultery as the foundation of the family. The dream of the prostitute Rosanette is to marry and be a respectable bourgeoise. And the easiest conquest for Frédéric is not the literal prostitute but the respectable Madame Dambreuse, who acquiesces with a facility he finds surprising. The coming and going of various "sentimental" objects that Arnoux brings to pass between his (changing) home and the (equally changing) rooms of Rosanette creates a blur between the spheres of legitimate marital life and illicit relations. The blur is extended, given Louise Roque's illegitimate birth and Monsieur Dambreuse's decision to leave his fortune to his illegitimate child, Cécile.

Politics, when it is not motivated by narrowly self-interested private concerns, is an arena for the displacement of equally private "sentimental" investments. Figures typically turn to politics out of personal pique or through a mystified longing for personal salvation. Rosanette's "commitment" to the Republic seems as strong or weak as anyone else's: she "declared herself in favour of the Republic, a position which had already been taken up by His Grace the Archbishop of Paris, and which was to be adopted with remarkable alacrity by the Magistrature, the council of State, the Institute, the Marshalls of France, Changarnier, Monsieur de Falloux, all the Bonapartists, all the Legitimists, and a considerable number of the Orleanists" (p. 293). Revolution itself becomes a drainpipe for private frustrations: "Frédéric consoled himself [over Madame Arnoux] by railing against authority, for like Deslauriers, he longed for a general upheaval, he had become so embittered" (p. 273). Both Frédéric and Deslauriers make "radical" speeches when they are carried away by the general madness (*démence*), and the appeal to crowd psychology with reference to their behavior seems appropriate, for it is something that comes over them like a contagious fever only to give way to another, perhaps seemingly opposed, orientation or point of view. Will in general—political will in particular—is reduced to mere velleity, indicating both the questionable status of will itself as the anomic ground of arbitrary activity and its insubstantiality in the absence of viable norms and commitments. The only alternatives to self-interest and vapid velleity in the novel are the self-righteous but quite unstable dogmatism of Sénécal, the naive class-collaborationist hopes of Dussardier, and the evangelical religiosity of one of the speakers at the Club of Intelligence where Frédéric makes his abortive bid for a political role. For this speaker, who receives the overwhelming endorsement of the crowd, "the time had come to inaugurate the reign of God. The Gospel led straight to 1789. After the abolition of slavery would come the abolition of the proletariat. The age of hatred was past; the age of love was about to begin" (p. 303).

At the Club of Intelligence one has the first reference to the *tête de veau*, the calf's head, whose significance will be explained by Deslauriers only at the very end of the novel. This custom of toasting the king by drinking from a calf's head began in England as a royalist ceremony, only to be parodied by "independent spirits" after the fall of the Stuarts and to be copied in turn by French terrorists after Thermidor. For Deslauriers it "shows that stupidity is catching" (p. 417), and as an imitation of an imitation, the *tête de veau* would seem to mark the ludicrous place in which politics in general ends up in the novel—a place it shares with love, as the final scene intimates.

It is by now commonplace to refer to *The Sentimental Education* as a *Bildungsroman* with the *Bildung* left out. The education of children simply finds no place in the novel, and that undergone by adults is tantamount to a process of hardening and drying up. "Process," however, is an inexact term, as there is less a development than a disclosure of what is already present in the characters. An earlier title Flaubert considered for the work was *Les Fruits secs*, and the *justesse* of this title can be appreciated from the fate of the child of Frédéric and Rosanette, for its death before the process of education begins literally leaves it in a state equivalent to that of adults after their putative sentimental education. The baby at birth is like an animated dried fruit, "a yellowish-red object, hideously wrinkled, which smelt unpleasant and was wailing" (p. 380). When it dies, covered with "whitish spots" that "looked like patches of mildew" (p. 395), Rosanette wants to have it embalmed, but the impracticality of this mummified romantic desire leads the parents instead to have it preserved and memorialized in the final painting of Pellerin.

The world of professions and occupations fares no better than those of politics and education. In this crucial sector of modern life one finds either the non-participation of the *rentier* who dreams dilettantishly of various avocations or the indiscriminate hustle and bustle of *l'homme à tout faire*, ready to take on any task that promises success or profit. Common to this lack and this excess of activity is the absence of vocation. Frédéric thinks only of maintaining or increasing his income as a *rentier* when he is not dreamily wondering whether he should choose to be a great novelist, painter, or politician. Deslauriers, after being dismissed as a prefect during the revolutionary period, "had been director of colonization in Algeria, secretary to a pasha, manager of a newspaper, and an advertising agent; and at present he was employed as solicitor to an industrial company" (p. 416). Arnoux, always the vulgar *bon enfant*, begins as a bastardized or dubiously hybridized purveyor of high art, for he seeks *"le sublime à bon marché"* ("the sublime at a popular price"; p. 50), and his dealings with good painters are mixed with shady affairs, the labor of hacks, and the journalistic promotion of art. His industrialization of art takes him to a pottery factory and then to the commerce in religious objects; he finally flees Paris in the face of prosecution for fraud. Pellerin, Flaubert's self-parodic exponent of pure art, himself ends up as a photographer "after dabbling in Fourierism, homeopathy, table-turning, Gothic Art [Arnoux's shop for religious objects is named *L'Art Gothique*], and humanitarian painting" (p. 416). The very serialization of activities—repeated time and again—tends to level them through a process of equalization and substitutability, and it attests to both the omnipresent role of commodification and the tendency of the characters to pass into one another even when they appear to be most opposed. For, like institutions, the characters whose life is in part shaped or disfigured by them tend to become disarticulated and to collapse into one another.

I have already mentioned the role reversal relating Rosanette and Madame Dambreuse. Indeed, Frédéric and the narrator put Rosanette's pregnancy "on hold" for twenty-five months while Frédéric has his affair with Madame Dambreuse, who thus appears as a prolonged interlude in the prostitute's attempt at domesticity. Yet Rosanette is herself a *passe-partout* in almost slapstick fashion as doors open and shut with the entrance and exit of a proliferating series of lovers and clients, and she reverts to prostitution when she is in need of money during her pregnancy. Louise Roque is to Frédéric as he is to Madame Arnoux, for he is her fetishized ideal and fixated object of phantasmatic investment. She has toward him the quasi-incestuous involvement of a younger to an older person that Frédéric replicates in his devotion to Madame Arnoux. The latter of course seems to be the polar opposite of Rosanette on the "sentimental" spectrum, yet she is a weak vessel for the ideal; it is unclear whether her beauty is anything out of the ordinary, and her mind is filled with bourgeois maxims (as is that of the prostitute). This may be interpreted to mean that Frédéric's devotion to her is one of pure art that transcends its "real" referent, but this interpretation simultaneously reduces pure art to pure illusion. And other features of Frédéric's relation to

Madame Arnoux are not accommodated by it. After Madame Arnoux is overcome by superstitious fears during the illness of her child and fails to appear at a prearranged rendezvous with Frédéric on a street corner (of all places), he of course sleeps with Rosanette, in the bed prepared for his ideal woman, as the revolution of 1848 breaks out in the streets of Paris. One has here a relation of substitutability between Madame Arnoux and Rosanette, and it is not limited to this politico-amorous incident. Madame Arnoux has not only had the bad judgment to marry the vulgar Arnoux; she has the bad taste to remain with him even when she discovers that Rosanette is his mistress. The continued proximity of Madame Arnoux and her husband threatens to lower the former in Frédéric's eyes. Frédéric must, moreover, evoke either Rosanette or Madame Arnoux to motivate love-making with Madame Dambreuse, and the prostitute and the ideal woman blend imperceptibly into each other in superimposed images in his mind. "The company of these two women made as it were two melodies in his life: the one wild, amusing; the other grave and almost religious. And the two continually and gradually intermingled, for, if Madame Arnoux merely brushed him with her finger, his desire immediately conjured up the image of the other woman, since in her case his hopes were less remote; while if, in Rosanette's company, his heart happened to be stirred, he promptly remembered his great love" (p. 149). It is also significant that the prostitute posing as a statue of liberty during the mob's invasion of the Tuileries is a Medusa-like parody both of the unattainable republican ideal and of the unapproachable Madame Arnoux. She appears elevated on a pile of clothes (p. 290), a seedy simulacrum of Madame Arnoux's arresting "*apparition*" on the bench aboard ship where Frédéric first beholds her.

Frédéric gets all of his women secondhand as other men's leftovers, and Deslauriers repeats this gesture: he tries to seduce Madame Arnoux, conspires with Madame Dambreuse, sleeps with Rosanette, and marries Louise Roque. Frédéric finds himself in other characters as well, notably in Arnoux, whose paternal patronage he willingly accepts and whose interests he strives to protect, in part (but not only) for the sake of his wife. Toward the end of the novel Frédéric is even described in terms that recall, in a more dismantled and discontinuous fashion, those used to characterize Arnoux near the beginning of the story: "He was a Republican; he had travelled; he knew the secrets of theatres, restaurants, and newspapers" (p. 16). Of Frédéric it is said, in the famous passage whose isolated treatment obscures the parallel with Arnoux:

> He travelled.
> He came to know the melancholy of the steamboat, the cold awakening in the tent, the tedium of landscapes and ruins, the bitterness of interrupted friendships.
> He returned. [P. 411]

I shall simply mention one more case of a character's lability: Pellerin, like Frédéric, parodies features of Flaubert himself. The inconstant defender of *l'art pour l'art* and critic of realism has painted only sketches by the age of fifty, and in the course of the novel he comes to execute three portraits: two of prostitutes—one private and one public—and the third of the abortive offspring of Frédéric and a prostitute. The first is of Rosanette, and to it is affixed a notice stating that it (she) is the property of Frédéric Moreau of Nogent. The second—a paragon of wayward displacement and free substitutability—"showed the Republic, or Progress, or Civilization, in the form of Christ driving a locomotive through a virgin forest" (p. 298). The third and last is a more abstract rendition of the dead baby: "Patches of red, yellow, green, and indigo clashed in violent contrast; the thing was hideous, almost laughable" (p. 400). Pellerin's trajectory, as I have intimated, not only intersects with Arnoux's in the banalization and commercialization of art; it also replicates the heterogeneous inconstancy of Arnoux's professional life and that of other characters as well.

In this mutable but basically unchanging world, the aleatory itself does not challenge existing structures, for structures—though rigid—are brittle and insubstantial, and the aleatory itself is ephemeral and ineffective; it readily veers toward insignificant nonsense and sheer absurdity or at best toward *"le sublime à bon marché."* The most memorable scene of *l'aléatoire politique* is the meeting of the Club of Intelligence culminating in Frédéric's fruitless attempt to gain a hearing while the patriot from Barcelona babbles on unintelligibly in a foreign language. Here there is no tense, mutually contestatory interaction between meaning and challenges to it; the aleatory goes slack, and the satiric import of the scene depends upon the importation of expectations from the reader. One may also mention the unmotivated image of the man on horseback near the beginning of the treatment of 1848—an epigonal figure who, again on the basis of imported expectations given little footing in the text, might be seen as a parody of the traditional solitary leader providing direction and purpose for the people (he might also be seen as a double of Frédéric himself at the Club of Intelligence): "In the middle of the crowd, above the swaying heads, an old man in a black coat could be seen on a white horse with a velvet saddle. He was holding a green branch in one hand and a piece of paper in the other, and he kept waving them stubbornly. Finally, giving up hope of making himself heard, he withdrew" (p. 286).

Perhaps the most provocative instance of the seeming opposition and disintegrative subsidence of the private and the public into one another may be found in the scenes concerning the bloody June Days in Paris and the escape of Frédéric and Rosanette to Fontainebleau. By the outbreak of the workers' revolt in June, Frédéric has become disillusioned with politics. Following his fiasco at the Club of Intelligence he feels the urge to see Rosanette: "After all that ugliness and bombast, her prettiness would be a relief" (p. 307). Yet Rosanette accuses him "of having started the Revolution" and, assuming the role of a homespun patriarchalist, invokes her own variant of the argument he would make to Deslauriers (which itself recalls passages in Flaubert's correspondence): "Come on! Use your noddle! A country has to have a master, just like a house; otherwise everybody does what he likes with the house-keeping money" (p. 308). Frédéric nonetheless believes he can find idyllic release with her on an excursion that takes him away from the street fighting in Paris. Yet the deadening process of deflation and equalization sets in not only in Paris itself but in its seemingly utopian alternative. In Paris,

> by and large the National Guards were merciless. Those who had not taken part in the fighting wanted to distinguish themselves; and in an explosion of panic they took revenge at one and the same time for the newspapers, the clubs, the demonstrations, the doctrines, for everything which had been infuriating them for the past six months. Despite their victory, equality—as if to punish its defenders and ridicule its enemies—asserted itself triumphantly: an equality of brute beasts, a common level of bloody atrocities; for the fanaticism of the rich counterbalanced the frenzy of the poor, the aristocracy shared the fury of the rabble, and the cotton nightcap was just as savage as the red bonnet. The public's reason was deranged as if by some great natural upheaval. Intelligent men lost their sanity for the rest of their lives. [P. 334]

If this deceptively evenhanded narratorial conception of the effects of violence, with its ideological invocation of an analogy to the role of natural forces, appears (as well it might) much too facile, it may be observed that it is qualified in a significant way. Immediately after it one has a scene of specifically upper-class frenzy as Roque shoots a prisoner pleading for bread. The old man "was furious at seeing his authority flouted," and his act "soothed him, as if he had been paid a compensation" for the damage the front of his building incurred during the insurrection (p. 335). And it is later in his discussion with Deslauriers that Frédéric both defends the complaints of the workers and issues his own equivocal appeal concerning the need for an aristocracy or a single man.

Less equivocal is the fact that the escape to Fontainebleau is itself fruitless, for in it one has a jarring contrast between the narratorial description of nature and the royal palace, on the one hand, and the reactions of Rosanette, on the other. Here description and dialogue undercut each other, most strikingly perhaps when what may anachronistically be called a magnificent Proustian passage on the "peculiar melancholy of royal residences" is punctured by a yawn from Rosanette, who is not only ignorant of the history inhabiting the palace but insensitive to its natural surroundings. The failure of escape and refuge within an idyll is epitomized in this remarkable one-sentence paragraph evoking a utopia (although its halting, "gasping-for-breath" quality is partially lost in the English translation that substitutes four commas for the original seven: "Debout, l'un près de l'autre, sur quelque éminence du terrain, ils sentaient, tout en humant le vent, leur entrer dans l'âme comme l'orgeuil d'une vie plus libre, avec une surabondance de forces, une joie sans cause" (Standing side by side on a hillock, and breathing in the wind, they felt their souls were filling with a sort of pride in a freer life, a surge of strength, an inexplicable joy; p. 323).

One may note the indefiniteness of the *quelque* that does not localize the promontory or hillock, as well as the brief *envolée lyrique* in the phrase referring to a freer life, which is not interrupted by commas. The reference to a surge of strength or, more literally, to a superabundance of force is of course quite gratuitous, since it is nowhere in evidence in the novel. Yet the inexplicable joy (or joy without cause) is all one can expect from so vague and empty an image of utopia. What is most striking, however, in light of the collapse of spheres, is that this deceptive utopian image evoked by nature has little to distinguish it from vague utopian hopes stimulated by political events. It could, for example, as readily have been written of Dussardier on the barricades. Indeed, Frédéric precipitately leaves Fontainebleau, for "sentimental" reasons that are at fragile odds with idyllic flight, when he learns that Dussardier has been wounded in Paris. "He was shocked by this selfishness, and he reproached himself for not being in Paris with the others. His indifference to the country's misfortunes had something mean and bourgeois about it. His love suddenly weighed upon his conscience like a crime" (p. 329).

This is perhaps the place to make a few brief observations about the style of *The Sentimental Education* before turning to its two famous concluding scenes. The novel, especially when compared with *Madame Bovary*, seems harder and drier stylistically, as if the narrator had already learned the "educational" lessons that are implicit in the lives of the characters. It is an exacting and brilliant treatment of exhaustion and boredom that incurs the risk of appearing exhausted and boring itself. One remarkable feature of the text is the prominence of narration, description, and dialogue with a relatively restricted, evanescent, and at times almost insignificant use of the free indirect style. The narrator is primarily ironic and objectivating, taking a marked critical distance from characters and events—at times even resorting to clipped *comptes rendus*. The interplay of proximity and distance, of irony and empathy allowed by the free indirect style, with its subtle interweaving of the perspectives of the narrator and the characters, is given somewhat confined space in which to deploy itself. The very tempo of its use by the narrator seems to replicate in its own way the fleeting and insubstantial quality of Frédéric's "sentimental" desires in love and politics. The sense of narratorial involvement in the story is thus curtailed, and with it that of the reader is also diminished. Indeed, the reader may be somewhat bewildered by the disparity between the seemingly impersonal objectivity of the narration and what he or she would like to believe is a hyperbolic intensification of the most negative and deadening features of modernity. If one can even speak of the transformative implications of the novel, they would seem to be dependent upon the response of the reader, whether the challenge is faced in the writing of the novel itself (as it was, say, by Proust, Joyce, and Beckett) or, more problematically, in social and political life. These narrative effects, which exacerbate the sense of collapsing spheres and absent articulations, will be carried even further in *Bouvard and Pécuchet*, to which the concluding scenes of the novel provide a rather pointed introduction. (In fact, the entire pattern of fleeting hope, heightened expectation, and rapid deflation that marks Frédéric's desires in both the political and the amorous realms becomes the very basis of the narrative itself in *Bouvard and Pécuchet*, giving that text the structure of a spastic soufflé.)

The last two sequences in the novel may be read as offset love scenes that repeat—or recognition scenes that echo—

each other. They cannot be (as they all too often are) discussed in isolation, for they are blatant displacements of each other. The first is situated in 1867, the second in the winter of 1867–68, as the novel passes in resounding silence over the entire course of the Second Empire from 1851 to 1867. It seems to me altogether problematic to interpret this silence as meaning that 1851 either is a decisive break in history or is absolutely inconsequential—indeed, this very opposition may be as inoperative as other oppositions inscribed or implied in the novel. It would also seem gratuitous to contend that Flaubert's interest in the Second Empire is revived during its final stage of relative "liberalization" before its collapse in the aftermath of the Franco-Prussian war of 1870.

In any case, in the first scene Madame Arnoux returns to see Frédéric:

> Towards the end of March, 1867, at nightfall, he was alone in his study when a woman came in.
> "Madame Arnoux!"
> "Frédéric!"

The relatively precise dating of the objective statement in this passage recalls the novel's first sentence: "On the 15th of September, at six o'clock in the morning, the *Ville-de-Montereau* was lying alongside the Quai Saint-Bernard, ready to sail, with clouds of smoke pouring from its funnel" (p. 15). But the initial passages of the novel continue in a narrative and descriptive vein, whereas in this penultimate scene impersonality and objectivity are interrupted by exclamations as the two characters briefly annotate their surprise by identifying each other by name. Then begins their elaborate *pas de deux* in which clichés of love, detached from present reality, are exchanged almost as if they were sacred objects, and the discoupled couple try to remember the past and to project it into a happier but unlived future anterior. Madame Arnoux even refers to the "Frédéric's bench" (*le banc Frédéric*), where she, in her retreat in Brittany, sits contemplating the sea—a sentimental object reminiscent of the bench on which he first saw her sitting on board the *Ville-de-Montereau*. But the role reversal implied in this reference goes further, for now Madame Arnoux is the more desirous suitor of the two, and Frédéric even suspects that she "had come to offer herself to him" (p. 415). When earlier a lamp illuminated the twilight obscurity and lit up Madame Arnoux's white hair, "it was like a blow full in the chest," and "to conceal his disappointment, [Frédéric] went down on his knees, took her hands, and started murmuring endearments to her" (p. 414). The exchange of these clichéd words, referring only to an illusory past, is indeed a ritual act, but one that is "contaminated" with a utilitarian value—to conceal disappointment and actively to suppress the awareness that the idol is at last ready (perhaps was always ready) to descend from a phantasmatic pedestal. To take the ritualistic exchange of clichés only as evidence of the liberation of the signifier or the transcendence of the referent would itself be to deny or to disavow the repeated process of separation and collapse of seeming opposites at work throughout the novel, including its mournful if not funereal final scenes.

Indeed, Frédéric's suspicion that Madame Arnoux has crossed the line to profanation and prostitution "filled [him] with desire, a frenzied, rabid lust such as he had never known. Yet he also had another, indefinable feeling, a repugnance akin to a dread of committing incest. Another fear restrained him—the fear of being disgusted later. Besides, what a nuisance it would be! And partly out of prudence and partly to avoid degrading his ideal, he turned on his heel and started rolling a cigarette" (p. 415). The heterogeneous series of feelings evoked in Frédéric prevent the emergence of a fully coherent explanation for his overdetermined response, and his "rabid lust" itself, while presumably novel in his experience, flares up only to die down rapidly, like the desires with little staying power that preceded it (and like the brief flare-up of the free indirect style itself in the reference to the nuisance value of transgression). The rolling of a cigarette is another appropriately misplaced gesture, for it here averts the act of love-making that it stereotypically follows (as in the case of Rodolphe and Madame Bovary). The scene ends anticlimactically, as "neither of them could think of anything more to say" (p. 415). Madame Arnoux, in an exhausted and grotesquely overplayed romantic gesture, lets fall her white hair and, cutting off "a long lock close to her head," gives it to Frédéric, then leaves. The scene ends with the words, "Et ce fut tout" [And that was all; p. 416]. These final words collapse the simile marking Frédéric's first "vision" of Madame Arnoux ("Ce fut comme une apparition") into an empty metaphor.

Narratively, however, that was not all, for one has a displaced replay of the exhausted love scene in Frédéric's final encounter with Deslauriers. The two *bonhommes* are "reconciled once again by that irresistible element in their nature which always reunited them in friendship" (p. 416). (Once again, the French is more suggestive: "reconciliés encore une fois, par la fatalité de leur nature qui les faisait toujours se rejoindre et s'aimer.") This last scene includes a mock rundown of the fate of other characters as well; they are despatched in a farcically rapid review made up of brief one-liners. After Deslauriers explains the parodic *bêtise* of the *tête de veau*, he also tries to explain the fate of Frédéric and of himself through brittle binary oppositions that fail to hold up and deliver meaning.

"They had both failed, one to realize his dreams of love, the other to fulfil his dreams of power. What was the reason?" (p. 417) One may initially note that the question itself is false in that its premise is inexact. Frédéric was not simply the passive man of love and Deslauriers the active seeker of power; they were very much each other's parodic alter egos. Early in the text, for example, we are told that "the same thought nearly always occurred to them at the same time" (p. 64), and their sentimental and political involvements are slightly out-of-phase repetitions of one another.

The two questers nonetheless seek reasons for their apparently different modes of failure.

"Perhaps it's because we didn't steer a straight course [C'est peut-être le défaut de ligne droite]," said Frédéric.

"That may be true in your case. But I, on the contrary, was far too rigid in my line of conduct [Moi, au contraire, j'ai peché par excès de rectitude], and I failed to take into account a thousand-and-one minor factors which were really all-important. I was too logical, while you were too sentimental."

Then they blamed chance, circumstances, the times into which they were born. [P. 418]

Nowhere else are Frédéric and Deslauriers closer to Bouvard and Pécuchet than in this final scene. With respect to both paradoxical pairs, the exact measure of excess and lack in relations cannot be neatly allocated. Frédéric has also showed an excess (not simply a lack) of *ligne droite* in his obsessive fixation on a fetishized object, and Deslauriers has been led by "sentimentality" in a thousand-and-one directions (reacting to Frédéric's failure to finance a desired newspaper, becoming obsessed with the section of the Civil Code that caused him to fail his law exam, running after the women with whom Frédéric became involved, and so forth). The failure of binary oppositions to explain the fate of the two friends is itself indicated by the turn to another heterogeneous series of nonexplanatory factors (chance, circumstances, the times), causing the quest for reasons to trail off on paths that lead nowhere.

Memory is the final note struck in the scene between Frédéric and Deslauriers. They refer to a scene that had already been evoked in allusive terms early in the novel when Deslauriers declaimed.

"Venus, queen of the skies, your servant! But Poverty is the mother of Conscience, and heaven knows we've been slandered enough about that!"

The reference to an adventure they had shared amused them. They roared with laughter as they walked along the street. [P. 30]

The boyhood visit to *la Turque* is, significantly, situated *hors texte*, before the beginning of the novel in 1840, for it occurs in 1837 and is referred to only in retrospect. The concluding reference to it thus returns to a displaced origin, a beginning before the beginning of the novel that never takes place within the novel itself. The earlier reference to it is made in the key of laughter—which, we recognize retrospectively, echoes a feature of the visit itself, while the elaboration of the traumatic event in the final scene takes on a more ambivalent coloration.

La Turque herself may be exotically misnamed, for on the basis of her proper name, Zoräide Turc, "many people actually believed that she was a Mohammedan from Turkey" (p. 418). Her bordello, the bane of respectable bourgeois, "was, of course, the secret obsession of every adolescent" (p. 419). The allusion to the East, here as elsewhere in Flaubert's work, may itself be misleading; the quest for the exotic "other" and the desire to escape the familiar typically lead to the "discovery" of the repetitive and the "same." Still, the perhaps mistaken or misleading allusion has the power to trigger a disclosure that was repressed in the novel to this point, for earlier prostitution itself paraded under a variety of masks and deceptive names. Here, through a curious reversal, it finally calls itself by its proper name.

The scene recalled by Frédéric and Deslauriers, in a shared sentiment one hesitates to call nostalgic, is that in which they, as youths, picked some flowers in Madame Moreau's garden and offered them to the prostitutes *chez la Turque*.

Frédéric presented his, like a lover to his betrothed. But the heat of the day, fear of the unknown, a sort of remorse, and also the very pleasure of seeing at a single glance so many women at his disposal affected him so powerfully that he turned deadly pale, and stood still, without saying a word. The girls all burst out laughing, amused by his embarrassment; thinking they were making fun of him, he fled, and as Frédéric had the money, Deslauriers had no choice but to follow him.

They were seen coming out. This caused a local scandal which was still remembered three years later.

They told one another the story at great length, each supplementing the other's recollections; and when they had finished:

"That was the happiest time we ever had [C'est là ce que nous avons eu de meilleur]," said Frédéric.

"Yes, perhaps you're right. That was the happiest time we ever had," said Deslauriers. [P. 419]

And so the novel ends. The heterogeneous "reasons" for Frédéric's mute embarrassment before the laughing girls are again not explanatory, and the scandal felt by respectable bourgeois is compounded but not rounded off by the scandal of a seemingly inappropriate romantic gesture in a house of prostitution. Yet the gesture may be quite fitting with respect to the relation between the still relatively naive and the accurately named—between youth and prostitution. One somehow suspects, however, that even this binary cannot withstand the weight deposited by all the others that have been proved wanting in the course of the novel. And it seems both fitting and unsatisfying that the novel should end with a literal, and movingly empty, repetition.

One purpose of this essay has been to argue for an approach to literature that is bivocal or even multivocal—one that does not simply reinsert a text in its empirical context but indicates how a text responds to its contexts. A novel is a historical event among other events, but it is not a mere document. It supplements empirical reality in variable ways that the inadequate notions of the ideological and the critical (one might add the potentially transformative) may at least aid us in understanding. Its supplementary status also indicates how it makes claims on the reader, demanding a "dialogical" response (or an interpretation not divorced from practice) that goes beyond the documentary use of the text as a source for facts and hypotheses about the times. Indeed, a novel's undeniable documentary aspects can be better appreciated when they are situated in a broader network of relations that articulate the precise manner in which documentary elements are textually embedded. The interaction among documentary, ideological, and critical components or forces can be quite intricate in the case of a novel such as *The Sentimental Education*, which at the very least forces upon the reader the question of what to do with a world marked by collapsing spheres and untenable mediations. I do not pretend to have answered this question; I have at most indicated how the novel may be seen as raising it with more or less hyperbolic insistence. Indeed one sense in which my reading is "dialogical" is that it attempts both to supplement existing interpretations by emphasizing what I think they under-play and to prompt further readings that may have a similar relation to the deficiencies of my own. My goal is thus neither exhaustiveness nor definitiveness.

I would nonetheless note that one prevalent interpretive in-ference—an inference whose very prevalence may itself have some "symptomatic" significance—is not entailed by the reading I have offered. I would not conclude that, since the novel does not deliver satisfyingly symbolic, cathartic, or re-demptive resolution of the problems it treats, it clearly fur-nishes a counsel of despair indicating the futility of all ac-tion—except perhaps the act of narrating failed meanings—an act that, through a melancholy paradox, acquires compelling if not compulsive "interest." Such a conclusion may attest more to one's own sense of impasse and formalistic minimalism than to any necessary implication of the text, and it ignores the varied possibilities opened by the text's own resistance to providing "intranovelistic" solutions to the problems it dis-closes and explores. The inference that action is futile would most plausibly apply only *within* the terms and assumptions of a sociohistorical and political context such as the one at issue in the novel. By contrast, one may read the novel as indicating the obvious need to change that very context, although the text itself says more about what not to do in this respect than about the more difficult and far from obvious matter of what is to be done. One may nonetheless interpret the resistance that the text offers to internally satisfying "symbolic" solutions as a provocative way of confronting the reader with the issue of coming to terms with analogous problems in his or her own context, just as one may "read" the attempt to "work through" a transferential relation in psychoanalysis as a way of bringing about a transformed response to sources of disorientation and impasse in social life.[7]

---

[7] I read Mark Conroy's excellent *Modernism and Authority: Strategies of Legitimation in Flaubert and Conrad* (Baltimore, 1985) only after having com-pleted this study. His understanding of *The Sentimental Education* and of larger problems in history and criticism generally converges with the approach

I have tried to take. Yet despite his emphasis upon the tenuousness of oppositions and his recognition of the two final scenes as repetitions of each other, Conroy tries to protect the ending from the process of collapse of evacuated binaries into each other. Amalgamating the approaches of Jonathan Culler (in *Flaubert: The Uses of Uncertainty* [Ithaca, 1974]) and Jean Baudrillard (in *For a Critique of the Political Economy of the Sign* [St. Louis, Mo., 1981]), he sees the two "epilogues" as affirmations of purely fictional or nonreferential uses of language that are exchanged ritualistically between protagonists in a gift (in contrast to a market) economy. Conroy insists that this process of seeming liberation of the signifier itself has a history, but he does not stress strongly enough the extent to which any such movement is counteracted by forceful tendencies in *The Sentimental Education* itself. It is significant that Conroy's own text becomes rather uncertain in its argument and unclear in its formulations when he interprets the two final scenes; he even departs from his own critical protocols by conflating the workings of the novel with selected quotations of the author's statements about pure art and the *livre sur rien*. My own view is that the two "epilogues" do not escape the critical work of the novel in disclosing the fragility of binary oppositions (including that between referential and nonreferential uses of language or between market and gift exchange in modern society). One need not deny the bizarre, beleaguered pathos of the concluding scenes, but one may nonetheless question the idea that the novel finally offers its readers a transcendental saving grace in the tenuous form of an "illusory" appeal to pure fiction and self-consciously formalistic secular ritual. Indeed, one might observe that the very pathos of these scenes (to the extent that it exists at all) derives in part from the problematic, "impure," well-nigh evacuated relation between ritual and the demystifying forces it resists. One might further suggest (as I have tried to do) that the degree to which *The Sentimental Education* itself resists purely symbolic (or satisfyingly "intranovelistic") closure with respect to unresolved sociopolitical and cultural problems is the degree to which it makes one vital connection with history and the issue of significant changes in it. (One may also compare my approach with Peter Brooks's stimulating discussion in *Reading for the Plot* [New York, 1984], pp. 171–215. I also read Brooks's book after having completed this study, but in response to his analysis I changed the final paragraph of this chapter.)

5

Mann's *Death in Venice*:
An Allegory of Reading

Thomas Mann employed henceforth, again and again, and ever more audaciously, this parodistic method whose secret is a premeditated and aesthetically mastered incongruity between the message delivered and the tone of voice in which it is delivered, between the outrageous tale and the conciliatory bearing of the language that does the telling. The outward literary gesture seems to ask challengingly: "Who, after this testimony, is prepared to suggest that the classical tradition of literature is seriously disturbed?", while the story, despite its being so decorously narrated, answers most emphatically: "I."

Nowhere is this kind of "parody" more successful than in *Death in Venice*, where content and form are at most skillfully arranged loggerheads. For the composition could not be more classical. It reflects what is *said* of Aschenbach: that he classically triumphed over the forces of formlessness and decomposition. Yet what is *shown* through this composition is the utter defeat of a classical campaign so disastrously waged out of season. The irony of this situation, profoundly moral and untouched by mockery, is Thomas Mann's way of acknowledging the tragically simultaneous presence of two incompatible forces within him: a conservative love of the classical literary tradition and the disruptive insight that, alas, this tradition has had its day.

Erich Heller

My epigraph is taken from Erich Heller's well-known essay "Autobiography and Literature."[1] As is his wont, Heller emulates Mann himself by playing a variation on the story he is discussing: he stresses the parodic and ironic dissonance between the seemingly perfect, classical narrative form in which *Death in Venice* is recounted and the unsettling content of the story told. His insistence on this dissonance seems correct or at least suggestive with reference to one important level of the text. So does his idea of what is shown: a fall from innocence and a failed quest for reborn innocence. But I think that this interpretation is too simple to account for the complexity of the text.

Heller's interpretation does not adequately address the role of doubling effects and attempts at transformative reversal in *Death in Venice*. Through these doubling effects, the text becomes more and other than the tale of a quest for lost innocence recounted in a parodic and ironic dissonance between form and content. And the problem of its relation to its pertinent contexts becomes both more insistent and more intricate. There are, for example, signs that the seemingly perfect narrative form is itself suspicious. And, as Heller himself indicates but interprets in a very classical manner, there is a hope of regeneration or renewal in Gustav Aschenbach's own quest for what Kenneth Burke translates as the "miracle of reborn ingenuousness"—what Heller interprets as innocence.

> The power of the word with which he here cast out the outcast announced the turn away from all moral skepticism, all sympathy with the abyss; it was the counter-move to the laxity of the sympathetic principle that to understand all is to forgive all— and the thing that was here well begun, even nearly completed, was that "miracle of reborn ingenuousness" which was taken up a little later in one of the author's dialogues expressly and not without a certain discreet emphasis. Strange coincidences! Was it as a result of this rebirth, this new dignity and sternness, that his feeling for beauty—a discriminating purity, simplicity, and

[1]In Thomas Mann, *Death in Venice* (1912; New York: Modern Library, 1970), 114–15. All page references in the text are to this revised edition of the authorized translation by Kenneth Burke with a critical essay by Erich Heller.

evenness of attack which henceforth gave his productions such an obvious, even such a deliberate stamp of mastery and classicism—showed an almost excessive strengthening about this time? But ethical resoluteness beyond knowledge, the knowledge that corrodes or inhibits moral firmness—does not this in turn signify a simplification, a reduction of the world to too limited terms, and thus also a strengthened capacity for the forbidden, the evil, the morally impossible? And does not form have two aspects? Is it not moral and amoral at once—moral in that it is the result and expression of discipline, but amoral, and even immoral, in that by nature it contains an indifference to morality, is calculated, in fact, to make morality bend beneath its proud and unencumbered scepter? [Pp. 16–17]

The German expression rendered as "miracle of reborn ingenuousness" is *Wunder des wiedergeborenen Unbefangenheit* and the problem is how to translate and interpret it. My question is whether, through doublings and reversals, Mann attempts to make irony and parody bend back on themselves and, in a serious jest, offer the possibility of a reborn *Unbefangenheit* that is not simply the repossession of a lost original innocence or ingenuousness.

In approaching this question, one can begin schematically by listing at least four sets of oppositions that are inlaid in the text through an intricate process of doubling and displaced repetition: form and content (to which I have already alluded); art and life (a recurrent theme in Mann); the Apollonian and the Dionysian (from Nietzsche); and civilization and its discontents (from Freud). The question is how the text inscribes and plays out these oppositions in offset parallels and displaced repetitions.

Let us begin with form and content, a pair which—as Martin Heidegger warns us in *The Origin of the Work of Art*—constitutes the most powerful and prevalent conceptual tool in the analysis of art. *Death in Venice* does not simply rely on this binary opposition but renders it problematic through doubling and reversal. Form is explicitly thematized as a problem, and its ambivalent moral-immoral nature has particularly troubling effects in art: "Even as it applies to the individual, art is a heightened mode of existence. It gives deeper pleasures, it consumes more quickly. It carves upon the faces of its votaries the mark of imaginary and spiritual adventures; and though their external existence may be as quiet as a monk's, in the long run it produces a fastidiousness, over-refinement, fatigue, and alertness of the nerves such as would not result from actual living, even if crammed with illicit passions and pleasures" (p. 19).

The content of the story seems negative and unsettling. Yet Mann seeks in a displaced and discreet way what eludes Aschenbach: the *Wunder des wiedergeborenen Unbefangenheit.* The problem of translation is crucial, and translation, as always, implies interpretation. *Unbefangenheit* is a doubly negative term. *Un* designates a lack or an absence. *Befangenheit* signifies constraint, self-consciousness, and also prejudice. I would suggest that the word *Unbefangenheit* does not refer to a lost original innocence but to an absence of constraint or of self-consciousness that is *achieved* and always subject to challenge or loss. It is a spontaneity derived in paradoxical fashion in and through culture and art. And whether one judges the quest for it to be yet another illusion or a higher-order naiveté will affect one's response to Mann in general.

Mann himself used the term *Unbefangenheit* in a play, *Fiorenza.* Florence as the center of authentic Renaissance culture is a city often contrasted with Venice, its overrefined and decadent counterpart. It is significant that in the first version of the play the term is *Naivität,* which is closer to the idea of original innocence, evoking Schiller's contrast between the naive and the sentimental. And in *Death in Venice* itself, we are told that a treatise of Aschenbach's is compared by critics to "Schiller's conclusions on naive and sentimental poetry" (p. 11).

In Schiller the term "naive" is apparently related to the original, the innocent, the unreflectively spontaneous. It is contrasted with the sentimental as the sophisticated product of self-conscious reflection. The term *Unbefangenheit,* substituted by Mann for "naive," might be argued to place in question the naive notion of the naive and the system of oppositions in which it functions.

The two English translations of *Unbefangenheit* in standard editions tend to settle the question of its meaning in symmetrically opposite, one-sided ways. Kenneth Burke translates it, as I have said, as "ingenuousness"—a translation close to Heller's idea of innocence and the Garden of Eden. H. T. Lowe-Porter translates the word as "detachment," which indicates distance in contrast with innocence, ingenuousness, or presence.[2] But one may note that the dictionary definition of "ingenuous" is itself a good example of Freud's idea of a term that develops toward an ambivalence:" (1) Of a superior character; noble; honorable. (2) Free from reserve, disguise, or dissimulation; open; frank; candid; also, naive, artlessly frank. (3) Erron. for ingenious."[3] The last, erroneous sense is close to "disingenuous."

I would suggest that the complexity of *Unbefangenheit* is best rendered in English by "unconstraint," and the question is how it is to be achieved or at least approached.

A second phrase in the passage referring to the miracle or wonder of reborn unconstraint is *seltsame Zusammenhänge*—the strange way things hang together. Again the two translations decide the issue of interpretation in symmetrically opposite but complementary directions. Burke renders *Zusammenhänge* as "coincidences"—thus favoring the side of the nonlinear, synchronic, associative, paratactic, and metaphoric. Lowe-Porter offers "sequences of thought"—a translation more on the side of the linear, diachronic, logical, hypotactic, and metonymic.

Both these sets of translations ("ingenuousness" and "coincidences"; "detachment" and "sequences of thought") tend to foreclose interpretation prematurely in a one-dimensional way. Mann's text, I think, goes to neither extreme but explores the complex interaction between the two sets of meanings. Indeed, the text in general inquires into relations and possibilities in a world displaced from pure origins and oppositions.

[2]*Death in Venice and Seven Other Stories*, trans. H. T. Lowe-Porter, (New York, 1930).
[3]*Webster's New Collegiate Dictionary* (Springfield, Mass., 1960).

A similar problem arises with respect to the inscription or internalization of autobiography and historical context in the novella. Heller stresses the autobiographical nature of the text, but he also notes a difficulty with this interpretation. Section 2, up to the concluding passages (p. 18), is autobiographical: Mann did or planned to do what is ascribed to Aschenbach, and it is this portion of the text that includes the passage on the "wonder of reborn unconstraint." But at the very end of section 2 there is a turn or twist in the narrative that upsets autobiographical expectations. Here it is said of Aschenbach that his wife died young and that they had only one child, a girl—unlike Mann, whose wife actually accompanied him on his trip to Venice. And the prose also changes pace to become dryly descriptive until the final paragraph of section 2. The sober portrait of Aschenbach recalls Gustav Mahler rather than Thomas Mann. But in the final paragraph on art and life, quoted above, the style shifts back to the more evocative mode, and a problem is posed that did preoccupy Mann himself: the relation of life and art. At the very least, these movements indicate that the relations between literary text and autobiography are complex and shifting.

The general historical context is also internalized in a complex way. The very first sentence strikes the chord of historical insertion: "When for several months the situation in Europe had been so menacing. . . ." Aschenbach tries through travel to escape a critical context that his own story doubles or replicates in its own manner. Perhaps too readily, Thomas Mann accepted the contextual interpretation of Georg Lukács, for whom it was significant that Aschenbach was the biographer of Frederick the Great of Prussia. The disintegration of Aschenbach is for Lukács emblematic of the instability of Prussia with its explosive combination of hollowed-out discipline and decadent destructiveness, its rigid form and suspect content.[4]

Yet such an interpretation, while not altogether beside the point, is somewhat too direct and literal. Like *Doctor Faustus,*

[4]Georg Lukács, "In Search of Bourgeois Man," in *Essays on Thomas Mann,* trans. Stanley Mitchell (New York, 1965), pp. 25–26.

Death in Venice makes its historical time or period a content of the story in terms of the offset parallel of the "artist problem." The individual artist is in significant respects a more elevated figure than the political regime, although in Aschenbach's case this may be true to a somewhat lesser extent than in Leverkühn's. And Aschenbach's time is itself less degraded than Leverkühn's. Yet Aschenbach is not simply ignoble, and his time is clearly one of crisis and disorientation. Both texts, moreover, raise the difficult issue of the relation of Mann as writer to the artist figure as well as the relation of the literary text to the problems it renders and situates.

In addition, *Death in Venice* displaces one's very notion of historicity in the direction of repetition with variation or change. And Mann interweaves events that actually happened to him during his own visit to Venice with quasi-mythical motifs. The result is a recurrence of events and figures that complicate the narrative through doubling and repetition. The first evanescent figure Aschenbach sees—the man with protruding teeth, a jutting Adam's apple, and red hair—is his own double as well as a figure of death and the diabolical. He connects the desire for travel with the erotic and deadly. Travel becomes a kind of displaced love affair that may court death, thus bringing together two forms of escape from the everyday and the habitual. There is also the suspicious, illegitimate ferryman who, like the mythical Charon, takes the souls of the dead to Hades. Aschenbach resists the ferryman's attempt to transport him. The old, rouged, and cadaverous pederast on the boat and the illustrious figure of Socrates are linked and also function as doubles of Aschenbach. Heller brings out a number of mythical motifs in the story, although he does not relate them to the process of doubling and repetition in the narrative.

The relation between form and content is further complicated by its implication in other oppositions that are not altogether pure—oppositions that also double or repeat each other. (1) Art and life: Art is supposed to enrich life and to be a form of discipline related to morality. But the fascination for form may be a tempting negation of life. "And what is nothingness if not a form of perfection?" (p. 40). (2) Apollonian and

Dionysian: Apollonian form that structures Dionysian desire may become autonomized and excessive, thereby stimulating the outburst of uncontrolled frenzy. (3) Civilization and its discontents: The works of civilization require repression and sublimation that may go too far, threatening to heighten the sense of guilt and to exhaust binding forms. One may then have the breakthrough of destructive forces.

Thus one has a set of oppositions that are displacements of one another, and each opposition is fully autonomous or pure neither internally nor externally. And the "artist problem" as an offset parallel of a crisis in modern history signals a further complication in all these inlaid, doubled oppositions. The oppositions do not refer to a simple primal scene where pure desire breaks through civilized forms in some original fall from grace. One does not have a naive allegory of the Garden of Eden. All the oppositions are already removed from a simple origin and implicated in doublings and repetitions. The context is one of advanced civilization and displaced origins. And the motif of doubling is insistent in the text. Aside from the instances I have already mentioned, there are two appearances of the old pederast on the boat, two references to strawberries, two allusions to tigers, two farewells of the guitar-playing musician (who doubles the first death figure in multiple ways), two dreams, and two extended Socratic interludes. Furthermore, all the opposites relate to "decadence" in which traditional forms are not only displaced from any origin but on the verge of sterility and exhaustion. "Decadence" is the extreme form of displacement from a putative origin—its penultimate name. Art faces the problem of "decadence" as does life, faces it in a heightened form. And the Dionysian itself is not pure instinct but threatens to be twice barbaric in that it comes with high or at least late culture. One has the problem of the latecomer or epigone who, burdened with knowledge, must try to create or invent in the context of nearly exhausted and redoubled forms, in a context where inventions or creations threaten to be hollow repetitions of one another.

Aschenbach himself is clearly a latecomer—a latecomer in a highly sophisticated culture and a latecomer to erotic desire.

He cannot go "all the way to the tigers" (p. 10). His desire is not pure erotic frenzy but an attenuated, "decadent" eroticism. His desire is aestheticized. And art for him is an erotic tease. Mann's own "artist problem" in the text is to try to make irony reverse or outwit itself—how?—by rendering the allure of "decadence" yet turning one's own rendition of it into a "wonder of reborn unconstraint," a wonder that is not and does not pretend to be a simple, apocalyptic return to lost innocence but an achievement of irony itself.

Let us look a little more closely at the complex movement of the text and then return to the question of Mann's relation to Aschenbach and of the narrative to the story it renders. Aschenbach is introduced as the extreme case of the civilized, Apollonian, neoclassical artist who becomes a hero of the times, given his self-controlled manner of laboring on the edge of exhaustion. He is the prototypical modern artist. He strives for the "wonder of reborn unconstraint" (the "modernist" break with the degraded past), but it eludes him as he becomes the epitome of the latecomer, the epigone (the typical "postmodernist" position). "Gustave Aschenbach was the one poet among the many workers on the verge of exhaustion: the overburdened, the used-up, the clingers-on, in short all those moralists of production who, delicately built and destitute of means, can rely for a time at least on will power and the shrewd husbandry of their resources to secure the effect of greatness" (p. 15). This is the image that caused anxiety in Thomas Mann, the possibility that he was like this poet and that he perhaps did not take enough risks in writing to enable him to attain greatness. Mann was not Nietzsche, and, with bittersweet acceptance, he knew it. The very absence of an anxiety of influence in his various and varying invocations of Nietzsche was perhaps a cover for a more deeply internalized anxiety about his own artistic venturesomeness. Mann's problem, posed in another way, was how to confront his own kind of anxiety with ironic poise and lightness of touch.

After a series of false starts, Aschenbach acknowledges the obvious but initially unnoticed fact that Venice is the place he seeks. One may even wonder whether this realization was itself at first repressed, for Aschenbach recognizes his destination "of a sudden, as a thing astounding and self-evident" (pp. 18–19). And there is a bewildering affinity between the erotic desire that arises in Aschenbach and the art form cultivated in a context of "decadent" civilization. Aschenbach's desire for the boy Tadzio is itself highly aestheticized; it is not the tiger's instinctual desire for meat. Indeed, Aschenbach is fascinated not so much by the real flesh of the boy as by the way in which beautifully graceful gestures have alighted on this young man. The boy's form is stylized; he is an *objet d'art,* an aestheticized fetish. We can never tell whether the boy possesses an extraordinary sensitivity and acts in a seductive way or whether Aschenbach projects his own fantasies and imaginings onto the boy in order to rationalize his obsessive desire.

Aschenbach perceives Tadzio through aesthetic analogies. The boy recalls (in a parody of Platonic *anamnesis*) "Greek sculpture of the noblest period," specifically "the ancient statue of the 'boy pulling out a thorn'" (p. 34). The boy's name has aesthetic qualities—an initially inarticulate musicality in the vowel sound "u" that ends the name when it is called out and seems to approximate it to the putative origin of language in the primal cry of the heart. But Tadzio doubles the problem of modern art, for he too is a beautiful form on a sickly foundation. The enamel of his teeth is too thin, and he has a white pallor that Aschenbach resists relating to anemia. In his own relation to the boy, Aschenbach remains a voyeur, never touching his object of desire. They are bound together by a desire that is blocked and stimulated by aesthetic distance. Aschenbach never even addresses Tadzio, although there is an indication that his frank expression of feeling might have cleared the air, brought a return to health, and "very possibly put things on a sound, free and easy basis" (p. 62).

As desire is aestheticized, there is also the reverse movement: art is eroticized—but not all the way. The art form teases desire until one has a fascinating but bewildering mingling of categories. The complex transitional passages near the beginning of section 4 (beginning on p. 58) deserve close attention in this respect. In them Mann rewrites Plato's *Phaedrus* and converts Socrates more fully into what is only suggested in Plato: Socrates, the quester for truth, may also sophistically mislead youth as he joins the poets and stimulates "decadent" desire. In Plato, Socrates is a suitor of Phaedrus but one who apparently tries to lead the boy from sensual love to the higher love of truth and beauty. Indeed, the crucial difference between the Socrates-Phaedrus and Aschenbach-Tadzio relationships is the absence of dialogue in the latter. The Socratic interludes are themselves fantasies or dream states that hover indeterminately between Aschenbach and the narrator. In Mann, moreover, the Socratic dialectic is derailed as Socrates turns into one who leads youth astray and heralds desublimation. The sun, the image of the higher truth, may itself beguile reason, blind the quester, and turn him toward the senses.

Prefiguring Socrates' more blatantly Dionysian but still "decadent" speech in section 5 is the Socratic interlude in section 4: "For beauty, my Phaedrus, beauty alone is both lovely and visible at once; it is, mark me, the only form of the spiritual which we can receive through the senses. Else what would become of us if the divine, if reason and virtue and truth, should appear to us through the senses? Should we not perish and be consumed with love, as Semele once was with Zeus? Thus beauty is the sensitive man's access to the spirit—but only a road, a means simply, little Phaedrus. . . ." (p. 60). Up to the ellipsis one has a "faithful" rendition of Socratic education as it is usually understood. But after it, Socrates takes an alluringly dubious turn, and the narrator simultaneously takes a critical distance on him: "And then this crafty suitor made the neatest remark of all: it was this, that the lover is more divine than the beloved, since the god is in the one, but not in the other—perhaps the most delicate, the most derisive thought which has ever been formed, and the one from which spring all the cunning and the profoundest pleasures of desire" (p. 60). Socrates here reverses and displaces the argument of Lysias that he engages in the Platonic dialogue, the argument that the nonlover is to be preferred to one who loves. But Socrates in

Death in Venice manipulates Lysias's argument with a comparable sophistic motivation to justify the desire of an old man for a young boy.

In the paragraph following the first Socratic interlude, the desire to write is stimulated by desire for the boy:

> Moreover, he would do the work in Tadzio's presence, taking the figure of the boy as a standard for his writing, making his style follow the lines of this body which seemed godlike to him, and carrying his beauty over into the spiritual just as the eagle once carried the Trojan shepherd up into the ether. Never had his joy in words been more sweet. He had never been so aware that Eros is in the word as during those perilously precious hours when, at his crude table under the canopy, facing the idol and listening to the music of his voice, he followed Tadzio's beauty in the forming of his little tract, a page and a half of choice prose which was soon to kindle the acclaim of many through its clarity, its poise, and its vibrant emotional tension. Certainly it is better for people to know the beautiful product only as finished, and not in its conception, its conditions of origin. For knowledge of the sources from which the artist derives his inspiration would often confuse and alienate, and in this way detract from the effects of his mastery. Strange hours! Strangely enervating efforts! Rare creative intercourse between the spirit and body! When Aschenbach put away his work and started back from the beach, he felt exhausted, or even deranged; and it seemed that his conscience was rebuking him, as if after a debauch. [P. 61]

To put things simply and somewhat reductively, we have here—along with the ironic warning about psychobiographical interpretation and the exclamatory transitional devices that recall the *seltsame Zusammenhänge!* of an earlier passage—the birth of the desire to write from erotic desire at a distance in the presence of Tadzio. And, more pointedly, we have the figure that unites the writing process with the body of the boy. The lines made by the pen seem almost to follow the contours of the boy's body. What this form of desire produces is the *miniature* art form that doubles or repeats at a distance the passion that inspires it. (Here one may recall Max Weber's contention that modern art is constrained to be miniature and that monumental art in modern conditions is always an abomination.) The overly obvious image I would offer for this "page and a half of choice prose" is that of the pearl in the oyster, the pearl that forms around the irritation caused by the grain of sand inside the oyster. This page and a half of choice prose is not itself the expression of the purely Dionysian. Nor does it seem to be the wonder of reborn unconstraint. It is a prelude to the *Liebestod*—the song of love and death.

In the next paragraph, the fascinated, intoxicated, and increasingly hopeless Aschenbach, fixated on the boy, follows Tadzio and is on the verge of touching him. Here one has the intimation that the expression of desire might have "put things on a sound, free and easy basis," might have restored Aschenbach to a "wholesome soberness," and unfixed fixation through a kind of talking cure. But Aschenbach utters the words "too late!"—too late to approach the boy and too late for Aschenbach.

Thus, in section 4, beginning with the first extended Socratic interlude, there is a transition or passage in the story in which a powerfully alluring but dangerously indiscriminate mingling of categories is on the verge of breaking down or passing into chaos, at least in an attenuated way. In section 5 there is further breakdown and a partial—only a partial—breaking loose of Aschenbach. A plague from the East—the land of the tigers—comes to Venice, and Aschenbach experiences a complicity with the plague, which he feels compelled to keep secret. Here, the eating of the overripe strawberries is a gesture that Heller compares to the eating of the apple in Eden. But, as I indicated earlier, any analogy with an original fall is displaced. Earlier in the story, Aschenbach had already eaten "large ripe" strawberries. And overripe strawberries are at best "decadent" apples. Aschenbach's eating them is close to Leverkühn's act (in *Doctor Faustus*) of seeking out a syphilitic prostitute and having sex with her.

In section 5 we have the repetition, in less censored form, of the hallucinatory dream that accompanied Aschenbach's desire to travel—not "all the way to the tigers," not to the East but to Venice, where tigers do not float in the canals. In the second dream, there is a Dionysian orgy complete with the eating of the steaming flesh of a victim. In section 5 we also have the second extended Socratic interlude, in which Socrates confesses that "we poets cannot take the road of beauty without having Eros join us and set himself up as our leader" (p. 95). Socrates, the paragon of light, clarity, and irony, goes over to the enemy: he joins the poets. And he asserts the indiscriminate mingling of his knowledge with the seduction of youth, perverse desire, and "a natural leaning toward the abyss" (p. 95). "But form and innocence, Phaedrus, lead to intoxication and to desire, lead the noble perhaps into sinister revels of emotion which his own beautiful rigor rejects as infamous, lead to the abyss—yes, they too lead to the abyss. They lead us poets thus, I say, since we cannot lift ourselves up, and can but let ourselves loose" (p. 96). At this point it seems that all roads lead to the abyss, even the quest for "a new rigor, form, and reborn innocence [*zweiten Unbefangenheit*]" (p. 96).

Near the end Aschenbach is looking for the last time at Tadzio who is engaged in a wrestling match—a tempting game that seems to have no rules or limits, an adolescently Dionysian game in which Tadzio is subjugated and pressed down under the weight of a heavier boy. This is a game like that which Aschenbach wanted to play but could never bring himself to envision beyond fantasy. And it is a game from which Tadzio escapes in a petulant, narcissistic, aesthetic movement. Tadzio wades to a sandbank teasingly situated between the boundless and the boundary, between the open sea and the shore. In isolation the boy makes a last beautiful gesture that Aschenbach cannot touch: "And suddenly, as though at some recollection, some impulse, with one hand on his hip and without shifting his basic posture, he made a lovely twist with the upper part of his body, and glanced over his shoulder toward the shore" (p. 98). Meeting this glance from afar, Aschenbach collapses; he dies in a mirrorlike relation to the narcissistic object of desire or the inward-turning trope. Tadzio's "lovely twist" at the end of section 5 responds as well to the "slow twisting movement" by which Aschenbach himself turns his palms upward at the end of section 3 in a dubious imitation of the martyr calmly welcoming death. And the open palm is of course contrasted with the closed fist that was presented in section 2 as the symbol of Aschenbach's excessive self-discipline and control.

Like Aschenbach, Mann as a writer faces the problem of the latecomer who must use nearly exhausted categories and forms in making art and trying to be inventive. For him the only possible spontaneity is one that is derived from a reuse and a working through of traditional givens. Mann resorts to irony and parody. Can they be played out to the point of critical affirmation and the regeneration of nearly empty forms? Does Mann in a text like *Death in Venice* succeed where Aschenbach seems to fail? The answer, I think, is both yes and no.

In one movement, one is tempted to say "no." At times Mann as a writer seems very close to Aschenbach, and the text renders Aschenbach's story in a compelling way. The more oneiric passages exert an almost hypnotic influence, and the text as a whole has the power to move the reader, perhaps to empathy. *Death in Venice* cannot be reduced to the theme of "decadence" in the ordinary negative sense. Yet the way the text is moving can leave the reader in doubt about the fundamental relations it agitates. The text itself seems dangerously close to the perfect narrative form or inward-turning trope that is narcissistically self-enclosed and able to induce a deadly fascination. Is this form like Tadzio's anemic body or like Aschenbach's miniature art that tries to build on unstable, sickly foundations? Is Mann himself a false Socrates, an unreliable narrator, a deceptive "high modernist"? Is any notion of reborn unconstraint an illusory naiveté or at best a rather transparent fiction?

In another movement (which cannot be given absolute priority or the privilege of closure), one is tempted to say "yes," at least in a qualified way. Mann as writer undertakes the risky venture of rendering Aschenbach's story in alluring tones. Yet the text of *Death in Venice* cannot simply be identified with Aschenbach's story, or Mann as writer with Aschenbach (or with the biographical Mann, for that matter). The text brings out the captivating side of Aschenbach's story, but it retraces it with marks of difference. At points the narrator draws back in critical fashion. The narrative voice is not fully participatory or empathetic. And the text does not fully conform to the opposites it explores. It is neither dreamlike nor sober and ironic but sets up a challenging interplay between oneiric and soberly ironic movements. And a measure of perspective is offered on all the opposites I mentioned earlier. Ironic and parodic gestures do seem close to outwitting themselves and suggesting a reborn unconstraint that is not a naive return to some original state but a cultural achievement. (Here, to strain the allegory, the absence of an absolute origin or foundation does not necessarily imply an uncontrolled free play of infinite signification but rather the possibility of an interaction or interplay of limits and excess, norm and transgression in discourse and practice.) The text of *Death in Venice* does not totally transcend the problems it explores, but neither does it replicate them in a fully symptomatic manner. In a double movement it enacts certain limiting possibilities and becomes a counteragent or antidote to them, for it shows how a complex use of irony and parody may both touch extremes and not be altogether consumed by them. In this sense, irony and parody are neither the figures of absolute impasse nor negative cultural items to be transcended in a refound innocence or state of salvation. Used in a certain way, they may, however problematically, be parts of a "reborn unconstraint."

Does *Death in Venice* provide any effective indication that sociopolitical transformation must be considered a vital part of any quest for "reborn unconstraint"? This rather dissonant question should be raised, although there are no easy answers to it. Ony may, I think, accord limited credence to Lukács's argument that *Death in Venice* critically discloses in its portrayal of the "artist-figure" a state of society and culture that are based upon an untenable combination of rigid form and volatile content. To argue that the text stylistically intimates a better articulation of seeming opposites in the body politic would be admissible only on the level of extended and perhaps forced allegory. A few years after the publication of *Death in*

Venice, Mann himself tried to formulate his relation to politics in his *Reflections of a Nonpolitical Man* (1918). In that tortured defense of the "nonpolitically" aesthetic imagination, which sees the world *sub specie necessitatis,* Mann himself seemed to replicate and legitimate the "deadly dichotomies" of modern German intellectual history. Indeed, his opposition of the authentic inwardness and profundity of German *Kultur* to the trivialities and politically committed enthusiasms of the Western *Zivilisationsliterat* seemed to identify a religion of art with ideology as the fatalistic naturalization of social and cultural conditions. And his "nonpolitical" stance was of course itself highly politicized and had crucial social and cultural implications. But in this work the manifest oppositions overlay a more compelling division within Mann himself—a division that at times became overt as the "ironic German" recognized his own contributions to critical analysis and the disruption of "conservative" *Kultur*—the ways he too was a writer on the side of civilization. It is these inner divisions that *Death in Venice* announces and accentuates in its own way. They become more pronounced in *Doctor Faustus* (1947), in which arguments of the *Reflections* are parodied—in the mouths of members of the Winfried and Kridwiss circles—and their protofascist possibilities disclosed; the very opposition between German *Kultur* and Western *Zivilisation* is both enacted and deconstructed in the intricate relations between the artist figure Adrian Leverkühn and the humanistic narrator Serenus Zeitblom.

How *Death in Venice* itself might be related practically to any larger conception of sociocultural and political change is moot. But the one inference to be drawn from my reading is that along with its critical presentation of a state of crisis, *Death in Venice* can be seen to imply that any mode of sociopolitical action must come to terms with problems in the use of language. To say this is not to advocate making an absolute of the so-called linguistic paradigm. It is, however, to indicate that the use of language is never a purely instrumental or utilitarian question. It is part of the end one seeks and inherently bound up with an estimation of the validity of any political endeavor or sociocultural order. The broad issue is the role of critical forces in helping to effect a desirable transformation—one embodying a certain relation between normative commitment and critique. In this respect, irony and parody are themselves not unequivocal signs of disengagement on the part of an apolitical, transcendental ego that floats above historical reality or founders in the abysmal pull of aporia. Rather a certain use of irony and parody may play a role both in the critique of ideology and in the anticipation of a polity wherein commitment does not exclude but accompanies an ability to achieve critical distance on one's deepest commitments and desires.

6

History, Time, and the Novel:
Reading Woolf's *To the Lighthouse*

> As I see it, the vast knowledge we possess should challenge
> us not to indulge in inadequate syntheses but to concentrate
> on close-ups and from them casually to range over the whole,
> assessing it in the form of aperçus. The whole may yield to
> such light-weight skirmishes more easily than to heavy
> frontal attack.
>
> Siegfried Kracauer, *History:*
> *The Last Things before the Last*

The complexity of modern literature—as well as our own
closeness to it and the problems it explores—rather than any
general methodological dictum, may lend a certain credence to
the quotation from Siegfried Kracauer that serves as my epigraph. Yet the desire to combine syntheses and closeups is
unavoidable; it characterizes the work of many of those whom
we today recognize as major critics. I would like to approach
Virginia Woolf's *To the Lighthouse* with a brief and selective
discussion of two such critics, Joseph Frank and Erich Auerbach: selective in that I focus upon their more synthetic views,
which I find to be somewhat vulnerable, and neglect their
close-ups, which are often insightful. (For example, Frank's
remarkable reading of Djuna Barnes's *Nightwood* is in no sense
exhausted by his general conception of spatial form.) My effort
may be seen as an attempt to decrease the distance between
"practical criticism" and larger views, however abbreviated or
even allusive the latter may remain in my own discussion.

Frank's seminal essay, "Spatial Form in Modern Literature," was first published in 1945, and an expanded version was included in his book *The Widening Gyre* in 1963.[1] Auerbach's *Mimesis* was first published in 1946.[2] Frank's essay does not mention Virginia Woolf, yet it is not difficult to see how his guiding concepts and analyses can be applied to her work. Auerbach devotes the famous last chapter of *Mimesis* to Woolf's *To the Lighthouse*. While both studies were published some time ago, it could be argued, I think, that they retain a high degree of canonical authority. Moreover, they share a comparable apprehension of the modern world as undergoing extreme crisis. Frank relies on world-historical theories postulating a correspondence of artistic styles ("naturalistic" and "non-naturalistic") with the degree of sociocultural equilibrium and confidence or disequilibrium and disarray; his primary emphasis, however, is on formal analysis and interaesthetic comparison. Auerbach is more circumstantial and tortured in his depiction of modern disorder. Yet both critics arrive at strikingly similar conclusions about the nature of modern literature, particularly with reference to the problems of time and history.

In his essay on spatial form, Frank explicitly takes the plastic arts as his reference point, especially in the light of Wilhelm Worringer's theories about them: "We shall take our point of departure from Worringer's discussion of the disappearance of depth (and hence of the world in which time occurs) in non-naturalistic styles" (Frank, p. 56). With this reference point in mind, he believes he is able to account for developments in literature: "Since modern art is non-naturalistic, we can say that it is moving in the direction of increased spatiality. The significance of spatial form in modern literature now becomes clear; it is the exact complement in literature, on the level of aesthetic form, to the developments that have taken place in the plastic arts" (Frank, p. 57). The nature of this complemen-

---

[1]Bloomington, Ind., 1968. All references are to this edition, hereafter cited as Frank.

[2]Princeton, N.J., 1968. All references are to this edition, hereafter cited as Auerbach.

tarity remains rather unclear. Is there a paradoxical mimetic relation of literature to the plastic arts in the departure from mimesis, representation, and naturalism? Is it a question of coordinate developments? Or is one dealing with a formal analogy? Frank never addresses or even distinguishes these questions, but from the perspective I shall try to elaborate, this may not be of great moment. The preliminary issue is the adequacy of the very concept of spatial form that provides the basis for Frank's account.

Frank, like Auerbach, appeals to developmental or evolutionary arguments to account for the departure in modern literature from developmental and evolutionary models. Indeed, such models are essential for his own unthematized conception of history and time. "The evolution of aesthetic form in the twentieth century has been absolutely identical. For if the plastic arts from the Renaissance onward attempt to compete with literature by perfecting the means of narrative representation, then contemporary literature is now striving to rival the spatial apprehension of the plastic arts in a moment of time. Both contemporary art and literature have, each in its own way, attempted to overcome the time elements involved in their structures" (Frank, p. 57).

Frank also maintains that the concept of spatial form overcomes the duality of form and content by shaping the very substance of literary works. In Proust, for example, the "use of spatial form arose from an attempt to communicate the extratemporal quality of his revelatory moments." Indeed, Proust's "ultimate value, like that of Plato, was an existence wrenched free from all submission to the flux of the temporal." Yet Pound, Joyce, and Eliot, while also drawn to epiphanies, are presumably more complex than Proust because they "all move out beyond the personal into the wider reaches of history—all deal, in one way or another, with the clash of historical perspectives induced by the identification of modern figures and events with various historical or mythological prototypes." Their work thus has a palimpsest effect in which "the chief source of meaning is the ironic dissimilarity and yet profound human continuity between the modern protagonists and their long-dead (or only imaginary) exemplars" (Frank, p. 58). One might assume, in the light of the relatively conventional categories Frank employs here, that he would classify a work such as *To the Lighthouse* as closer to the "personal" concerns and neo-Platonism of Proust than to the offset mythicohistorical parallelism he locates in Pound, Joyce, and Eliot.

Crucial in spatial form for Frank is the technique of juxtaposition. It is the alternative to chronological, linear, developmental time as represented in the classical narrative. All the modern literary works he has discussed maintain, for him "a continual juxtaposition between aspects of the past and the present so that both are fused in one comprehensive view." Moreover, through this juxtaposition of past and present, "history becomes ahistorical; now it becomes a continuum in which distinctions between past and present are wiped out." Thus there is a hyperbolic movement whereby offset parallels lead to the obliteration of distinctions and the creation of a continuum. Again one has a putative parallel with the plastic arts, for in them "the dimension of historical depth has vanished. . . . Past and present are apprehended spatially, locked in a timeless unity that, while it may accentuate differences, eliminates any feeling of sequence by the very act of juxtaposition" (Frank, p. 59).

Extending his own hyperbolic conception of spatial form even further into the voiding of distinctions, Frank asserts that "what has occurred, at least as far as literature is concerned, may be described as the transformation of the historical imagination into myth—an imagination for which historical time does not exist, and which sees the actions and events of a particular time only as the bodying forth of eternal prototypes." Appealing to the authority of Mircea Eliade, Frank affirms that modern thought in general recurs to "cosmic, cyclical, infinite time" (p. 60). In fact, for Eliade, the work of writers such as Eliot and Joyce "is saturated with the nostalgia for the myth of eternal repetition and, in the last analysis, for the abolition of time" (quoted in Frank, p. 60). Thus, in Frank's view, observations (speculations?) from anthropology and the history of religions confirm his own conclusion that "modern literature has been engaged in transmitting the time world of history into the timeless world of myth. And it is this timeless world of myth, forming the common content of modern literature, that finds its appropriate aesthetic expression in spatial form" (Frank, p. 60).

One might object that this seemingly critical study of the obliteration of distinctions in modern literature has culminated in a crescendo of indistinction whereby differences among myth, history, and the arts tend to collapse in a global, diffuse apprehension of modern thought. What is most striking about Frank's procedure is an unproblematic reliance upon a simple logic of identity and difference to bolster the unexamined use of the most commonplace concepts. Frank simply assumes that we know full well what space and time, history and myth, temporality and intemporality are. At the very least, they are pure binary opposites, totally different from one another and internally homogeneous. That temporality may involve spacing, or that historicity may not be identified with linear, chronological, developmental time or narrative in general with a certain conception of temporality seems to be entirely beyond Frank's ken. Nor is there an apprehension that the very literary works he treats in such summarily authoritative fashion may be placing in question the very assumptions and modes of conceptualization he employs to account for them.

In Auerbach we encounter a more subtle mode of analysis and a thicker level of description, yet he too strives to center his account on the themes of time and consciousness, and in certain respects he fills out Frank's conception of spatial form. What was a suggestive sketch becomes a three-dimensional statue.

In an extensive explication of his initial quotation from the fifth section of part I of *To the Lighthouse*, Auerbach continually notes the difficulty in ascribing narrative voice or point of view to any specific figure in a clear-cut, unambiguous way. Voice or viewpoint seems to mutate in delicately modulated, ironic-empathetic movements. Yet when he comes to summarize his explication, he reverts to a simplistic developmental model and relies on the binary opposition between objectivity and subjectivity in a typical misinterpretation of free indirect style or *Erlebte Rede* as a rendition of the consciousness of characters in the words of the author: "The writer as narrator of objective facts has almost completely vanished; almost everything stated appears by way of reflection in the consciousness of the dramatis personae" (Auerbach, p. 534).

A comparable reductive gesture occurs in his attempt to collapse the problem of language into that of consciousness and to link consciousness with a certain conception of time. Obscured in the process is the manner in which modern techniques of narration challenge the identification of language with consciousness and, particularly with respect to the seemingly random event, broach the questions of unconscious dimensions of language use and the interplay between the aleatory and the constrained. "These are the characteristic and distinctively new features of the technique: a chance occasion releasing processes of consciousness; a natural and even, if you will, a naturalistic rendering of those processes in their peculiar freedom, which is neither restrained by a purpose nor directed by a specific subject of thought; elaboration of the contrast between 'exterior' and 'interior' time" (Auerbach, p. 538). It is curious that whereas Frank stresses the nonnaturalistic nature of modern literature, Auerbach here stresses a natural and even naturalistic rendering of putatively conscious processes. Even more curious is the invocation of this term when there is no natural model that can be imitated, and one must rely upon the language used to have any access to its object. Yet this move is concordant with Auerbach's seeming assumption that consciousness has a fully independent status, which is simply rendered or represented by language. A binary is of course also at work in the opposition between "interior" and "exterior" time, though some of Auerbach's own discussions indicate that such a binary is being challenged in certain modern texts.

While Auerbach and Frank seem to have similar pre-understandings of the nature of historical time (chronological, linear, developmental), they tend to construe its contrasting term somewhat differently. Instead of spatial form, Auerbach emphasizes the random moment as the epiphanous gateway to the intemporal. Yet before he reaches his final, strangely disconcerting apostrophe to it, he follows a tortuous route in delineating the vaster contextual implications of modern literature. For he begins in Lukácsian tones, only to modulate toward a voice akin to that of Serenus Zeitblom in Mann's *Doctor Faustus* and then to take an almost mandarin turn in apprehensively intimating the hope and despair of a common life in the form of a leveling threat to *Bildung* and high culture.

There is, Auerbach intimates, "a good deal to be said" for the view that "a method which dissolves reality into multiple and multivalent reflections of consciousness" is "a symptom of the confusion and helplessness . . . a mirror of the decline of our world."

> There is in all these works a certain atmosphere of universal doom: especially in *Ulysses*, with its mocking *odi-et-amo* hodgepodge of the European tradition, with its blatant and painful cynicism, and its uninterpretable symbolism—for even the most painstaking analysis can hardly emerge with anything more than an appreciation of the multiple enmeshment of the motifs but with nothing of the purpose and meaning of the work itself. And most of the other novels which employ multiple reflection of consciousness also leave the reader with an impression of hopelessness. There is often something confusing, something hazy about them, something hostile to the reality they represent. We not infrequently find a turning away from the practical will to live, or delight in portraying it under its most brutal forms. There is hatred of culture and civilization, brought about by means of the subtlest stylistic devices which culture and civilization have developed, and often a radical and fanatical urge to destroy. Common to almost all of these novels is haziness, vague indefinability of meaning: precisely the kind of uninterpretable symbolism which is also to be encountered in other forms of art of the same period. [Auerbach, p. 551]

This passage, which could find its place in Lukács's *Destruction of Reason* (and which is similar in nature to "humanistic" attacks upon certain variants of contemporary criticism), is followed by a shift in tone. Modern literature is not simply symptomatic, indeed aggravating, with regard to the worst aspects of modern society and culture at large: "Something entirely different takes place here too. Let us return again to the text which was our starting point." *To the Lighthouse* is not entirely exempt from Auerbach's strictures; it too "breathes an air of vague and hopeless sadness" (Auerbach, p. 551). Yet "it is one of the few books of this type which are filled with good and genuine love but also, in its feminine way, with irony, amorphous sadness, and doubt of life" (Auerbach, p. 552). The reader may notice that allowance is made for a relative exception, and even then the terms of contrast with those other modern texts are not terribly strong; indeed, they are bizarrely prejudicial in their masculine way. The moment of apocalyptic hope seems very weak, and the promise of an upbeat ending remote. In fact, the final recognition scene is one of the most disconsolate consolations in modern criticism or literature:

> It is precisely the random moment which is comparatively independent of the controversial and unstable orders over which men fight and despair; it passes unaffected by them, as daily life. The more it is exploited, the more the elementary things which our lives have in common come to light. . . . It is still a long way to a common life of mankind on earth, but the goal begins to be visible. And it is most concretely visible now in the unprejudiced, precise, interior and exterior representation of the random moment in the lives of different people. So the complicated process of dissolution which led to fragmentation of the exterior action, to reflection of consciousness, and to stratification of time seems to be tending toward a very simple solution. Perhaps it will be too simple to please those who, despite all its dangers and catastrophes, admire and love our epoch for the sake of its abundance of life and the incomparable historical vantage point it affords. But they are few in number, and probably they will not live to see much more than the first forewarnings of the approaching unification and simplification. [Pp. 552–53]

As I turn to Woolf's novel,[3] I cannot promise a more congenial ending than Auerbach's, but I would like to suggest a reading that may perhaps have different implications for our understanding of certain techniques in modern literature.

The interpretations of Auerbach and Frank depend upon the idea of a breakdown of developmental time in the modern period and the emergence of the random or aleatory event as the debris of temporality. The novelist attempts to transvalue or transubstantiate this debris into a redemptive moment—what Benjamin termed the *Jetztzeit* or now-time—that becomes a portal to the intemporal and transhistorical. Although Auerbach and Frank do not explicitly make this point, their views are in certain respects compatible with the argument that the so-called "autonomization" of art in the modern period reached its apogee in the "high-modernist" aestheticism of figures such as Woolf—an aestheticism that, for some later analysts, involved the codification of an art-for-art's-sake ideology and the radical departure from realistic representation and social commitment.[4]

While these interpretations are extremely appealing, the view I would like to offer is somewhat different. Auerbach and Frank assume a dichotomy between the intemporal and time, whether the latter is construed as a succession of random now-points or as an ordered, sequential development. (Walter Benjamin is more complicated in this respect, for a careful reading of his "Theses on the Philosophy of History" would, I think, support certain features of my argument.) I want to maintain that *To the Lighthouse* problematizes this dichotomy, as well as the other binary oppositions that attend it in the accounts of Auerbach and Frank. In the novel, the seeming fixation of the

---

[3]Virginia Woolf, *To the Lighthouse* (1927; New York: Harcourt, Brace & World, 1955). All references are to this edition and page numbers are cited in the text.

[4]See, e.g., Peter Bürger, *Theory of the Avant-Garde* (1974), trans. Michael Shaw, with foreword by Jochen Schulte-Sasse (Minneapolis, 1984). See also Fredric Jameson, "Postmodernism, or the Cultural Logic of Late Capitalism," *New Left Review* 146 (1984):53–92.

moment is a retrospective effect of a process of repetitive temporality that cannot be construed as simple juxtaposition and that undercuts the opposition between linear time and the intemporal. Given the dearth of social institutions that may collectively shape repetitive temporality into a viable rhythm of social life, the discourse of the novel attempts to inquire into the possibilities of such a temporality in language. In the process, memory makes the pathos-charged but impossible attempt to stop time as a movement of repetition with change. Particular events recur with more or less significant variations (for example, the attempt to go to the lighthouse in part I occurs with a modification in part III). And the discourse of the novel both marks and fills in the wavelike gaps or intervals (the "spacings") between events through a fluid exploration of shifting perspectives and quicksilver modulations of narrative voice.

The accompanying diagram attempts to represent the narrative movement of the novel.

The horizontal level refers to the "diachronic" movement of "outer" events in "real" historical time as it is conventionally understood. (But the novel is contesting this conventional understanding of time.) On this horizontal level are such ordinary projects as bringing clothes to people in the lighthouse. This level also includes so-called epochmaking events like war in collective life or marriage in personal life. Time in this dimension is a matter of change that can be chronicled in terms of a succession of now-points. The vertical level refers to the more "synchronic" and structural dimension. On this level, an aesthetic immobilization and perception in depth of the random event or moment *seems* to provide a fleeting passage outside time and a reconciliation between "inner" experience and the impersonal symbolic form. Yet the interaction between the diachronic and the synchronic in terms of a quasi-ritualistic, repetitive temporality is complex. It problematizes the epi-phanous moment of insight without entirely destroying it. Thus time is not simply spatialized, and the moment is not simply eternalized. Rather, events recur with variations, and the sense of timelessness is an ex post facto (or *nachträglich*) effect—a sense that always comes in the past tense.

Let us look a little more closely at the two levels and how they interact. There are at least two kinds of "outer" event on the "diachronic" level of ordinary time. First and most impor-tant, there is the apparently insignificant, random, contingent event. The bulk of the novel concerns aleatory events of this sort and what may be revealed in the spaces or intervals be-tween them (for example, knitting a stocking or making a trip to the lighthouse). I shall return to this kind of event.

A second kind may be labeled the "history-making" event in social or personal life; these make for major changes, typically in destructive and violent ways, and pose the severest chal-lenge to the work of art as Virginia Woolf conceives it; they are disruptive. An interesting question is that of how events of this sort—those ordinarily seen as major historical occurrences— are treated in the novel. How does the novel inscribe or tex-tualize the important context of events (such as war and death) that make for basic and often violent change in individual and collective life?

The answer to this question must include a discussion of the function of brackets and parentheses in the novel; see, for ex-ample, the significant use of the bracket in part II. As explicit marks of punctuation, brackets represent the way in which major and often negative forces of ordinary time and history are self-consciously contained, in a sense suppressed. But they are not simply silenced, eliminated, or avoided through un-selfconscious repression, denial, and escapism. Major events of war, death, birth, marriage, and violence are explicitly bracketed. Minor disruptive events often occur in parentheses: for example, the movement of knitting needles or the killing of a fish. In short, events not socially controlled in a viable way through collective institutions and rituals in the modern world are disruptive and hence bracketed in the art of Virginia Woolf;

punctuation serves as an explicit policy of containment. Note that, along with the scandal of ordinary history, the erotic also tends to be bracketed and treated with extreme discretion. (Here one may mention the etymology of bracket from the Latin *brachae,* "breeches," and the French *braguette,* "codpiece.")

On page 201 of the novel, World War I and the death of Andrew Ramsay from the explosion of a shell take place in brackets (here one has a book in which the First World War occurs in brackets!), as does the death of Mrs. Ramsay on page 194:

> Mr. Ramsay, stumbling along a passage one dark morning, stretched his arms out, but Mrs. Ramsay having died rather suddenly the night before, his arms, though stretched out, remained empty.

The setting of the novel is in keeping with the bracketing of disruptive historical events and forces. The misty island in the Hebrides facilitates scenes of contemplation and reverie. There is not, for example, the threat of urban reality to be found in *Mrs. Dalloway.* Yet both novels have as their social setting the hothouse environment of upper classes largely closed off from other sectors of society and leading an extremely sublimated existence. In one sense, this might be seen as a limitation.

In another sense, however, the use of brackets to frame "history-making" events constitutes a reversal and transvaluation of ordinary or conventional perspectives. Conventionally, the events that make history form the substance of the text; the accidental and the aleatory may be relegated to brackets or footnotes. In this novel, epochal events are self-consciously represented as extraneous to the main story. Marginal incidents become crucial if not central, and liminal states or processes of transition—threshold phenomena—are explored and rendered. Contingent, insignificant events—those that many historians might consider non-events, such as knitting a stocking or going to a lighthouse—are promoted to prominence. The emphasis on little things in life recalls Nietzsche's assertion that great politics really concerns things we generally ignore, like digestion and climate—that great politics is a politics of everyday life. Could one then assert that, by implication, a critical comment is made about the conventional organization and understanding of what is important?

Yet the disruptive and violent events are not simply outside the novel as its "unthought." They are included in certain tactful, subtle, and perhaps potentially transformative ways. And periodically, violent events threaten to burst their brackets and erupt catastrophically. The control of them is a matter of tact and style in the largest sense, for violence is always just below the surface and transgression on the threshold.

The dimension of history that is unbracketed and renewed in the novel is the microlevel of seemingly insignificant happenings. Here small mutations flash by, and one has the importance of what transpires in the intervals between events—intervals traced in mutable novelistic discourse. The little ordinary events repeat one another both in erosive ways and in ways art may transform into something remarkable. Repetition suggests the ambivalence of ordinary, contingent events, their existence in two registers: they are simply there materially; they are possibly allegorical. The lighthouse itself is an installation on a rocky island inhabited by people with ordinary needs, and it is perhaps something else again—an "attempt at something," in the words of the novel. Note also the dual sense of repetition in the recurrent fall of the waves, which provide both reassuring meaning and a sense of terrifying emptiness. They emblematize repetitive temporality itself.

The monotonous fall of the waves on the beach, which for the most part beat a measured and soothing tattoo on her thoughts and seemed consolingly to repeat over and over again as she sat with the children the words of some old cradle song, murmured by nature, "I am guarding you—I am your support," but at other times suddenly and unexpectedly, especially when her mind raised itself slightly from the task actually at hand, had no such kindly meaning, but like a ghastly roll of drums remorsely beat the measure of life, made one think of the destruction of the island and its engulfment in the sea, and warned her whose day had slipped past in one quick doing after another that it was all ephemeral as a rainbow—this sound which had been obscured and concealed under the other sounds suddenly thundered hollow in her ears and made her look up with an impulse of terror. [Pp. 27–28]

The novel is also double in its realistic and its lyrical, evocative movements. On one level, it provides a realistic characterization of individuals and a depiction of social manners. There is a pointed portrait of upper-class English academic society on vacation. (What could be more disheartening!) One has daily life outside the workaday round but repeating certain of its concerns and complexities as if in a crucible or a hothouse. Leisure time seems to immobilize and intensify the standing tensions of everyday life. And there is a forceful sense of the threat that ordinary reality, once it is liberated from brackets, poses for the aesthetic imagination. On another level, the transformative power of art is affirmed—but only on the verge of apprehensive insight into empty spaces, blank stupidity, incipient violence, and darkness at the core of things.

One may also note that there is at least a minimal plot structure of the conventional linear sort superimposed upon the repetitive events, inner scenes, mobile voices, and protean perspectives. In one sense, the end of the story is in the beginning: the project of going to the lighthouse, conceived and frustrated in part I, is realized in part III. But there is little real suspense in the novel on this literal level. Interest shifts to the spaces between the events and the recurrent movements to the lighthouse on other levels. The very project of going to the lighthouse becomes implicated in a kind of displaced and secularized ritual process reconceived in art. And it shifts in perspective with the shift in the image of the lighthouse itself—a shift that relates image and "reality" in a nonreductive manner.

In part I the lighthouse, as an imaginary object of a quest, is largely on the side of wish, dream, and childhood. It is linked to the wish of a male child (James), a wish that the mother encourages but the father blocks or cuts off. In part III the lighthouse still has this aspect but it is also a commonplace reality, a lighthouse on a rocky island that is arrived at by boat.

On the second—the vertical or synchronic—level I referred to, the novel seems quite allegorical. The characters are close to archetypes. One has the beautiful, imaginative, sensitive, fecund female and mother, Mrs. Ramsay. And one has the philosophical, soberly realistic and logical, sterile male and father, Mr. Ramsay. On this level, the random moment or banal event may seem to be immobilized as a meaningful passage to an evanescent aesthetic vision of permanence and presence. Yet things are never quite what they seem to be or are never simply one thing and not another. Mr. and Mrs. Ramsay are not pure opposites—the one creative and life-giving, the other negative and deadly. And the perfect moment or epiphany of aesthetic insight is never a secure possession or an unproblematic saving grace.

Indeed, the novel itself begins before its literal beginning, and its ending is enigmatic. The first words—"'Yes, of course, if it's fine tomorrow,'" said Mrs. Ramsay, 'but you'll have to be up with the lark'"—presuppose (as Erich Auerbach has noted) an earlier question that remains unstated, an empty space or trough in the waves. And this wavelike motion from space to event is repeated throughout the text. The novel is not divided into chapters but organized almost musically as a three-part invention. Part I, "The Window," covers in outer time a few hours on a September evening in the summerhouse, yet it is the longest segment. Part II, "Time Passes," covers ten years, yet it is the shortest section. It is a lyrical tour de force (could it possibly be longer?) in which the voice of the narrator paradoxically evokes the state of nature after the passage of human beings and their voices. The house is both devastated and purified by natural forces, wind and sand. The only voice of a character that breaks the silence is that of a being on the margin of human communication, the witless caretaker Mrs. McNab. And the folds of Mrs. Ramsay's shawl hanging over the boar's skull in the children's room are loosened by natural forces.

In part I there is a thematic and perspectival interplay of

largely unreconciled opposites, movements, and possibilities—a vast dialogic interchange of voices and views. Mrs. and Mr. Ramsay seem to be polar opposites, and the table of other characters is like a force field organized around them. But, as I noted, the opposites are not pure. Mrs. Ramsay tries to organize life as a work of art with people as flowers in her bouquet. She is in every way a matchmaker. Yet at times she interferes in the lives of others and makes mistaken matches— the wedding of Paul and Minta, for example. She can be destructive in her interventions. Mr. Ramsay is an analytical philosopher with a linear mentality. He has written a book about "subject, object, and the nature of reality," which his son Andrew captures for Lily Briscoe in the image of a cleanly scrubbed table. His logic is linear: how to get from Q to R. Yet he has a touch of madness and eccentricity as he storms around the house reciting "The Charge of the Light Brigade."

Unlike her husband, Mrs. Ramsay is sensitive to the feelings of others, but she too can be domineering, though she gives in excessively to Mr. Ramsay's demands. In contrast to the literal-mindedness of her husband, she sees that one thing is never simply itself but also something else. This point is evoked in the beautiful image of the shawl and the boar's skull. Mrs. Ramsay comes into the children's room where shadows cast by a boar's skull are frightening the little girl Cam. But the boy James wants the boar's skull to remain where it is. Here the mother is in a double bind, confronted with the contradictory demands of her children. Through an incantatory use of language, Mrs. Ramsay transforms the skull into an imaginary object for Cam—a pretext for a fairytale. After covering the skull with her shawl, she "said how lovely it looked now; how the fairies would love it; it was like a bird's nest; it was like a beautiful mountain" (p. 172). But to James "she whispered" that "the boar's skull was still there; they had not touched it; they had done just what he wanted; it was there quite unhurt" (p. 173). Through the shawl or veil of language, the boar's skull both is and is not in the same place at the same time. Mr. Ramsay would not understand this logic of noncontradiction between incompatibles. Yet in trying to convert life into art,

Mrs. Ramsay goes too far in her own way and is both too imposing and too permissive. Her beneficial effect is greatest after she dies and serves as a memory in part III.

In part III, the two children who bore traits of their parents are also dead: Prue, who had her mother's beauty; Andrew, who had his father's brains. Gone as well are Mr. Bankes, Lily Briscoe's chance for love in life; and Mr. Tansley, Mr. Ramsay's parodic double, who is writing his dissertation about the influence of something on somebody. Present is the catlike, silent, lyrical poet, Mr. Carmichael, who is now famous but rather dissipated. Also present are Lily Briscoe, Mr. Ramsay, James, and Cam.

The "real" trip to the lighthouse undertaken by Mr. Ramsay, James, and Cam—its completion anxiously anticipated on shore by Lily and Mr. Carmichael—is in one sense a ritual act: Mr. Ramsay offers his dead wife a memorial act of atonement, acceding to the undertaking he refused in part I. He simultaneously moves toward his children and helps James to work through a grudge he has borne against his father for ten years because his hopes about going to the lighthouse were dashed by paternal authority. James also comes to see the doubleness of the lighthouse: "James looked at the lighthouse. He could see the white-washed rocks; the tower, stark and straight; [. . .] he could see windows in it; he could even see washing spread on the rocks to dry. So that was the lighthouse, was it? No, the other was also the lighthouse. For nothing was simply one thing" (Pp. 276–77).

One is tempted to say that James has learned Mrs. Ramsay's lesson. But the lesson is ambivalent in the manner of a Heideggerian statement. Nothing is simply one thing and one thing only—say, death. Nothing is simply one thing; it is also something else—say, death and life.

In this scene, Mr. Ramsay does not go all the way to his children but maintains an element of aloofness and reserve. For the first time in his life he congratulates James for doing something well—steering the boat—but he does not reciprocate the desire of the children to do something for him: "Both wanted to say, Ask us anything and we will give it you. But he did not ask them anything" (pp. 307–8). There is no full cycle of reciprocity (and no incest) but a gesture toward the children that remains asymmetrical.

Lily maintains a fruitful distance from Mr. Ramsay and limits his assertions by not giving in to all his demands. Here she differs from Mrs. Ramsay, whose place she takes with this significant modification. Yet Mrs. Ramsay as a memory or a revenant is important for Lily in part III. Indeed, Lily's memory of Mrs. Ramsay indicates the retrospective role of an epiphanous insight into reality, and it does so with a gentle touch of irony and pathos (together).

> "Like a work of art," she repeated, looking from her canvas to the drawing-room steps and back again. She must rest for a moment. And, resting, looking from one to the other vaguely, the old question which traversed the sky of the soul perpetually, the vast, the general question which was apt to particularize itself at such moments as these, when the released faculties that had been on the strain, stood over her, paused over her, darkened over her. What is the meaning of life? That was all—a simple question; one that tended to close in on one with years. The great revelation had never come. The great revelation perhaps never did come. Instead there were little daily miracles, illuminations, matches struck unexpectedly in the dark; here was one. This, that, and the other; herself and Charles Tansley and the breaking wave; Mrs. Ramsay bringing them together; Mrs. Ramsay saying, "Life stand still here"; Mrs. Ramsay making of the moment something permanent (as in another sphere Lily herself tried to make of the moment something permanent)—this was of the nature of a revelation. In the midst of chaos there was shape; this eternal passing and flowing (she looked at the clouds going and the leaves shaking) was struck into stability. Life stand still here, Mrs. Ramsay said. "Mrs. Ramsay! Mrs. Ramsay!" she repeated. She owed it all to her. [Pp. 240–41]

One should also try to read the parentheses in this passage, and one might compare it to another passage, of which I shall quote only a portion: "One wanted, she thought, dipping her brush deliberately, to be on a level with ordinary experience, to feel simply that's a chair, that's a table, and yet at the same time,

It's a miracle, it's an ecstasy" (pp. 299–300). Here the duality is expressed in the form of a demand or a want, and it remains unclear whether the demand is answered.

In the final passages of the book, one has a last rendering of the elusive hope that imagination and reality may be brought together in fleeting moments of aesthetic vision. The landing at the lighthouse connects with the simultaneous realization of Lily and Mr. Carmichael on shore that the boat must have reached the lighthouse. This echolike repetition or recognition scene is empty or tautological but not entirely senseless. The last paragraph returns to Lily's painting:

> Quickly, as if she were recalled by something over there, she turned to her canvas. There it was—her picture. Yes, with all its greens and blues, its lines running up and across, its attempt at something. It would be hung in the attics, she thought; it would be destroyed. But what did that matter? she asked herself, taking up her brush again. She looked at the steps; they were empty; she looked at her canvas; it was blurred. With a sudden intensity, as if she saw it clear for a second, she drew a line there, in the centre. It was done; it was finished. Yes, she thought, laying down her brush in extreme fatigue, I have had my vision.

In part I, Lily's painting fails to come right. It is an abstract portrayal of an imaginary object: Mrs. Ramsay framed in the window. Here at the end, with a shift toward the lighthouse, Lily seems to get it right. Yet Lily seems to see things clear only for a second when she draws a line in the center and divides it, splitting the focal point. The phrase "in the centre" is itself separated by a rather ungrammatical comma from the preceding "she drew a line there." Then there is an aftereffect of vision—a *nachträglich* epiphany—conveyed conditionally in the past tense: "as if she saw it clear for a second." And Lily has had her vision in the past perfect tense. The completion of Lily's painting with its line-crossed center—its divided moment of recognition, if you like—coincides with, and would seem to be a metaphor for, the completion of the novel with its attempt at something. Yet this attempt is far from a naive quest for presence or a simple perception of eternity, and the inferences one might draw about what to do with events once they are released from brackets are not foregone conclusions.

One is nonetheless tempted to draw inferences, and I shall hazard a few. In the text, the problem of the status of art in modern society is at least partially addressed thematically and stylistically. The problem of art is thematized in the treatment of Lily Briscoe's painting. This painting is not autonomized but closely implicated in the movement of social relations in the novel. The painting fails to take in part I, as social relations themselves remain out of focus and are held together only abstractly by the polarities of Mr. and Mrs. Ramsay. The painting is itself out of the picture in part II. It returns in part III, and at the very end Lily seems to get it right. But we are not told precisely how or why. In this part of the novel itself, moreover, there are some indications of a shift in social relations toward a more livable, tense balance, with the memory of Mrs. Ramsay serving as a tutelary spirit or partly beneficent revenant. Lily is able to place limits on the demands of Mr. Ramsay in ways his wife proved unable to do. And the remaining children come to a new rapport with their father—a rapport far from perfect but significantly different from the earlier relation. With these gains, there are also irrecuperable losses in the deaths or absences of certain characters from part I.

Stylistically, something has been attempted as well, and it has been at least partially attained. But its communication remains, and in a sense must remain, indirect and allusive. Still, it too has import for social relations, which can never be exhaustively codified but can possibly be housed in institutions that regulate repetitive temporality. A desirable interaction between viably articulated social institutions and provocative challenges to them, however, is marked primarily by its relative unavailability in the world thematized or represented in the novel. Yet it is suggested as a possibility by the novel's very use of language—a use relating a desire for stability to retrospective illuminations and liminal overtures. This novel may thus suggest how written texts and institutions can be seen as displacements of one another, with the attempts and partial accomplishments of the former having limited but not insignificant implications for the critique and transformation of the latter.

7

History and the Devil

in Mann's *Doctor Faustus*

> We make naught new—that is other people's business. We
> only unbind, only set free. . . . What [the artist] in classical
> decades would have without us, certainly, that, nowadays,
> we alone have to offer. And we offer better, we offer only the
> right and true—that is no longer the classical, my friend,
> what we give to experience, it is the archaic, the primeval,
> that which long since has not been tried. Who knows today,
> who ever knew in classical times, what inspiration is, what
> genuine, old, primeval enthusiasm, not infected by critique,
> paralyzing good sense, or deadly rational control—who
> knows the divine raptus? I believe, indeed, the devil passes
> for a man of destructive criticism? Slander and again slander,
> my friend! Gog's sacrament! If there is anything he cannot
> abide, if there's one thing in the whole world he cannot stom-
> ach, it is destructive criticism. What he wants and gives is
> triumph over it, is shining, sparkling, vainglorious unreflec-
> tiveness! . . .
> We lay upon you nothing new, the little ones make noth-
> ing new and strange out of you, they only ingeniously
> strengthen and exaggerate all that you already are.
> The devil to Adrian Leverkühn in Thomas Mann,
> *Doctor Faustus*

Who is the devil in *Doctor Faustus?* This is an embar-
rassingly insistent but unanswerable question, no doubt—one
that invites psychological and sociological reduction or, more
generally, "cultural" explanations of which the devil himself

is the potent and wily critic in spite of his distaste for criticism. But let us start by calling him names, a classical apotropaic device. The names with which we shall hesitantly begin are repetitive temporality; repetition as displacement; the parodic and hyperbolic voice of the unconscious that deceptively promises the transcendence of parody and the breakthrough to the old, the inspired, the original: revolution as reaction, the return of the repressed. But this beginning is not decisive, for the names we have chosen are not identical. They have somewhat different valences. Indeed they threaten diabolically to displace while repeating one another and to be caught up in the wily one's game, the game *Doctor Faustus* itself tries to play and work out without giving full sympathy to the devil.

The interposed narrator, Serenus Zeitblom—the discursive intermediary between Thomas Mann and the "diabolical" modern genius Adrian Leverkühn—himself has difficulty in beginning. He quite improperly addresses the reader while deferring his formal introduction and the disclosure of his name until the beginning of the second chapter. He spends the first chapter thematizing and enacting the problem of beginning, and he enunciates his fear that he may "be driven beyond [his] proper and becoming level of thought and experience an 'impure' heightening of [his] natural gifts" in undertaking the task of narrating the uncanny story he is driven to tell.[1] He compulsively begins an endless series of excuses for premature anticipations of characters and events which, along with retrospective allusions, mark his far-from-linear account. He repeats and repeats his "sense of artistic shortcomings and lack of self-control" (p. 4). Yet his story is very much "about" repetition, its variations, and the difficulties in coming to terms with it.

On the simplest and most obvious level, the narrative structure involves a tangled web of relations linking Mann as writ-

---

[1]Thomas Mann, *Doctor Faustus*, trans. H. T. Lowe-Porter (1947; New York: Vintage Books, 1971), p. 5. All references are to this edition; however, I have at times modified the translation, which combines excellence with some incredible lapses where meaning is distorted or wordplay lost.

er, Zeitblom as narrator, Leverkühn as seemingly central figure, Germany as the diabolically hyperbolic embodiment of
modernity, and the reader as implicated witness to the story
told. Mann has himself referred to his montage technique in
piecing together or grafting into the context of the novel components from various literary and existential sources—the
Faust chapbooks, letters, theological treatises, recent events,
his own earlier writings, and so forth—in a heady interplay of
fact and fiction. As is well known, Theodor W. Adorno, who
had studied with Schoenberg, was Mann's "privy councilor" in
musical matters. And the novel itself interweaves narration,
commentary, and theory. It comments on itself and offers theoretical reflections on its problems in ways that threaten, as
Erich Heller has wryly observed, to reduce the commentator to
plagiarism in his or her discussion of it.[2] But the text does not
become "autonomous" or self-referential in a narcissistic
sense that would repress or deny a specific engagement with
history. Indeed, it thematizes the problem of the "autonomy"
of modern art and its relation to historical issues. The question
it opens, in ever so intricate a form, is that of the precise manner in which the novel relates to its relevant contexts without
being simply reducible to them.

Zeitblom as narrator is both mediator and supplement as
well as a kind of buffer zone positioned between Mann and
Leverkühn. He is also situated between Mann and the reader.
Zeitblom represents one aspect of Germany often lost sight of
in discussions of the Nazi period. His name combines the Latin
and the Germanic: *Serenus*, serene; *Zeitblom*, time with a hint
of *Blume*—flower of time. He is a Catholic, a humanist, a child
of the Enlightenment and of civilization. In certain ways he is
like Settembrini of *The Magic Mountain*, who now acquires a
narrative voice and must confront even more severe challenges
to his values. He is manifestly not a dominant figure; neither is
he an insignificant one. But he is clearly not up to the demands
of the times and is even occasionally overwhelmed by them.
He is pathetic yet noble in the face of problems that are too big

[2]See *The Ironic German* (Boston, 1958), p. 277.

for him to handle, given his ideology and his intellect. He has the courage to resign his teaching position when the Nazis come to power, but he can do little to prevent or effectively oppose their rise and their appeal. At times he passively goes along with protofascist views that repel him, and when he does speak out against them, he tends to be reduced to humanistic and rationalistic nostrums. He is not the simple opponent or adversary of revolution as reaction. He is himself infected by the currents of the time; he even threatens to replicate them. The fact that he, like Nietzsche (one model for Leverkühn), is a philologist is one small sign of the complications in his personality. From earliest childhood he has a genuine love for Leverkühn; in his adulthood his love is reinforced by a commitment to his friend and his musical experiments—a commitment that remains steadfast even when it is sorely tested by doubts and the suspicion of affinities between the devilishly disconcerting art form and the frenzied sociopolitical disorientation of the period. Yet he too is at times attracted to extremes, gets carried away, loses control, and succumbs to the excesses from which he tries to keep a critical distance.

I shall later quote references to Germany that should be read as hyperbolic outbursts and indeed are so marked by "alienation effects" in the text. Here I shall simply mention the problem of the relation of the narrator to anti-Semitism. Zeitblom's family name might be seen to have Jewish overtones, and his attitudes toward Jews have at least traces of Jewish self-hatred. His very outrage at the blatant idiocies of Nazi propaganda does not bring with it a full escape from "racial" prejudice and stereotyping. Even as he takes his distance from the Nazis, he lets slip ways in which their ideology is infectious: "I have never, precisely in the Jewish problem and the way it has been dealt with, been able to agree fully with our Führer and his paladins; and this fact was not without influence on my resignation from the teaching staff here. Certainly specimens of the race have also crossed my path—I need only think of the private scholar Breisacher in Munich, on whose dismayingly unsympathetic character I propose in the proper place to cast some light" (p. 8). The suspect reference to "specimens of the race" itself is made in a proleptic remark that attests to an absence of full, classical narrative control. Chaim Breisacher himself represents the paradox of the protofascist Jew who espouses a radical, modernistic, archaicizing "conservatism" that is as offensive to traditional conservatives as it is to liberal bourgeois. And he makes repeated appearances—in the Schlaginhaufen salon, "where the social ambitions of the hostess brought people of every stripe together" (p. 279); in the Kridwiss circle (itself a "mature" repetition of the youthful Winfried society), where the indiscriminate mingling of categories is made to serve the ideological forces of reaction; and finally in the group called together to hear the last words of Adrian Leverkühn where Breisacher (unlike many others) stays to the bitter end, though the reader is given no indication of his reaction to the disquieting event.

An even more complicated and bewildering stereotype of the Jew is provided by the devil himself, for the "Great Adversary" has internalized certain stereotypical and prejudicial features of the Nazi's scapegoated "other." Since Zeitblom recedes from the narrative scene in the central "dialogue" between Adrian and the devil, Mann as writer may be implicating himself here as well. Early in the exchange, the devil objects to the name *Dicis et non facis* on the grounds that he delivers on his promises "more or less as the Jews are the most reliable dealers" (p. 226). In his second metamorphosis as a refined intellectual, "writer on art, on music for the ordinary press, and theoretician and critic, who himself composes, so far as thinking allows him" (p. 238), he has a hooked nose and black, woolly hair. Later in the text, Saul Fitelberg is an avatar of the devil who at times literally repeats the devil's temptations, but in the mask of the mass-market impresario he tries vainly to convince Adrian to take his show on the road and capitalize on it. Yet Fitelberg is not a representative of crass commercialism (in the manner of, say, Recktall Brown in Gaddis's *Recognitions*). He is genuinely ingratiating and insinuating; he has an intimate knowledge of music and can *causer musique* with someone like Leverkühn. He is a cultured European, and he is Jewish. And it is difficult to decide whether the stereotype he embodies, as well as its affiliates in the text, are symptomatic expressions of prevalent ideological prejudices or critical disclosures of the very fact of their prevalence and the need to counteract them in oneself, not simply in discrete others.

An axial narrative technique of the novel is dependent upon the fact that—except in the central chapter 25—we see Leverkühn only through Zeitblom's words. Thus the "genius" is perceived by the reader only in the indirect lighting provided by the discourse of one who loves, fears, and does not fully understand him. Given this narrative technique, Adrian, the center of the novel—its ideological "dominant"—is decentered. Even in the central chapter, in which the narrator has simply transcribed Adrian's own notes made on sheets of music, the central figure is doubled by his parodic, diabolical alter ego. To this extent, the novel emulates the atonal, nonhierarchical, serial music that Adrian Leverkühn fictively invents. But the return of the polyphonic in the atonal is also countered by the harmonizing and humanizing role of parody in Zeitblom's narrative. The novel is written in intentional parody of a pompous, stuffy, academic style not up to the events it relates and the problems it treats. Yet the parody of this style is telling and at times even moving, and the style itself is not the object of nihilistic attack or radical dismemberment.

For Leverkühn, however, the problem of modern art and of culture in a thoroughly problematic time would seem to pose itself in terms of the transcendence of parody. Yet Leverkühn seems to live to the utmost intensity the extremity of paradox, and parody itself is enmeshed in the unreconciled meeting of incompatible extremes. While the pact with the devil is made to enable the composer to transcend parody and achieve a total breakthrough, his ordinary life falls increasingly into a self-parodic repetition compulsion. And the artistic breakthrough itself courts both existential breakdown and the return to the oldest but now neobarbaric sources of immediate, unconstrained creativity. Leverkühn is thus a "representative" figure insofar as he embodies a parodically and paradoxically unmediated meeting of the extremes that divide modernity, but he is not a simple representative. The one way in which he does seem to get beyond if not entirely transcend parody—at least to drive it to its explosive limit—is in his own uncompromising tragedy, while his historical context descends beneath parody to filthy, self-deceived, and bloody farce. In and of itself, however, his tragedy redeems nothing; it provides no symbolic recompense, either for the characters or for the reader, but remains unsettling both in its indirect relation to history and in its disquieting implications for any present time that has not transcended the basic problems to which it bears witness.

Leverkühn seems a singularly Germanic figure: modeled on Nietzsche, unintentionally reminiscent of Wittgenstein, he provoked Schoenberg (perhaps assuming the role of *Pierrot lunaire*) to accuse Mann of plagiarism. Yet he is a singularly Germanic figure only insofar as the Germanic is itself a hyperbolic manifestation of modern crisis and extremity—a hyperbole within the hyperbole. He is thus a highly ambivalent figure, a question mark. The very oppositions he embodies are especially troubling because they are not pure opposites. They—like everything with which he comes in contact—are displacements of one another that allow neither for dialectical reconciliation nor for viable interplay and mutual contestation.

Leverkühn experiences a pathos of distance, at times an icy detachment from things. Yet he longs for human closeness, communication, and love. In his life, these forces meet only in an impenetrably obscure economy. In his music the "dehumanization" of art encounters its expressive counterpart only in the most problematic of ways. For him parody seems to be irrevocably on the side of the icy and the distant, and the breakthrough seems to require the transcendence of parody.

As a child Leverkühn is marked by an uncanny precociousness. In an extremely unchildlike manner, he learns so quickly that he becomes bored with everything. His boredom bespeaks the exhaustion of traditional forms and canonical gestures that seem fit only for parody or for a life of unself-conscious self-parody. Phenomena that elicit childlike awe or sacred respect from others—such as the prescientific, quasi-magical attempts of his father to "speculate the elements"—bring forth laughter from him. But his laughter and sense of the ridiculous are eerie rather than carnivalesque. They recall at a slight remove a story from St. Augustine's *De civitate Dei*—the story of the laughter of Ham, "son of Noah and father of Zoroaster the magian . . . the only man who laughed when he was born— which could only have happened by the help of the Devil" (p. 85). This reversal of what occurs at the time of the ordinary infant's "breakthrough" thus moves to the side of the devil and prefigures the later pact. Adrian retains a joking relation with others throughout his life, but it is a relation in which intimacy and commitment are either deferred or engaged at a disastrous price.

Even in Leverkühn's early life, nature itself is not the setting for innocence and authenticity. It cannot be the simple alternative to problems of culture. It poses in its own displaced manner the problems of simulation, dissimulation, and parody. There is, for example, the case of the fluctuating boundary between the organic and the inorganic suggested by his father's experiments with an erotic "devouring drop." And there is the edible butterfly, nature's charlatan, that cunningly imitates or deceptively simulates another beautiful but distasteful and poisonous butterfly in order to escape predators—a phenomenon that evokes Leverkühn's chilling laughter.

If the boundary between nature and culture is unsettled, a related boundary is recurrently questioned as well: that between culture and cult. Zeitblom would like to disestablish the sharp opposition between culture and civilization as well as the tendency of culture to be belittled in relation to cult. By Leverkühn's time, the opposition of Germanic *Kultur* to Western *Zivilisation* was becoming a mainstay of modern German intellectual history, and the demand that true culture be grounded in prereflective cult was taking the defense of culture from conservative to radical rightest and even protofascist extremes. Early in the text, Zeitblom informs the reader that he often "explained to [his] pupils that culture is in very truth the pious and regulating, I might say propitiatory entrance of the dark and uncanny into the service [*Kultus*] of the gods" (pp. 9–

10); the translation of course loses the wordplay between *Kultur* and *Kultus*, wherein a change of one letter signifies a break between two world views. Zeitblom's humanistic attempt to tame or domesticate cult in the interest of a civilized understanding of culture is resisted, in different but perhaps related ways, by experimental art and by reactionary politics, both of which reaffirm the cultic in its pagan or barbaric force—but a barbaric force that has become, deceptively and questionably, neobarbaric precisely because it comes after and along with a long and intricate history of civilization. For the young Leverkühn, however, the entire system of oppositions upon which Zeitblom would rely calls for deconstruction. After one of the lectures of Leverkühn's music teacher, the enigmatic stutterer Wendell Kretzschmar (the "z" in his name that evokes an affinity with Nietzsche is for some unexplained reason dropped in the English translation), Zeitblom recounts this exchange:

> What principally impressed [Leverkühn], as I heard while we were walking home, and also next day in the school courtyard, was Kret[z]schmar's distinction between cult epochs and cultural epochs, and his remark that the secularization of art, its separation from divine service, bore only a superficial and episodic character. . . . That the cultural idea was a historically transitory phenomenon, that it could lose itself again in another one, that the future did not inevitably belong to it, this thought he had certainly singled out from Kret[z]schmar's lecture.
>
> "But the alternative," I threw in, "to culture is barbarism."
>
> "Permit me," said he. "After all, barbarism is the opposite of culture only within the order of thought which it gives us. Outside of it the opposite may be something quite different or no opposite at all. . . . For a cultural epoch, there seems to me to be a spot too much talk about culture in ours, don't you think? I'd like to know whether epochs that possessed culture knew the word at all, or used it. Naïveté, unconsciousness, taken-for-grantedness, seems to me to be the first criterion of the constitution to which we give this name. What we are losing is just this naïveté, and this lack, if one may so speak of it, protects us from many a colourful barbarism which altogether perfectly agreed

with culture, even with very high culture. I mean: our stage is
that of civilization—a very praiseworthy state no doubt, but also
neither was there any doubt that we should have to become very
much more barbaric to be capable of culture again. Technique
and comfort—in that state one talks about culture but one has
not got it. Will you prevent me from seeing in the homophone-
melodic constitution of our music a condition of musical civilization—in contrast to the old contrapuntal polyphone
culture?" [pp. 59–60]

Leverkühn thus seems to regress from the attempted deconstruction of one "humanistic" opposition to the affirmation of another opposition—the "deadly dichotomy" between
culture and civilization that performed conservative if not reactionary ideological functions in the celebration of the German nation. The latter binary was of course the very opposition Mann himself tried to defend in a tortured and partially
self-questioning way in his early *Reflections of a Nonpolitical
Man* (1918), only to criticize it in his later polemical writing.
Leverkühn himself does not simply rest upon this opposition
in his thoughts about culture and modernity but tries in a
secularized or displaced theological mode to return to cultic
polyphony; he even retains a fascination for the attempt of the
religious utopian Beissel to coordinate musical and social pat-
terns, to the extent of conceiving of "master" and "servant"
notes. The culture-cult motif is struck in the section on the
youthful Winfried Society, and it is elaborated in the section
on the Kridwiss circle—an especially significant section, since
it forms part of the same threefold chapter as Leverkühn's penultimate masterwork the *Apocalypsis cum figuris.* But it receives its most rending rendition in the exchange with the
devil in which Leverkühn is promised his own version of the
felix culpa:

You will lead the way, you will strike up the march of the future,
the lads will swear by your name, who thanks to your madness
will no longer need to be mad. On your madness they will feed in
health, and in them you will become healthy. Do you understand? Not only will you break through the paralysing difficul-

ties of the time—you will break through time itself, by which I mean the cultural epoch and its cult, and dare to be barbaric, twice barbaric indeed, because coming after the humane, after all possible root-treatment and bourgeois raffinement. Believe me, barbarism even has more grasp of theology than has a culture fallen away from cult, which even in the religious has seen only culture, only the humane, never excess, paradox, the mystic passion, the utterly unbourgeois ordeal. But I hope that you do not marvel that "the Great Adversary" speaks to you of religion. Gog's nails! Who else, I should like to know, is to speak of it today?—Surely not the liberal theologian! After all I am by now its sole custodian! [P. 243]

Kretzschmar, whose stutter, indicating the difficulty of culture in transcending nature, is another reminder of the devil, himself poses the problem of "historical exhaustion and the vitiation of the means and appliances of art, boredom and the search for new ways" (p. 135). His lectures are supported from a public fund, yet they are attended by very few and understood by even fewer, perhaps only by Leverkühn. The topic of one of them is why Beethoven did not write a third movement for his piano sonata Opus 111. The suggested answer is that the sonata form had been exhausted by the second movement and that the third movement would have been superfluous.

Leverkühn does not use the intimate form of address—*du*— even with close friends such as the narrator Zeitblom. Yet he wants to be *per du* with humanity—on an intimate footing with it. He also seeks an art that is *per du* with humanity. The formulation of his goals, in the context of a discussion with his closest friends, expresses another variation of the crisis of modernity and the hope of overcoming it.

We spoke of the union of the advanced and the popular, the closing of the gulf between art and accessibility, high and low, as once in a certain sense it had been brought about by the romantic movement, literary and musical. But after that had followed a new and deeper cleavage and alienation between the good and the easy, the worth-while and the entertaining, the advanced and the generally enjoyable, which has become the destiny of art. Was it sentimentality to say that music—and she stood for them all—demanded with growing consciousness to step out of her dignified isolation, to find common ground without becoming common, and to speak the language which even the musically untaught could understand, as it understood the Wolf's Glen and the Jungfernkranz and Wagner? Anyhow, sentimentality was not the means to this end, but instead and much sooner irony, mockery; which, clearing the air, made an opposing party against the romantic, against pathos and prophecy, sound-intoxication and literature, and forged a bond with the objective and elemental—that is, with the rediscovery of music as an organization of time. . . .

It was mostly Adrian who talked, only slightly seconded by us. . . . Schildknapp had given expression to his disbelief in the deromanticizing of music. Music was after all too deeply and essentially bound up with the romantic ever to reject it without serious natural damage to itself. To which Adrian:

"I will gladly agree with you, if you mean by the romantic a warmth of feeling which music in the service of technical intellectuality today rejects. It is probably self-denial. But what we called the purification [or refinement: *Läuterung*] of the complicated into the simple is at bottom the same as the winning back of the vital and the power of feeling. If it were possible—whoever succeeded in—how would you say it?" he turned to me and then answered himself: "—the breakthrough, you would say; whoever succeeded in the breakthrough from intellectual coldness to a touch-and-go world of new feeling, him one would call the saviour of art. Redemption." [Pp. 320–21]

Thus the evacuation of pathos, demanded by an ascetically technical intellectuality, would, with the refinement of complexity into simplicity, bring an achieved spontaneity and the breakthrough to a renewed feeling. Yet the desire to be *per du* with humanity involves a paradoxical cross-cultural play on words that marks one instance where the translation actually enriches the text. *Per du* (not used in the original German) means in German to be intimately related; in French *perdu* means "lost." And the condition of Leverkühn's pact with the devil is that twenty-four years of creativity (one for each chapter or section after the central chapter) are to be acquired at the price of isolation and the renunciation of human intimacy and love. Yet Leverkühn's pact was initially sealed early in the novel when he (in imitation of a putative act of Nietzsche) intentionally sought out a syphilitic prostitute—the Hetaera Esmeralda, whose name recalls the name of a butterfly and becomes an obsessive motif in his music. His own obsession with her began when she brushed by his cheek, causing him to blush like the marking on the wing of the butterfly, as he sat bewildered, next to a piano in the bordello. He was taken there under false pretenses by a porter, who resembles another of his teachers, who in turn resembles the devil: one Schleppfuss, or drag-foot, professor of theology. But his aleatory encounter turns out to be fatal and to elicit what was in him: the need for a diabolical engagement induced by a sexual act in which human mediation between flesh and spirit in love is hinted at only to be exceeded by blind and almost sacred fascination beyond all calculations of prudence.

Anyone with whom Adrian becomes involved will also be *perdu*. One of these is Rudolf Schwerdtfeger, the violinist who seduces Adrian into composing a concerto for him and toward whom Adrian displays an "ironic eroticism." Schwerdtfeger's name sounds much like that of another close friend of Leverkühn's, Rüdiger Schildknapp. They have similar relations to the composer Leverkühn and are to that extent displacements of each other: Schwerdtfeger as an interpreter and performing artist, and Schildknapp as a translator who is somewhat disgruntled by what he sees as a derivative activity. While the sounds of their names erosively induce the reader to run them together, the meanings bear at least a tenuous difference: Schwerdtfeger as one who himself rubs away hard edges through a facile virtuosity; Schildknapp as a shield bearer whose escutcheon is threatened with effacement by the fall of the hero whose shield he would bear. Schildknapp himself is plagued with the weight of a bridge supported by progressively rotting teeth, while Schwerdtfeger is shot by a jilted lover as he prepares to go off with a woman whom Leverkühn had halfheartedly tried to engage by using Rudi as an *entremetteur.* (The woman's voice, needless to say, reminds Adrian of his mother's.) But the relations with Schildknapp and Schwerdtfeger are only dress rehearsals for Leverkühn's final, disastrous attempt to cheat the devil in his relation with his little nephew, Echo.

Chapter 25, involving Leverkühn's dialogue with the devil, is the displaced center of the novel. And the novel in general enacts a serioparodic relation to numerology. Leverkühn himself has a magic square above his piano; adding numbers in it in any serial direction always gives the same result—thirty-four. The magic square is atonal like the form of music Leverkühn fictively invents; the latter breaks through the dominant key signature and away from hierarchy, yet it offers a strict rule of order whose acoustic result may appear chaotic from a classical perspective. In the organization of the novel itself there are twenty-four chapters before the central one and twenty-four chapters or sections after it. One chapter—appropriately enough, chapter 34—is divided into three sections to indicate the affinity but not the full identity (in other words, the repetitively displaced relation) between its parts (the Kridwiss circle, preceded by a discussion of the biographical context and followed by an "internal" analysis of the *Apocalypsis cum figuris*).

What is the nature of Leverkühn's dialogue or internally dialogized monologue with the devil in chapter 25? The devil parodies the concerns of Leverkühn by practicing a strategy of citation. He literally quotes the unconscious of the genius and thus renders explicit what Leverkühn tries to repress. Leverkühn himself is both the devil's adversary and his advocate who argues with an internalized diabolical other. But the devil is himself up on modern psychology as well as sociology (at the very least he has read the critiques of T. W. Adorno), and he shows the superficiality of attempts to deny what he stands for by simply seeing him as a projection of a sick mind or a sick society: "Don't blame it on social conditions. I am aware you tend to do so, and are in the habit of saying that these conditions produce nothing fixed and stable enough to guarantee the harmony of the self-sufficient work. True, but unimportant.

The prohibitive difficulties of the work lie deep in the work itself. The historical movement of the musical material has turned against the self-contained work" (p. 240).

Or again: "We are entering into times, my friend, which will not be hoodwinked by psychology. . . . This *en passant*" (p. 249). The devil seems to insist upon a status that is neither quite cultic nor altogether secularized—in any case, a status that cannot be explained away. He demands a durability or iterability in and through differences. In his exchange with Leverkühn he changes appearances in an apparent parody of the devil who tempts Christ in the desert, but he retains the same voice in his displaced repetitions. As I have already said, one of the topics of the conversation is, of course, parody.

> I [Leverkühn]: "A man could know that [i.e., that it is all up with the classical tradition] and recognize freedom above and beyond all critique. He could heighten the play, by playing with forms of art out of which, as he well knew, life has disappeared."
> He [Devil]: "I know, I know. Parody. It might be fun, if it were not so melancholy in its aristocratic nihilism. Would you promise yourself much pleasure and profit from such tricks?"
> I (retort angrily): "No." [P. 241.]

Leverkühn's attempted breakthrough beyond parody to renewed objectivity and feeling reaches its highest forms in his last two masterworks, which are intricate displacements of each other: the *Apocalypsis cum figuris* and the *Lamentation of Dr. Faustus*. They are separated by Leverkühn's attempt to cheat the devil through love for his nephew Nepomuk, nicknamed Echo. Leverkühn seeks the love of a seemingly innocent child. His own love is innocent, since he cannot help himself. But it is also guilty because he knows the condition of his pact and the harm he will bring to one he loves. Thus he does not fully master his fate, but he nonetheless feels answerable for it. The child, the seeming embodiment of innocence transcending parody, is himself at least somewhat equivocal, however. He has an undeniable charm and is able to evoke the sincere affection of those around him. But he is almost too perfect to be credible, and he bears the suspect nickname Echo—a name that denies innocence. Reversing the relations in the myth, the child is very narcissistic and even rather affected in his poses. The echo effect itself marks the equivocal place of the human being in nature. An echo, in which the human voice is returned by nature, seems to intimate intersubjectivity and dialogical reciprocity with the other. Yet the only thing the human gets back is the distorted sound of his or her own voice. The revenge of the devil on Adrian is to have the child die cruelly and painfully of spinal meningitis—a disease that is itself a vicious echo or parody of Leverkühn's own syphilis of the meninges.

The composition that precedes Echo's appearance also in paradoxical and obscure ways anticipates it. And in the only tripartite chapter in the novel, which treats the *Apocalypse*, Mann himself explores the relation between thematic contextualization and formal analysis of the artwork. Zeitblom takes the "speechifying" of the Kridwiss circle to heart because it constitutes "a cold-blooded intellectual commentary upon a fervid experience of art and friendship . . . a work which had a peculiar kinship with, was in spirit parallel to, the things I had heard at Kridwiss's table-round" (pp. 372–73). Like the myth-hungry, antimodern, and reactively revolutionary ideologists of the Kridwiss circle, enamored of such works as Georges Sorel's *Reflections on Violence*, Adrian, in his extremely experimental work epitomizing the entire apocalyptic tradition, was also seeking "a state of mind which, no longer interested in the psychological, pressed for the objective, for a language that expressed the absolute, the binding and compulsory, and in consequence by choice laid on itself the pious fetters of pre-classically strict form" (p. 373). The reproach to which Leverkühn's work "did perhaps expose itself . . . in its urge to reveal in the language of music the most hidden things, the beast in man as well as his sublimest stirrings" was "the reproach both of blood-stained barbarism and of bloodless intellectuality" (p. 374). Zeitblom is deeply sensitive to this reproach, which involves the unmediated meeting and mingling of extremes, for he has "experienced in his very soul how near aestheticism and barbarism are to each other: aestheticism as the herald of barbarism" (p. 373). The very attempt to arrive back at cult through the sacrificial dismemberment of culture has for him its dangers; it requires a pact with the magical and the ritual, which are out of place in a profane epoch.

Adrian's *Apocalypse* courts these dangers especially in its relatively indiscriminate use of his preferred glissando effect— "a naturalistic atavism, a barbaric rudiment from pre-musical days . . . the gliding voice . . . a device to be used with the greatest restraint on profoundly cultural grounds" (p. 375). The glissando is "extremely uncanny" in its orchestral uses, but it is "most shattering" in its application to the human voice, for with it the voice loses touch with the human and with meaning to merge with subarticulate noise, particularly in the formless form of howls and shrieks. The *Apocalypse* is not punctuated by orchestral interludes; rather, the orchestra and voices "merge into one another, the chorus is 'instrumentalized,' the orchestra as it were 'vocalized,' to that degree and to that end that the boundary between man and thing seems shifted: an advantage, surely, to artistic unity, yet—at least for my feeling—there is about it something oppressive, dangerous, malignant." Indeed, "the whole work is dominated by the paradox (if it is a paradox) that in it dissonance stands for the expression of everything lofty, solemn, pious, everything of the spirit; while consonance and firm tonality are reserved for the world of hell, in this context a world of banality and commonplace" (p. 375).

Thus Adrian's reversal and generalized displacement of given assumptions invites an extremely serious reproach, one that approximates experimental art and protofascism—a reproach, Zeitblom tells us, "whose plausibility [he] admit[s] though [he] would bite [his] tongue out sooner than recognize its justice: the reproach of barbarism" (p. 377). But before Zeitblom will indicate, in however qualified a manner, what it is in the work that resists the reproach, the halting textual movement first intensifies that reproach by pointing to "a certain touch, like an icy finger, of mass-modernity in this work of religious vision, which knows the theological almost exclusively as judgment and terror: a touch of 'streamline,' to venture the insulting word. Take the *testis*, the witness and narrator of the horrid happenings: the 'I, Johannes' . . . whose chilly crow, objective, reporterlike, stands in terrifying contrast to the content of his catastrophic announcements." Zeitblom presses even further in disclosing the complicity of the work with the degraded forms of mass culture it seems to transcend. He offers another "example of easy technical facility in horror, the effect of being at home in it: I mean the loud-speaker effects (in an oratorio!)" (p. 377)—effects which (although Zeitblom refrains from mentioning the point) cannot but recall to the reader the easy technical facility of another manipulator of loud-speaker effects: Hitler. But then Zeitblom draws back at the brink of the abyss and reveals how the work itself resists too facile a conflation with sociocultural and political resonances:

> Soullessness! I well know this is at bottom what they mean who apply the word "barbaric" to Adrian's creation. Have they ever, even if only with the reading eye, heard certain lyrical parts—or may I only say moments?—of the *Apocalypse:* song passages accompanied by a chamber orchestra, which could bring tears to the eyes of a man more callous than I am, since they are like a fervid prayer for a soul. I shall be forgiven for an argument more or less into the blue; but to call soullessness the yearning for a soul—the yearning of the little sea-maid [in Hans Christian Andersen's story about a mermaid who painfully desires human legs—another obsessive motif in Leverkühn]—that is what I would characterize as barbarism, as inhumanity! [P. 378]

This bolt from the blue is, however, followed by concluding paragraphs in which Zeitblom, in extremely disconcerting fashion, reveals how the work does not transcend parody and even prefigures later events and the final composition motivated by them. For he turns to the question of how the diabolical laughter in the first part of the *Apocalypse*—"an overwhelming, sardonically yelling, screeching, bawling, bleating, howling, piping, whinnying salvo, the mocking, exulting laughter of the Pit"—has its "pendant" [*Gegenstück*] in "the truly extraordinary chorus of children which, accompanied by a chamber orchestra, opens the second part: a piece of cosmic music of the spheres, icily clear, glassily transparent, of brittle dissonances indeed, but withal of an—I would like to say—inaccessibly unearthly and alien beauty of sound, filling the heart with longing without hope" (p. 378). Thus in the music that is Adrian Leverkühn "utterly," the unrestrained laughter of hell "as repetition no longer recognizable" is displaced and merges undecidably with the heavenly chorus of children in a sublime echo effect.

Leverkühn's last work, the *Lamentation of Dr. Faustus*, returns to the echo effect, now given supplementary weight through the death of his nephew; and it seems to indicate, at least to Zeitblom, how longing without hope may engender a glimmer of hope nonetheless. The echo effect, we are told, was a favorite of baroque masters such as Monteverdi, and it is intimately related to the mournful, melancholic theme of lament. With this work, Adrian seems clearly to recognize how the breakthrough must combine tradition and critique. Yet his disarmingly "original" project (so like many others in the modern period) is to invert and take back Beethoven's Ninth Symphony with its culminating ode to joy. The death of a child reveals to him that one no longer deserves the Ninth Symphony, and so he must revoke or erase it, with joy reversed into lament. Beginning chorally and ending orchestrally, the piece plays variations on the words of Faustus: "For I die as a good and a bad Christian." The twelve syllables correspond to the twelve notes or tones used in the composition. The series they form "is the basis of all the music—or rather, it lies almost as key behind everything and is responsible for the identity of the most varied forms—that identity which exists between the crystalline angelic choir and the hellish yelling in the *Apocalypse* and which has now become all-embracing: a formal treatment strict to the last degree, which no longer knows anything unthematic, in which the order of the basic material becomes total, and within which the idea of a fugue rather declines into an absurdity, just because there is no longer any free note. But it serves now a higher purpose; for—oh, marvel, oh, deep diabolic jest!—just by virtue of the absoluteness of the form the music is, as language, freed" (pp. 487–88). Through the moving inexactness of words evoking music, the final work of Leverkühn seems to achieve the tense unity of objective intellectuality and formal strictness not only with the aleatory but also with expressive "warmth and sincerity of creature confidence" (p. 485) in and through the paradoxical medium of lament. Yet after completing this work, Leverkühn calls together a heterogeneous assemblage of friends and acquaintances and, in Reformation German, discusses his composition in the form of a Faustian confession of his sins in allying himself with the devil. At the end of his parodically inverted but genuinely anguished re-citation of Christ's own agony, he (recalling Nietzsche) utters a wailful lament, collapses into madness, and—in childlike dependence—must be tended by his mother.

The issue that has been active, either manifestly or latently, in my entire discussion is how the text of *Doctor Faustus*, through modulations of repetitive temporality, itself relates to its historical contexts. That relation is largely a matter of displaced or offset parallels. One of the most questionable of them is between pre-Nazi Germany and the Reformation or *Lutherzeit*. It is assumed in Adrian's use of old German, particularly in his exchange with the devil and in his "mad" confession to his assembled friends and acquaintances. It is explicit, yet marked as perhaps special pleading in the mouth of a humanist and Catholic, in Zietblom's occasional and at times unbalanced comments. He is even led to ask "whether the reformers are not rather to be regarded as backsliding types and bringers of evil. Beyond a doubt, endless blood-letting and the most horrible self-laceration would have been spared the human race if Martin Luther had not re-established [or cured: *wiederhergestellt*] the Church" (p. 88).

The relation between the rise of the Third Reich and Adrian's experimental art is a more pointed but still controversial matter. German history has for Mann perhaps the most concentrated and forceful expression of the problems and paradoxes of modern civilization—the paradoxical meeting of the best and the worst. Yet the way this history relates to the novel is intricate, and it is obvious that the parallel between Adrian and the rise of Hitler's Germany is indirect, in certain ways not a parallel at all. The Nazis themselves condemn Adrian's work as "cultural Bolshevism," and as in the case of the use and abuse of Nietzsche, the Nazi period is for Mann a vicious and low-grade parody of the artist-figure in whom problems attain more genuinely tragic dimensions. Indeed, it is when one tries to make the tragic exception into a rule of putative collective redemption in a time of crisis that one degrades and cheapens tragedy into senseless barbarism.

One form of more direct reference to German history in the novel is through Zeitblom's outbursts where he loses self-control and repeats in his response the excesses of the time that he condemns. What is significant is that these direct references are clearly situated textually as outbursts. Such is the case with the following moving—indeed, all too moving—passage:

> We are lost. In other words, the war is lost; but that means more than a lost campaign, it means in very truth that *we* are lost: our character, our cause, our hope, our history. It is all up with Germany, it will be all up with her. She is marked down for collapse, economic, political, moral, spiritual, in short all-embracing, unparalleled, final collapse. I suppose I have not wished for it, this that threatens, for it is madness and despair. I suppose I have not wished for it, because my pity is too deep, my grief and sympathy are with this unhappy nation, when I think of the exaltation and blind ardour of its uprising, the breaking-out, the breaking-up, the breaking-down; the purifying and fresh start, the national new birth of ten years ago [1933], that seemingly religious intoxication—which then betrayed itself to any intelligent person for what it was by its crudeness, vulgarity, gangsterism, sadism, degradation, filthiness—ah, how unmistakably it bore within itself the seeds of this whole war! My heart contracts painfully at the thought of that enormous investment of faith, zeal, lofty historic emotion; all this we made, all this is now puffed away in a bankruptcy without compare. No, surely I did not want it, and yet—I have been driven to want it and will welcome it, out of hatred for the outrageous contempt of reason, the vicious violation of the

truth, the cheap, filthy backstairs mythology, the criminal degradation and confusion of standards; the abuse, corruption, and
blackmail of all that was good, genuine, trusting, and trustwor-
thy in our old Germany. For liars and lickspittles mixed us a
poison draught and took away our senses. We drank—for we
Germans perennially yearn for intoxication—and under its spell,
through years of shameful deeds, which must now be paid for.
With what? I have already used the word, together with the word
"despair" I wrote it. I will not repeat it: not twice could I control
my horror or my trembling fingers to set it down again. [Pp. 174–
75]

Mann, with his own intense love-hate relation to Germany,
seems very close to Zeitblom in this madly passionate outburst. But then there comes an antidote to the poison draft of
intoxicated outrage in the form of an ironic alienation effect.
For the passage above is immediately followed by three asterisks and the observation: "Asterisks too are a refreshment
for the eye and mind of the reader. One does not always need
the greater articulation of a Roman numeral, and I could
scarcely give the character of a main section to the above excursus into a present outside of Adrian Leverkühn's life and
work" (p. 175). The more considered attitude toward Germany,
modulated and intense at the same time, as well as the supreme ambition of the novel itself, comes in the offset parallel
between the passage in which Zeitblom describes the effect of
the ending of the *Lamentation*, on the one hand, and the ending of *Doctor Faustus*, on the other:

At the end of this work of endless lamentation, softly, above the
reason and with the speaking unspokenness given to music
alone, it touches the feelings. I mean the closing movement of
the piece, where the choir loses itself and which sounds like the
lament of God over the lost state of His world, like the Creator's
rueful "I have not willed it." Here, towards the end, I find that
the uttermost accents of mourning are reached, the final despair
achieves a voice, and—I will not say it, it would mean to dis-
parage the uncompromising character of the work, its irremediable anguish to say that it affords, down to its very last note, any

other consolation than what lies in voicing it, in simply giving sorrow words; in the fact, that is, that a voice is given the creature for its woe. No, this dark tone poem permits up to the very end no consolation, appeasement, transfiguration. But take our artist paradox: grant that expressiveness—expression as lament—is the issue of the whole construction: then may we not parallel with it another, a religious one, and say too (though only in the lowest whisper) that out of the sheerly irremediable, hope might germinate? It would be but a hope beyond hopelessness, the transcendence of despair—not betrayal to her, but the miracle that passes belief. For listen to the end, listen with me: one group of instruments after another retires, as the work fades on the air, in the high G of a cello, the last word, the last fainting sound, slowly dying in a pianissimo-fermata. Then nothing more: silence, and night. But that tone that vibrates in the silence, which is no longer there, to which only the spirit hearkens, and which was the voice of mourning, is no more. It changes its meaning; it abides as a light in the night. [Pp. 490–91]

"Though only in the lowest whisper": this affirmation on the margin of silence reverses while replicating the hushed tones of the exchange with the devil. Compare the high G of the novel itself (which also recalls the painting of the Last Judgment mentioned toward the end of the first section on the *Apocalypse* as well as the recurrent Hetaera-Esmeralda motif):

Germany, the hectic on her cheek, was reeling then at the height of her dissolute triumphs, about to gain the whole world by virtue of the one pact she was minded to keep, which she had signed with her blood. Today, clung round by demons, a hand over one eye, with the other staring into horrors, down she flings from despair to despair. When will she reach the bottom of the abyss? When, out of the uttermost hopelessness—a miracle beyond the power of belief—will the light of hope dawn? A lonely man [*Mann*] folds his hands and speaks: "God be merciful to thy poor soul, my friend, my Fatherland." [P. 510]

Adrian cannot achieve in his personal life what is at least intimated in his music, for existentially the breakthrough is ironically reversed into compulsive repetition leading to tragic

172

breakdown. Yet the musical ambition is itself displaced onto the narrative with indirect implications for historical life, thereby ironically recalling the devil's promise that Adrian's venture would enable others (Zeitblom? Mann himself?) to create without madness. Here one may make a pertinent chronological point in the midst of repetitive temporality, its reversals and displacements. Zeitblom like Mann narrates his story during the Second World War, but he speaks of Adrian's life before the First World War and until May 1930, when the musician goes mad and continues a vegetating existence until 1940. Curiously, there is a three-year gap between Adrian's madness and Hitler's accession to power. Does this mean that the game was up in 1930, or that there was still a chance for Germany in that three-year interval? The text provides no answer. Indeed, it even leaves in doubt whether Zeitblom's interpretation of the "high G" of the *Lamentation* is his own projective wish-fulfillment, which resonates with his (Mann's?) concluding prayerlike invocation to Germany, Leverkühn, and the reader.

Nonetheless, it would be questionable to read the final lines as a simple apology for quasi-religious quiescence and fatalistic or apathetic withdrawal. Mann, in other texts written or spoken during the period in which he wrote *Doctor Faustus*, was asserting the need for active commitment to democratic values and opposition to fascism in ways that might be read, to some limited extent, as the counterpart to what he attempts in the novel. Nor should one ignore the fact that Zeitblom, despite his desire for moderation, can assert that "ethically speaking, the only way a people can achieve a higher form of communal life is not by a foreign war, but by a civil one—even with bloodshed" (p. 300) and even that "the dictatorship of the proletariat begins to seem to me, a German burgher, an ideal situation compared with the now possible one of the dictatorship of the scum of the earth" (pp. 339–40)—outbursts indeed, but not modulated by irony. But the most unsettling dimension of the novel—its hyperbole, perhaps its hubris, in any event a sign of both its power and its limits—may be that it almost leads the reader to look at the Nazi period as an offset and distorted displacement of the life and work of Adrian Leverkühn rather than vice versa. It is of course at this point that the novel reaches its limits and, in its seeming attempt to break through them, courts disaster.

One should, however, perhaps end by finally striking the note of Thomas Mann's own skillful use of parody in the novel—a use that cannot be conflated either with Zeitblom's unskilled narrative or with Leverkühn's explicit conception of parody as a chilling dead end. By contrast, Mann's parody, in its liminal position between humane care and diabolical play, is both mediation and supplement relating the interposed narrator's inept but endearing self-parody and the *Tonsetzers* demonically antithetic theoretical reflections and ambivalently poignant musical practice. Nor can Mann's parody be identified with an evasive strategy of containment or with the contorted attempt of a transcendental ego to pat itself on the back for its putative ability to bracket the world and view it from a safe aesthetic perspective. Rather, it is a complex narrative mode involving both implication in the story and critical distance from it: a mode of indirect, self-reflective discourse which, far from becoming fully autonomized or narcissistically speculative, may be one of the most compelling ways to address (by displacing)—possibly to work (if not break) through—certain problems, including one's relation to the demonic, the nearly exhausted, and the compulsively repetitive.

8

Singed Phoenix and Gift of Tongues:
William Gaddis, *The Recognitions*

> And thus it is my conclusion that *The Recognitions* by
> William Gaddis is not merely the best American novel of our
> time, but perhaps the most significant single volume in all
> American fiction since *Moby Dick*, a book so broad in scope,
> so rich in comedy and so profound in symbolic inference
> that—
>
> David Markham, *Epigraph for a Tramp*

At the beginning of the introduction to his invaluable *Read-er's Guide to William Gaddis's "The Recognitions,"* Steven
Moore quotes the lines that serve as my epigraph. They come
from a late 1950s potboiler in which they are found by a detec-
tive on a page in a typewriter—a page from a literature class
essay in progress. Moore notes:

A citation from a trashy thriller may seem an odd place to begin a
discussion of what may indeed be the most significant American
novel since *Moby Dick* except that it illustrates a curious point
concerning the literary reputation of *The Recognitions*: that the
strongest praise has come from such odd quarters as the twenty-
five-cent potboiler above, pseudonymous Jack Green's unpunctu-
ated, hand-mimeographed *newspaper*, a handful of articles
mostly in unheard-of journals, and a half-dozen Ph.D. disserta-
tions, but largely from the private enthusiasm of a small (but
growing) number of readers, many of whom apparently (including myself) are outside the walls of academe. (At one point there

was even a small club in Cleveland that met for the sole purpose of discussing *The Recognitions*.) The novel is still ignominiously branded a "cult" novel by many, as if its concerns were those only of a small band of literary eccentrics with special tastes rather than—as I believe—of anyone and everyone with a serious interest in American literature.[1]

The only qualification I would make to Moore's comment is that the novel should not be restricted to those with an interest in American literature, for *The Recognitions*, while a profoundly "American" work, engages larger European and world traditions, and its satire of modern culture and society has acquired increasingly broader relevance since the novel's original publication in 1955. And *The Recognitions*, if not a "cult" phenomenon, is assuredly a demanding and difficult text: Moore's own guide could be usefully supplemented with a critical edition, which would be of value not only to students but to any and every reader. The novel's very length (some thousand pages more or less, depending on the edition) is not only intimidating; it is one reason why the work has tended to be excluded from canons. It seems not only too arcane but too unwieldy to teach in literature or intellectual history courses. At the very least, one would have to devote three weeks to it, thus jeopardizing the "manageable" structure of a course and threatening to lose many students along the way. Furthermore, the novel seems to fall between two stools. It is too experimental to be read without the extensive critical commentary (and controversy) it has yet to receive (thus it is not generally classified with so-called "high modernist" texts like *Doctor Faustus*

[1] *A Reader's Guide to William Gaddis's "The Recognitions"* (Lincoln, Neb., 1982), p. 1. To my knowledge, the only other booklength publication devoted to Gaddis is a collection of essays, *In Recognition of William Gaddis*, ed. John Kuehl and Steven Moore (Syracuse, N.Y., 1984); the bibliography is especially valuable. According to the notes on contributors, Steven Moore has been "recuperated" for academe, for he is there listed as a graduate student at the University of Denver. Jack Green's vitriolic and funny history of the critical reception of *The Recognitions* from 1955–62, including his own assessment of its value, is titled—with barbed reference to critics—"fire the bastards!" (*newspaper*, nos. 12–14, 24 February, 25 August, 10 November 1962).

or *Ulysses*) yet not quite experimental enough to be assimilated to so-called "postmodernist" anticanons (in a sense it is to Gaddis's own *J R* of 1971 as *Ulysses* is to *Finnegans Wake*); hence more "experimental" writers, even when they have derived a great deal from it, have little motivation to take up its cause and disseminate it to at least a wider "educated" audience.

Seen from another perspective, however, the ambivalent status of *The Recognitions* can itself be taken as one of its challenges or even as one of its virtues. For one thing the work is able to do in an overwhelmingly insistent manner is to join limited experimentalism with gripping pathos—pathos of the sort one prefers not to evacuate. It is thus a work whose experimental techniques, allusory riddling, and self-referential—indeed, metafictional—cross-hatching rarely become mere exercises in acrostic acrobatics or self-indulgent pyrotechnics. All I shall attempt in this essay—at the risk of seeing things awry and abetting the process of canonization—is to scratch a few of the surfaces of *The Recognitions* and show (like the troll king in Ibsen's *Peer Gynt*) that a seemingly "ugly" object may, through altered vision, appear, if not "fine and brave," then at the very least deserving of further study. For the face it shows is a more critical, possibly transformative image of our own.

It would be deceptive to establish too exact a chronology for the events of the novel; it is, on the contrary, significant that chronology is left indefinite. It would be equally deceptive to rely on the date of publication and to reduce the novel to a document of the 1950s. Both procedures would curtail overmuch the novel's critical range and its ability to address contemporary readers. For *The Recognitions* provides a devastating, encompassing, and often hilarious critique of modern society and culture—of the manipulativeness, hucksterism, commodity fetishism, and self-congratulatory scientism epitomized in the United States but far from restricted to it. Its critique is not narrowly "presentist"; it excavates the genealogy of present discontents, and it discloses actual and formal connections among various traditions and sociocultural residues. Nor does the novel claim a total lack of complicity with its objects of criticism or venture to provide a symbolic resolution of the crises and impasses it explores. Rather its technique is that of the antidote which makes use of the sources of illness in combatting its prevalence and spread, recurrently running the risk of mistaking its object or the right dosage in curing it. It works through its materials, disclosing relations that are not immediately obvious and effecting variations that may convert repetition into a regenerative re-petitioning.

The Recognitions might even be taken as the epitome of Mikhail Bakhtin's notion of the significant novel as the polyphonic orchestration of the heterogeneous, fragmentary, often chaotic, at times cacophonous discourses of the times into a seriocomic, provocatively ambivalent *agon* or carnival of contending "voices" and dissonant possibilities in society and culture. For any given element—event, character, development—is never simply univocal or one-sided but generally has two or more valences: it is serious and ironic, pathos-charged and parodic, apocalyptic and farcical, critical and self-critical. The novel itself is an immense, encyclopedic counterworld, seemingly exhaustive in its range of references and cross-references, yet it also questions its own limits of possibility and the very feasibility of an encyclopedic quest. Stylistically, it relies on modified repetitions to bring out a reserved retinue of finer shades and hesitant possibilities; characters, events, developments, exchanges, and even sentences themselves are subtly varied iterations of one another, with more or less marked differences attendant upon such modified repetitions.

The plural of the title is itself significant. It echoes that of a third-century "theological romance" attributed to Clement of Rome. A quotation from Book V of the Clementine *Recognitions* serves as an epigraph to part II, chapter II, and it strikes the note of the problematic relation between recognition and misrecognition: "This is as if a drunk man should think himself to be sober, and should act indeed in all respects as a drunk man, and yet think himself to be sober, and should wish to be called so by others. Thus, therefore, are those also who do not know what is true, yet hold some appearance of knowledge, and do many evil things as if they were good, and hasten to destruction as if it were salvation."[2] The reference is picked up later in the chapter during a telephone conversation of Basil Valentine, which includes one of the self-reflexive allusions to the novel and its author:

> A novel? But . . . yes, perhaps he can, if he thinks it will do any good. But you can tell your friend Willie that salvation is hardly the practical study it was then. What? . . . Why, simply because in the Middle Ages they were convinced that they had souls to save. Yes. The what? The *Recognitions?* No, it's Clement of *Rome*. Mostly talk, talk, talk. The young man's deepest concern is for the immortality of his soul, he goes to Egypt to find the magicians and learn their secrets. It's been referred to as the first Christian novel. What? Yes, it's really the beginning of the whole Faust legend. But one can hardly . . . eh? My, your friend is writing for a rather small audience, isn't he? [Pp. 372–73]

The plural of the title has a bearing on salvation or redemption and on the obsessive motif of origin, forgery, invention, and diabolical pact. "Recognition" in the singular would imply a pure, unmediated return to, or repetition of, an absolute origin—the hope of full identity and (encyclopedic) wholeness. This impossible, phantasmatic desire in its most extreme, uncompromising form is a source of pathos in the text, but it is not named as such. It is not, for example, codified in terms of the Platonic form or the Jungian archetype as the name of the origin (despite the importance of Plato and Jung, among so many others, for the novel). Traditions which themselves convey a suspicion of names or images of the origin are active—notably Calvinistic, puritanical Christianity and pagan or syncretic Gnosticism—but never as simple lodestars or reference points. In their insistence on radical transcendence, these traditions preserve the inviolability of the origin in its very ineffability and unapproachability. For them there is a radical di-

[2]William Gaddis, *The Recognitions* (New York: Harcourt, Brace & World, 1955), p. 343. All references are to this edition. The book is currently available from Viking Penguin.

vide between spirit and matter, and any attempt to imitate or emulate the origin or its creations is sinful. All art, from this perspective, is forgery, and all imitation bears the taint of hubristic invention. In league with the devil, it always involves an attempt to provide illumination that does not derive entirely from a higher, external source. This is the message that his paternal aunt May conveys to the young Wyatt, and it makes his childish paintings diabolical invocations from the very beginning.

The novel suggests an affinity between extreme sectarian Christianity and Gnosticism, however—only one variant of the many linkages it intimates between seemingly incompatible traditions. Indeed, there is a further correlation between these outlooks and aestheticism with its cult of the transcendent artwork and its distance from matter and human needs. The auratic work of art is itself a displaced religious object, heir to the sacred value of the "original." In his notes Gaddis makes the following remarks about the character Basil Valentine, a sophisticated and internally complex avatar of the devil:

> Basil Valentine, is the gnostic presumption . . . is finally stricken down with insomnia, for his very refusal to realize and grant the worth of matter, that is, of other people. The essence of his gnosticism is largely an implacable hatred for matter. It is that element of aescetecism [sic] common in so many religious expressions turned, not upon the self, but upon humanity. And it is his very inability to accomplish this hatred entirely, and to entirely refuse love (which he can only understand as power over the object loved, over all, in the theory of which he works; over Wyatt, who denies and escapes it himself . . .) that undoes him, that leaves him as exhausted as Esther [Wyatt's wife], as awake as she is asleep.[3]

Whether as a slip or as an intentional neologism, Gaddis's misspelling of "aescetecism" as a portmanteau word brings out the relation between aestheticism and asceticism in the novel.

[3]Quoted in Moore, *Reader's Guide*, p. 142, from Peter William Koenig, "Splinters from the Yew Tree: A Critical Study of William Gaddis' *The Recognitions*" (Ph.D. diss., New York University, 1971), p. 93.

The plural *Recognitions,* however, indicates another approach to origins that supplements and contests the quest for an absolute. Here recognitions are recurrent concordances achieved in and through displacements—metaphors not of perfect identity but of recurrence in difference. They cannot be fixated once and for all in some unique source, and at the limit they intimate that the origin is itself a fiction or a forgery. They also suggest a different status for forgery—forgery in the dual sense of a counterfeit or simulacrum and of something that is forged or worked out. (The same dual sense is of course at issue in Joyce's *Portrait of the Artist as a Young Man.*) A recurrent motif of *The Recognitions* is that of the *semper aliquid haeret:* something [of the self or of invention] always sticks, even to the most perfect imitation or copy. Hence even the perfect forgery says something about its own time and its fashioner, thus drawing an internal limit to the quest for a return to the "original." In the modern world, moreover, "originals"—both religious and artistic—are implicated in a context that degrades them to the level of commercialized wares, instruments of advertising hype, and self-promotional pawns.

Jung in his *Psychology and Alchemy* (1944) suggested an elective affinity between the figure of Christ and the philosopher's stone of the alchemists in the light of their redemptive power.[4] In a commodity system, one might suggest an inversion of this affinity: that is, a correlation between the philosopher's stone and the commodity form itself, which is able to transform everything into gold (or its substitute, money) through the damnable power of universal equivalence. Hence the forgery, in its masked fraudulence, simply gives people what they want from fetishized originals, and it multiplies the sources of pleasure and profit. (This is the perspective of the cruder, capitalistic avatar of the devil: Recktall Brown.) Seen in another way, however, the forgery can itself emulate the original in a manner both mystified and perhaps necessary as a "stage" on the way to a more generalized transformation of cultural possibilities. It may be the highest form of aesthetic

---

[4]Collected Works, vol. 12 (Princeton, N.J., 1968).

activity possible in a degraded context—not an end term but a necessary "diabolical" reversal of ordinary assumptions within a broader process of possibly regenerative repetition.

Here, moreover, the hermetic and alchemical heritage acquires a positive connotation, not as a simple alternative to other traditions but at least as their necessary if ill-accommodated supplement. For despite its important affirmation of the need for human contact and understanding, the novel does not hold out a one-dimensional humanism as the promised land or the object of the quest. A certain humanism, combined with a self-assured scientism, takes the rest of nature as humankind's scapegoat—something with which one may experiment if doing so serves specifically human interests.

> Anti-histamine, streptomycin, penicillin, and 606 [Paul Erlich's remedy for syphilis]: few may question but that Theophrastus Bombastus von Hohenheim ("better known as Paracelsus") was right. It was Paracelsus who emerged from the fifteenth century (castrated by a hog, so they said, in his childhood) to proclaim that the object of alchemy was not at all the transmutation of base metals into gold, but the preparation of medicines, thus opening the way for the hospitalized perpetuation of accident which we triumphally prolong, enlarge upon, finance, respect, and enjoy today. [. . .] For unlike progressive revelation, the enlightenment of total materialism burst with such vigor that there were hardly enough hands to pick up the pieces. Even Paracelsus was left behind (dead of injuries received in a drunken brawl); and once chemistry had established itself as true and legitimate son and heir, alchemy was turned out like a drunken parent, to stagger away, babbling phantasies to fewer and fewer ears, to less and less impressive derelicts of loneliness, while the child grew up serious, dignified, and eminently pleased with its own limitations, to indulge that parental memory with no doubt but that it had found what the old fool and his cronies were after all the time. [P. 132]

What a scientistically conceived science does not retain from its alchemical parent, and what the novel attempts in its own way to rehabilitate, is at least twofold: to complete Christ's redemption of humanity with the redemption of all matter (for which the conversion of base metals into gold was at most emblematic); to see science (as well as art) as a vocation and a spiritual exercise in which the soul of the subject is as relevant as any "objective" discovery or power of prediction and manipulation.

One rather impressive derelict of loneliness to whom alchemy (along with much else) babbles is the displaced center of the novel, the quester and artist-figure who goes unnamed for hundreds of pages in the grotesquely bulging middle sections. In the beginning he is named Wyatt, and in the penultimate chapter is called Stephan and then is willing to call himself Stephen. His mother dies when he is a small child, the victim of a shipboard operation by a false surgeon who is actually a fugitive counterfeiter (Frank Sinisterra, who resurfaces at later points in the novel). His father, Gwyon, is a Protestant minister who becomes increasingly captivated by his study of primitive cults, meshing *The Golden Bough* with the Bible and ultimately reviving Mithraism, to the dismay of his initially bewildered and then scandalized parishioners. His distance from his son is bridged by his inclination to recount to the boy a strange medley of stories from various arcane texts treating archaic religions, hermeticism, patristic thought, and the lives of the saints. When Wyatt is dying from a disease that doctors are unable to treat, Gwyon sacrifices the Barbary ape he brought back with him from Spain—an ape that serves as a surrogate for the mother, who was buried in Spanish soil. Late in the novel, when Gwyon has entered more fully into the cult of Mithra, he sacrifices a bull and is sent to an asylum; there— in a reversal of the Christian story—he, the father, is apparently crucified by a crazed anatomist who himself has gone mad after having been "appointed by the Congregation of the Sacred Rights, at the Vatican, to investigate early methods of crucifixion" (p. 712). Gwyon is replaced by a more "with it" modern minister named Dick, "as this young man encouraged people to call him, since his Christian name was Richard" (p.

710), who at his own expense sends Gwyon's ashes in an oatmeal box to a monastery in Spain that Gwyon had earlier visited.

Wyatt is raised by his paternal aunt, "a barren steadfast woman, Calvinistically faithful to the man who had been Reverend Gwyon before [Wyatt's father]. She saw her duty in any opportunity at Christian umbrage" (p. 3). Wyatt assimilates much of Aunt May's guilt-ridden "No Cross No Crown" philosophy of life, as well as her attitude toward art. In one of her more memorable declamations, she tells the child:

> Lucifer was the archangel who refused to serve our Lord. To sin is to falsify something in the Divine Order, and that is what Lucifer did. His name means Bringer of Light but he was not satisfied to bring the light of Our Lord to man, he tried to steal the power of Our Lord and to bring his own light to man. He tried to become original, she pronounced malignantly, shaping that word round the whole structure of damnation, repeating it, crumpling the drawing of the robin in her hand,—original, to steal Our Lord's authority, to command his own destiny, to bear his own light! That is why Satan is the fallen angel, for he rebelled when he tried to emulate Our Lord Jesus. And he won his own domain, didn't he. Didn't he! And his own light is the light of the fires of Hell! Is that what you want? Is that what you want? Is that what you want?
>
> There may have been, by now, many things that Wyatt wanted to do to Jesus: emulate was not one of them. He made drawings in secret, and kept them hidden, terrified with guilty amazement as forms took shape under his pencil. [P. 34]

Aunt May's influence is moderated, however, by Wyatt's maternal grandfather, the Town Carpenter, a ribald, carnivalesque figure who is anathema to Aunt May but outlives her. Wyatt is obsessed by the image of his dead mother, which is displaced into the figure of the Virgin in his forged paintings (as well as into an act of "incest" with the model Esme when she appears with bleeding ears, wearing, as the mother did, large gold earrings); he is also obsessed by the desire for understanding ("recognition") vis-à-vis the distant father. Wyatt

himself begins by studying for the ministry, and art for him is
invested with displaced and disfigured religious values. When
he returns after years away from home, in a serioparodic Second Coming, he is misrecognized by those remaining: for the
Town Carpenter, he is Prester John; for the housemaid Janet,
he is Christ himself; for his father, he is apparently a Mithraic
messenger; and he introduces himself to the ladies of the Use-
Me Society as the Reverend Gilbert Sullivan. His father can
provide none of the answers he seeks, particularly in the quasi-
apocalyptic scene when he demands: "Am I the man for whom
Christ died?"

Wyatt, especially after he is divested of his name, is less a
character in any traditional sense than a blank space into
which other characters project their desires for redemption. As
a kind of sacrificial figure, he is dismembered and dissemi-
nated into those around him. His wife Esther makes demands
he cannot fulfill, yet after his departure she retains his memory
as an addled saving grace. (After an affair with Otto Pivner, she
settles down with Ellery, an advertising man for "Necrostyle,"
which specializes, among other products, in a sleeping pill
shaped like a communion wafer and sponsors a radio version of
the lives of the saints.) With her as with others, Wyatt has an
inordinate sense of privacy and of distance, a *noli me tangere*
attitude that bespeaks both his apartness and his lack of
human warmth and connection. If he is a Christ figure, he
seems to lack the exoteric and popular mission of Christ in
attempting to redeem all who would believe in him. His words,
however broken and in search of their own meaning, nonetheless have the proverbial ability to become encased in the hear-
er's mind and to be recycled almost as clichés.

The young Otto Pivner is his parodic ape, and the play Otto
writes and loses (it is never mentioned past a certain point,
upsetting the reader's expectations for its recovery in one form
or another) reads like a plagiarism, although no one can put his
finger on a specific source; it regurgitates and disperses Wyatt's
words only to disappear in the manner of the true cliché. Otto
as a partial Wyatt seeks his father, whom he has never met (we
hear nothing about his mother). The proposed meeting of fa-

ther and son never comes off; it is dislocated by a series of false recognitions.

Mr. Pivner is himself less a character than the consummate media man—the pathetic vehicle for information and fantasies purveyed by the newspapers and the radio; he almost randomly chooses a substitute son (the office boy Eddie Zefnic) and supports his education as an experimental psychologist. Treasury agents mistakenly pick up Mr. Pivner for counterfeiting while he and Eddie are making the vain attempt to listen to a radio broadcast of *The Messiah*, which "was trying to squeeze through an infinitesimal aperture" left by competing broadcasts, including a quiz program where a Mr. Crotcher wins a house in Arshole Acres (from the Latin *ars*, meaning art). To cure him of counterfeiting, Eddie convinces Mr. Pivner to undergo a lobotomy and writes to him of the justness of the decision in a semiliterate letter describing his own work. Eddie is making use of electric shock to induce anxiety attacks in "a whole bunch of kids (ha ha I mean little goats) . . . and everything is recorded real close by the lab and then we go over all that and try to get them out of it [the anxiety neurosis which is a breakdown], you can see it's real interesting and how much good it will do" (p. 933). The counterfeit money traced to Mr. Pivner is that used by Otto to buy his father a robe; Otto received the "queer" money from Frank Sinisterra, whom he mistook for Mr. Pivner. (The scene between Otto and Frank Sinisterra is a truly riotous comedy of errors).

Rather than give in to the temptation to discuss both the large array of characters and seriocomic scenes, I would simply note that the two figures with aesthetic views closest to Wyatt's own are the musician Stanley and the counterfeiter Frank Sinisterra. Stanley is attached to his dying mother, who progressively loses various parts of her body (we hear nothing of his father). When she dies, the object of his quest is to play in her memory a composition, which centuries earlier would have been a requiem mass, on the giant organ (donated by an American) in the church in Fenestrula. Like Wyatt, Stanley rejects the commercialization of art; he wonders: "How could Bach have accomplished all that he did? and Palestrina? the

Gabrielis? and what of the organ concerti of Corelli? Those were the men whose work he admired beyond all else in this life, for they had touched the origins of design with recognition" (p. 322). Frank Sinisterra's counterfeiting is also a labor of love. He reads the *National Counterfeit Detector* looking for "reviews" of his work as an artist might read the *Collectors Quarterly*. In fact, the return on his investment is less than 3 percent, for he uses bleached dollar bills for counterfeit twenties, and he receives only eight dollars for every hundred of "queer" money. He detests his own good-for-nothing son, Chaby, and toward the end of the novel, in Spain, he "adopts" the nameless Wyatt in an attempt to atone for what he did to Wyatt's mother. He provides Wyatt with a Swiss passport under the name of Stephan Asche ("ashes") and continually calls his recalcitrant companion "Stephan" for no reason other than to make him used to the new name.

Wyatt makes his Faustian pact with the devil when he agrees to paint forgeries of the fifteenth-century Flemish masters for the commercially minded impresario, Recktall Brown. He in fact began his career as a forger when, as a boy, he copied Bosch's *Seven Deadly Sins*—which was in his father's possession—and sold the original, for almost nothing, to Brown. Yet, as I intimated, the figure of the devil is cloven, with the other half assumed by Basil Valentine: art critic, spy, former seminarian, homosexual, and cultivated aesthete. Valentine himself bears the name of an alchemist who was said to have been charged with poisoning monks, the fifteenth-century author of *The Trimphal Car of Antimony*, a work that discussed an agent used to free gold from its impurities, the etymology of which was falsely derived from the Greek *anti* and *monos* (against monks): "*The Triumphal Car of Antimony.* Now I remember your name. Basil Valentine, the alchemist who watched pigs grow fat on food containing stibium, wasn't it . . . you tried it on some fasting emaciated monks and they all died" (p. 384). While Valentine resembles Wyatt in his distance from others and his distaste for human contact (he obsessively washes his hands), he also distinguishes himself from the artist in a telling way: "I know that I hate [people], where you wish you could love them" (p. 386). Yet, as we shall see, neither Valentine nor Brown are purely negative figures.

The society that Brown exploits, Valentine detests, and Wyatt withdraws from is demotically diabolical: an Age of Publicity whose rule of spirituality with respect to instances of artistic and cultural attainment is an inverted one: if you can't rise to their level, you can at least drag them down to yours. Its Bible is Dale Carnegie's *How to Win Friends and Influence People*—the age's answer to *The Pilgrim's Progress*. Carnegie's *"action* book" serves as a recurrent reference point in the novel and becomes a veritable sign of the times—an epitome of its common culture.

> It was written with reassuring felicity. There were no abstrusely long sentences, no confounding long words, no bewildering metaphors in an obfuscated system such as he feared finding in simply bound books of thoughts and ideas. No dictionary was necessary to understand its message; no reason to know what Kapila saw when he looked heavenward, and of what the Athenians accused Anaxagoras, or to know the secret name of Jahveh, or who cleft the Gordian knot, the meaning of 666. There was, finally, very little need to know anything at all, except how to "deal with people." College, the author implied, meant simply years wasted on Latin verbs and calculus. Vergil, and Harvard, were cited regularly with an uncomfortable, if off-hand, reverence for their unnecessary existences. ("You don't have to study for four years in Harvard to discover that," Mr. Pivner read, with a qualm of superiority, for he understood that Otto had, indeed, gone to Harvard.) In these pages, he was assured that whatever his work, knowledge of it was infinitely less important than knowing how to "deal with people." This was what brought a price in the market place; and what else could anyone possibly want? [P. 499]

(The novel itself includes some coy toying with the Harvard-Yale rivalry, for the Ivy League has taken over the advertising industry, and most of the ad men seem to have gone to Yale, where languages such as Latin and Italian are, to their knowledge, not taught.)

Carnegie's tract for the time makes its last grotesque appearance in the mouth of Father Eulalio, translator for the Spanish "Royal Monastery of Our Lady of Another (or Second) Time." This is the monastery that Gwyon visited and that serves as the setting for Wyatt's final scene. Eulalio, the parodic possessor of the gift of tongues, dreams only of typewriters and other commodities, and he asks the fatuous but famous writer Ludy whether he has the book Eulalio so wanted, *How to Procure for Friends and Vanquishing of Everybody* (p. 862).

The line between symptomaticity and resistance is often hard to draw in the pervasively insinuating, indeed ingratiating, society and culture that the novel renders. In the long and tortuous letter from Agnes Deigh (*Agnus Dei*) to an unknown dentist in an adjoining set of rooms, whom she sees from her window beating a girl who turns out to be his daughter (thus making Agnes herself liable to a suit for the false accusation that leads to the arrest of the good doctor!), she—on her way to increasing distraction, culminating in a suicide attempt that fails because she falls on a mailman—parodies Herbert Marcuse as she observes: "We are the great refusal, doctor" (p. 757). The novel at times reads like a more sophisticated analogue—both more modulated and more bold—of Marcuse's *One-Dimensional Man*, a resister's critique of society's lack of resistance that itself threatened at times to replicate the one-dimensionality of its objects of criticism.

While it is certainly hyperbolic in its grotesque realism, outlandish parody, and bitter response to the times, *The Recognitions* is only infrequently close to one-dimensionality itself. Yet there are a number of areas in which the novel, in disclosing the limits and limitations of society and culture, also threatens to fall prey to them. While it offers an astounding array of religious heritages and debris, it devotes relatively little attention to specifically Judaic traditions or to the problem of anti-Semitism. The latter appears as background noise in cocktail party chit-chat or as passing slurs. This status perhaps reflects accurately what all such prejudice or stereotyping should amount to, but it hardly does justice to its prevalence, virulence, and scapegoating potential in modern history. Except for an unnamed onanistic critic, there is but one black in the novel: Fuller, Recktall Brown's manservant, who tends the black poodle that is Brown's familiar. Fuller suspects the dog of spying on him and finally kills it, as Wyatt stabs Valentine after Brown himself has fallen to his death (in the suit of armor Fuller repeatedly polished), thus rendering unnecessary the literal realization of the act of murder Fuller so often enacted ritually against his master. But Fuller is largely a comic grotesque, and his level of ideological awareness often seems close to that of Rochester on the Jack Benny show.

Homosexuality is everywhere in the novel, yet the connotation it carries seems largely negative. Valentine is the most striking homosexual figure, and he seeks domination of Wyatt or at least the ability to make the artist recognize their affinity. The group of homosexuals around Agnes Deigh is an object of sustained parody, and her attachment to them is a sign of her own deficiencies. Wyatt himself is unable to acknowledge and come to terms with the homosexual component in himself other than through denial and disavowal. He is extremely upset when his wife Esther touches upon the subject, and we learn toward the end of the novel, in a scene in which it is difficult to distinguish between phantasm and memory, that in North Africa he killed the homosexual friend of his Munich days and thenceforth began a life of wandering. (A long section on Wyatt's period in Munich with Han was apparently cut from the novel at an editor's request; only a number of fleeting, tangled allusions remain.)

The use of homosexuality primarily as a negative symbol of sterility and decadence may have been prompted in part by Robert Graves's views in *The White Goddess* (1944), which was an important "source book" for Gaddis. Graves provided one variant of the absolute original, here located in age-old pagan culture: "My thesis is that the language of poetic myth anciently current in the Mediterranean and Northern Europe was a magical language bound up with popular religious ceremonies in honour of the Moon-Goddess, or the Muse, some of them dating from the Old Stone Age, and that this remains the language of true poetry—'true' in the nostalgic modern sense of 'the unimprovable original, not a synthetic substitute.' "[5] In Graves's schema of world history, "true" poetry, myth, and ritual were disrupted by both Greek philosophy and Christianity. If, for Nietzsche, Christianity was Platonism for the masses and Socrates the figure of the divorce between Apollonian form and Dionysian frenzy, then for Graves, Greek philosophy and Christianity conspired to undo the poetic-mythic past, and the figure of Socrates was antithetical to the fascination of the White Goddess. Socrates was not only distant from women; he did not even practice sodomy. For Graves his "ideal homosexuality was a far more serious moral aberrancy—it was the male intellect trying to make itself spiritually self-sufficient" (*White Goddess*, p. 12). Basil Valentine is himself a largely "Socratic" figure in Graves's sense.

But while there is much use of the symbolism of sun, moon, and trees discussed by Graves, there would seem to be no literal feminine analogue of the White Goddess in *The Recognitions*. The obsessive image—which Wyatt ultimately tries to transcend—is that of the Virgin Mother, and women in the novel are either displacements of her or vessels for men (or both, in the case of Esme). The portrayal of Esther tends to remain one-dimensional, and while it is easy to see why she and Wyatt drift apart, it is more difficult to appreciate what attracted them to each other in the first place. Characters such as Hannah, Adeline, Maude Munk, and Mrs. Deigh are chiefly caricatural cameos. The two relatively complex figures are Agnes Deigh and Esme, yet it is significant that when they become most intricate, they tend to merge with the narrative voice (Esme in a rather jarring manner, given her usual level of foglike floating if not subarticulate stupor).

Yet it is significant that the very style of the text, which effects a many-sided interplay of voices and ideological perspectives, serves to mitigate the reduced nature of certain characterizations. The larger world in which the characters move is teeming with unrealized possibilities, both disastrous and regenerative. The novel's treatment of the cocktail party is par-

[5]*The White Goddess* (New York, 1966), pp. 9–10.

ticularly striking in this regard, for it becomes the scene of a vast and often misguided carnival of the half-baked, mutually attractive or repellent, at times flippant discourses and ideologies of the day. (It is the prelude to the great bonfire of modern dialogue in *J R*.) One technique carried to near perfection in *The Recognitions* is that of the subtly altered repetition: one could do an entirely stylistic study of the astonishing use of this technique. And the technique is of course not purely technical, for it responds to the very understanding of temporality in the novel. On both the level of dialogue and the level of description and narrative, one has a delicately articulated array of displaced repetitions and modulated recurrences. An exchange between Esther and Otto or one of Wyatt's sayings (or silences) reappears cunningly transformed (contextually if not verbally) in an exchange between Brown and Valentine or an encounter between Otto and Esme. These displacements are spots of time for possible or missed—perhaps empty—"recognitions."

One instance, of especially remarkable poetic density, occurs very early and very late in the novel:

> False dawn past, the sun prepared the sky for its appearance, and there, a shred of perfection abandoned unsuspecting at the earth's rim, lay the curve of the old moon, before the blaze which would rise behind it to extinguish the cold quiet of its reign. [P. 15]

> In the false dawn, the sun prepared the sky for its appearance; but even now the horned moon hung unsuspecting at the earth's rim, before the blaze which rose behind it to extinguish the cold quiet of its reign. [P. 700]

The waning moon illuminates a counterfeit dawn, but it is in the first passage also a shred of perfection. The sun, like the phoenix, extinguishes the old order of night to give rise to a new day, but in the movement from the first to the second passage there is an omission or consumption of the shred of perfection, intimating an economy of gains and losses in which any form of transcendence never comes without a cost. The curve of the moon also turns into a horn, approximating the

Mithraic bull sacrificed by Gwyon (itself a symbol of the sun) and indicating the hidden affinity between seeming opposites (sun and moon, day and night, male and female, enlightened reason and creative imagination, and so forth).

I intimated earlier that neither Brown nor Valentine is a purely negative figure. Brown marks the mutation of the American dream into a nightmare and an object of gallows humor, but he has a bizarre paternal relation toward Wyatt that is not devoid of genuine affection. His brash and unvarnished exploitation of art is, moreover, less hypocritical than the sly complicity of the false critics and connoisseurs over whom he reigns. When Wyatt threatens to expose his "originals" as forgeries, Brown seems to court suicide and to push the noses of the "critics" into the scarcely dried paint of the forged masterpieces whose counterfeit nature it is not in their interest to recognize. There is no common ground for mutual understanding between him and Wyatt, only a commercial pact, but from his own grossly materialist end of the spectrum Brown is as distant from pseudocritics as is Wyatt given his compromised but intransigently "mystical" dedication to art. In his own perverse manner, Brown is willing to die for his relation to art.

Under Brown's tutelage, Wyatt forges the works of fifteenth-century Flemish masters: Memling, Bouts, van der Weyden, Jan van Eyck. He rejects the "romantic" myth of originality as novelty and "self-expression," remembering the words of his art teacher in Munich, Herr Koppel:

That romantic disease, originality, all around we see originality of incompetent idiots, they could draw nothing, paint nothing, just so the mess they make is original. . . . Even two hundred years ago who wanted to be original, to be original was to admit that you could not do a thing the right way, so you could only do it your own way. When you paint you do not try to be original, only you think about your work, how to make it better, so you copy masters, only masters, for with each copy of a copy the form degenerates . . . you do not invent shapes, you know them, auswendig wissen Sie, by heart. [P. 89]

When Basil Valentine accuses Wyatt of calumniating through his forgeries the art he respects, the agitated Wyatt stammers out his sense of what it is to forge in the right way:

> I . . . when I'm working, I . . . Do you think I do these the way all other forging has been done? Pulling the fragments of ten paintings together and making one, or taking a . . . a Dürer and reversing the composition so that the man looks to the right instead of left, putting a beard on him from another portrait, and a hat, a different hat from another, so that they look at it and recognize Dürer there? No, it's . . . the recognitions go much deeper, much further back, and I . . . this . . . the X-ray tests, and ultra-violet and infra-red, the experts with their photomicrography and . . . macrophotography, do you think that's all there is to it? Some of them aren't fools, they don't just look for a hat or a beard, or a style they can recognize, they look with memories that . . . go beyond themselves, that go back to . . . where mine goes. [P. 250]

When Wyatt attempts to tell the critics that their originals are forgeries, he does so not simply to expose Brown but to disclose that he, Wyatt, is their "creator"—not in any absolute sense but in that he has realized certain unrealized possibilities in the "originals" and reproduced them in overwhelmingly adverse sociocultural and spiritual conditions. His forged emulations may in this sense surpass their original models, for they do more and do something different precisely to the extent that they are faithful to the originals and carry to perfection what may only be intimated in them. (One recognizes here what may anachronistically be called the "Pierre Menard" factor.) Yet Wyatt's emulation is attended by a nostalgic cult of the past and the atmosphere of spirituality in which the Flemish artists created their seemingly auratic works. In this respect, Basil Valentine plays a fruitful demystifying role, and his words to Wyatt remain imprinted in the latter's mind. Thus Valentine's seemingly diabolical negation helps to bring about a significant shift in the artist's orientation:

Vulgarity, cupidity, and power. Is that what frightens you? Is that all you see around you, and you think it was different then? Flanders in the fifteenth century, do you think it was all like the Adoration of the Mystic Lamb? What about the paintings we've never seen? the trash that's disappeared? Just because we have a few masterpieces left, do you think they were all masterpieces? What about the pictures we've never seen, and will never see? that were as bad as anything that's ever been done? And your precious van Eyck, do you think he didn't live up to his neck in a loud vulgar court? In a world where everything was done for the same reasons everything's done now? for vanity and avarice and lust? [. . .] These fine altarpieces, do you think they glorified anyone but the vulgar men who commissioned them? Do you think a van Eyck didn't curse having to whore away his genius, to waste his talents on all sorts of vulgar celebrations, at the mercy of people he hated? [. . .]

Yes, I remember your little talk, your insane upside-down apology for these pictures, every figure and every object with its own presence, its own consciousness because it was being looked at by God! Do you know what it was? What it really was? that everything was so afraid, so uncertain God saw it, that it insisted its vanity on His eyes? Fear, fear, pessimism and fear and depression everywhere, the way it is today, that's why your pictures are so cluttered with detail, this terror of emptiness, this absolute terror of space. Because maybe God isn't watching. Maybe he doesn't see. Oh, this pious cult of the Middle Ages! Being looked at by God! Is there a moment of faith in any of their work, in one centimeter of canvas? or is it vanity and fear, the same decadence that surrounds us now. [Pp. 689–90]

It is interesting that Valentine's words echo in their own register the more balanced and suasive tones of Johan Huizinga in *The Waning of the Middle Ages* (1924), another of Gaddis's "source books" for the novel.[6] In fifteenth-century Flemish art, "a *horror vacui* reigns, always a symptom of artistic decline" (*Waning*, p. 248). Huizinga notes the apparent contrast between "barbarous manifestations of arrogant pomp and the

---

[6]Garden City, N.Y., 1954; hereafter cited as *Waning*.

pictures of van Eyck, Dirk Bouts, and Rogier van der Weyden, with their sweet and tranquil serenity" (*Waning*, p. 250). But he goes on to mitigate if not erase the contrast. The painters were closer to the culture of the court, the nobles, and rich bourgeois than to the *devotia moderna* (*Waning*, p. 260), and their piety was no simple matter.

> In the piety interpreted by the art of the fifteenth century, the extremes of mysticism and of gross materialism meet. [. . .] By using the term primitive to designate the masters of the fifteenth century we run the risk of a misunderstanding. They are primitive in a purely chronological sense, in so far as, for us, they are the first to come, and no older painting is known to us. But if to this designation we attach the meaning of a primitive spirit, we are egregiously mistaken. For the spirit which the art denotes is the same which we pointed out in religious life: a spirit rather decadent than primitive, a spirit involving the utmost elaboration, and even decomposition, of religious thought through the imagination. [. . .] Instead of heralding the advent of the Renaissance, as is generally assumed, this naturalism is rather one of the ultimate forms of development of the medieval mind. The craving to turn every sacred idea into precise images, to give it a distinct and clearly outlined form, such as we observed in the *Roman de la Rose*, in Denis the Carthusian, controlled art, as it controlled popular beliefs and theology. The art of the brothers van Eyck closes a period. [*Waning*, pp. 262–64]

Wyatt's understanding of the Flemish masters and of his own quest undergoes a mutation toward the end of the novel. He is occupied in the monastery in the ultimate form of "restoration": the return of paintings to the state of blank canvases. His act of erasure, however, is undertaken with the same care and delicacy of touch as were his incomparable imitations of the masters. He has been followed to his retreat by the writer Ludy, and as Ludy names himself for the first time, the nameless artist rejoins, "People I've never seen before in my life call me Stephen" (p. 867). Actually, Frank Sinisterra had been calling him Stephan, and the change in one letter, perceptible only in the written form, is (whether intentional on Gaddis's part or not) noteworthy as marking the assumption of the name by the artist himself. The last name on the passport, "Asche," is an obvious indicator of the phoenixlike possibility of regeneration from one's ashes in an ambivalent act of destruction and renewal. The regeneration of Stephen is not total, as the final scenes in which he appears make evident, but it is significant in the transformational possibilities it suggests. "Stephen" was in fact the name originally intended for him by his parents. They "had agreed, if it were a son, to name him Stephen; and not until months after their son was born, and Aunt May had peremptorily supplied the name Wyatt from somewhere in the Gwyon genealogy, did they remember. Or rather, Camilla [his mother] remembered, and though it might have been a safe choice, for the name's sake of the first Christian martyr, even to Aunt May, neither of them mentioned it to her, for baptism had already taken place" (p. 27). Stephen's own recognition of the name, as he erases past masters and unknowingly eats bread made from the ashes of his father—thereby communing with and simultaneously eliminating the paternal ghost—is one sign of his movement toward a different status. So is his invocation of the name of Titian in his exchange with Ludy, who increasingly becomes aware, with growing anxiety and the desire to flee, of precisely what the artist's activity of restoration requires.

> Yes, he studied with Titian. That's where El Greco learned, that's where he learned to simplify, Stephen went on, speaking more rapidly—that's where he learned not to be afraid of spaces, not to get lost in details and clutter, and separate everything. [. . .] Separateness, that's what went wrong, you'll understand . . . or,— Everything withholding itself from everything else. [. . .] Painters who weren't afraid of spaces of . . . cluttering up every space with detail everything vain and separate affirming itself for fear that . . . fear of leaving any space for transition, for forms to . . . to share each other and . . . in the Middle Ages when everything was in pieces and gilding the pieces, yes, to insure their separation for fear there was no God . . . before the Renaissance. [Pp. 872–75]

Stephen recognizes the need for both spaces and connections and turns from the waning Middle Ages to the Renaissance in words that are themselves broken, groping, and punctuated with repeated ellipses. The sharing intimated in his own transition or transfiguration does not lead to total, self-assured identity, but it does bring with it a decision to go on and to begin again. As he speaks to Ludy, he notes the presence of the silent porter in the doorway, the man who raped and killed an eleven-year-old girl but who was allowed to atone as porter in the monastery. There is an easy familiarity between Stephen and the porter, for each accepts with compassion the crimes of the other—the porter permitting Stephen's work of "restoration," and Stephen seeing the fittingness of the porter's occupation. As Stephen observes, "There's a permanence of disaster here, left where we can refer to it, the towers of the Moors lie where they fell, and you'll find people living in them, whole cities jealous of the past, enamored parodies weighed down with testimonial ruins, and they don't come running to bury the old man, but give him the keys to the church, and he rings the bells. He says she comes to him carrying lilies that turn to flames when he takes them. You see how I trust him" (p. 876). Stephen and the old porter exchange a smile that is described in terms that repeat and vary earlier descriptions of an enigmatic expression upon the artist's face: "A smile commenced to break the lines on [the porter's] face, pressing the disease scars away until they were almost out of sight in the flesh. But the smile stopped there: the lines restrained it, and the scars showed out" (pp. 875–76). Stephen's smile meets the porter's across the figure of the panic-stricken Ludy. "Nonetheless Stephen's smile stopped where the other did, unrestrained by deep lines and scars, but it stopped" (p. 876). The narrator thus marks the limits of transfiguration in healing wounds, for history remains a process of reading the scars of the past, however modified they may be by changes or possibilities in the present.

Stephen appears for the final time as he encounters Ludy, who has gone for a "meditative walk" (p. 892). Stephen again refers to the story of the porter, and he intimates that the quest for redemption must be inflected toward a healing process of repeatedly "living through" the traumatic ruptures of the past. He also takes a distance from the desire for an absolute origin and the wish to become a perfect imitation of Christ as well as a pure artist, and he points the way to a need for recurrent attempts to come to terms with recurrent difficulties.

> If somewhere I've . . . done the same thing [as the porter]? And something's come out of it, something . . . like . . . he has. While I've been crowding the work alone. To end there, or almost end running up to the doors there, to pound on the doors of the church, do you see why he sent me on? Look back, if once you're started in living, you're born into sin, then? And how do you atone? By locking yourself up in remorse for what you might have done? Or by living it through. By locking yourself up in remorse with what you know you have done? Or by going back and living it through. By locking yourself up with your work, until it becomes a gessoed surface, all prepared, clean and smooth as ivory? Or by living it through. By drawing lines in your mind? Or by living it through. If it was sin from the start, and possible all the time, to know it's possible and avoid it? Or by living it through. I used to wonder, how Christ could really have been tempted, if He was sinless, and rejected the first, and the second, and the third temptation, how was He tempted? . . . how did He know what it was, the way we do, to be tempted? No, He was Christ. But for us, with it there from the start, and possible all the time, to go on knowing it's possible and pretend to avoid it? Or . . . or to have lived it through, and live it through again, and deliberately to go on living it through. [P. 896]

Stephen catches a bird in his hand as it flies up before the startled Ludy (who has an obsessive fear of birds close at hand). He keeps it locked in his grip for the remainder of the conversation, with an intensity indicative of the proximity between life and death. Images of birds, merging the Christian paraclete, the pagan phoenix, and the bird that may be simply a bird, recur in various forms throughout the novel. Stephen quotes the Bishop of Hippo to Ludy, who misrecognizes the reference to Saint Augustine: "*Dilige et quod vis fac* . . . Love and do what you will" (p. 899). Ludy misses the point even when the statement is translated, and he (recalling Otto) makes a note to check what it might mean. Stephen quotes a translation of the Hungarian inscription on Valentine's cigarette case, and liberates the bird. "Yes, much I pondered, why you came here to ask me those questions, Stephen laughed above him, stepping away. He opened his hand. The bird struck it and went free.—Hear . . . ? Bells sounded, far down the hill there.—Goodbye."

The liberation of the bird repeats and reverses the killing of the wren committed by Wyatt as a child—the act he could not confess to his father until it emerged in "broken, disjointed fashion" during his severe illness. Upon hearing the confession, the father rejoined that early Christian missionaries used to have the wren hunted down and killed, for it was to them a king and "they couldn't have that, . . . around Christmas . . . they couldn't have that" (p. 47). The wren thus combined a pagan and a paternal symbolism, and the liberation of the bird has as one of its implications the working or living through of both Oedipal and interreligious conflict. Stephen departs from Ludy with "the old man ringing [him] on"; he reaffirms the need to simplify and to live deliberately, but he gives no specific idea of where he will go or what he will do.

The final scenes with Wyatt-Stephen would seem to constitute the dramatic high point of the novel, its moment of transformation or even transfiguration. But they are not its conclusion. The last chapter is a kind of satyr play in which the fate of the other characters is resolved in a parodic rendition of the traditional novelistic wrap-up. The scenes between Stephen and Ludy are not devoid of their own parodic and farcical moments, and the departure of Stephen is followed by the portrait of Ludy back in his room, trying to puzzle out the meaning of the misrecognized quotation from Augustine, as a bird flutters across the room and the mirror reflects "the face of a man having, or about to have, or at the very least valiantly fighting off, a religious experience" (p. 900). The reader, moreover, is aware that the eleven-year-old girl raped and killed by the porter was slated for canonization but had been mistakenly replaced by the corpse of Wyatt-Stephen's own mother, the girl's corpse having been stolen by Frank Sinisterra and converted, with Stephan's aid, into a counterfeit mummy. In the final chapter, many elements of the dramatic scene between Stephen and Ludy are parodied. Otto assumes the new name Gordon (that of the hero in his lost play) and is repeatedly told by Dr. Fell (who failed to cure Wyatt as a child) that since all his money has been stolen, he will have to start all over again; the Angelus rings in the background. Don Bildow also attempts to put off the old man and put on the new as he purchases a suit of clothes, which—he discovers, after destroying his old suit to avoid paying customs duties on the new—turns out to be a sailor suit for a seven-year-old boy.

The last chapter, which marshals all the characters for a final appearance, is a forceful indication of the novel's attempt to join the serious and the parodic, both in its critique of the dominant culture and in its self-reflexive relation to itself. In other words, the novel strives for a destructive-regenerative ambivalence—one in which the resurgent phoenix and the dialogic interplay of tongues do not emerge unscathed but do bring about significantly critical and potentially transformative effects. The serious and mock apocalyptic fate of Stanley is emblematic in this respect. It both parallels Stephen's course (Stephen the martyr was stoned to death) and is a metaphor for the work of the novel itself; indeed, it might be seen as the final if displaced self-reflexive reference to *The Recognitions*.

Stanley is finally able to play his work on the giant organ of the church at Fenestrula. He arrives there not as he thought he would, through the ministrations of Agnes Deigh's mother, but through the good offices of Father Martin. This priest knew Wyatt when the latter was studying for the ministry and made a series of brief, chance appearances in Wyatt's life, always as the cleric was in the process of rushing to catch a train. In the final chapter Father Martin is leading pilgrims to Italy, and after hearing Stanley's confession, he is shot by Valentine's associate. It is noteworthy that the scene of Stanley's confession is itself a brief, serious interlude that seems uninterrupted by other forces—except the echo effects (patent-pat-patient-compassion) and the retrospective role of situational irony as we realize the implications of Father Martin's arranging for Stanley's solitary performance at Fenestrula. "Father Martin listened to him, and talked to him, with an extraordinary gentleness and sternness at once, with a calmness which was never complacent, a strength of understanding (though he never said he understood), an interest which was not patent curiosity to excuse pat answers (for he gave none), and a patient sympathy with the figures Stanley spoke of, a quality which showed itself the deepest aspect of his nature, the most hard earned and rarely realized reality of maturity, which was compassion" (pp. 951–52).

Putting on his best suit for his visit to the church, Stanley discovers moth holes around the crotch. "There was nothing, absolutely nothing, the way he had thought it would be" (p. 955). In church a priest in a hurry to be off somewhere tells him in Italian, which he does not understand, not to use too much bass and to avoid strange combinations of notes because the church is so old that the vibration could be dangerous. Oblivious of the warning, Stanley pulls out all the stops of the organ and strikes a "chord of the devil's interval from the full length of the thirty-foot bass pipes. [. . .] The walls quivered, still he did not hesitate. Everything moved, and even falling, soared in atonement. He was the only person caught in the collapse, and afterward, most of his work was recovered too, and it is still spoken of, when it is noted, with high regard, though seldom played" (p. 956).

The last words, in their serioparodic, apocalyptic resonance, could of course apply to the novel itself, which is well worth the reading even if it unsettles a few walls.

Epilogue

> Epilogue. 1. A speech, short poem, or the like, addressed to the spectators, and spoken after the conclusion of a play; also, the speaker or speakers of this. 2. A concluding section, as of a novel, serving to complete the plan of the work.
> Webster's New Collegiate Dictionary

> *Epiloguer.* 1. To carp, to cavil (*sur*, at). Fam. To speechify, to enlarge (*sur*, upon); to make a fuss, to waffle (*sur*, about).
> Larousse Modern French-English Dictionary

In the light of the preceding chapters, I would like to return to some of the issues raised in the Introduction, at times in a contrapuntal manner that stresses different points or supplements the earlier argument. Specifically, I want to draw out some of the general protocols of reading that inform this study and—without pretending to provide either a "grand theory" of the novel or a fully satisfying sense of closure for my own account—to state more systematically and didactically my understanding of how to investigate a text's relation to history and politics.

The texts I have selected range over five national cultures and stretch across more than a century in time. On the one hand, this fact impedes a more coherent understanding of determinate sequences, not simply in the developmental or successive-stage format that I question but even in the mode of displacement or repetitive temporality that I argue is active in modern novels themselves. On the other hand, this very diversity helps to test both generalizations about the novel and protocols in reading it. One obvious but significant context that is inscribed with more or less pronounced differences in these texts is the context furnished by an apprehension of modern society and culture as undergoing multiple crises, notably a crisis of legitimation. The "crisis" metaphor has of course become somewhat hackneyed, but one feature of significant modern texts is to renew our sense of its pertinence, indeed its virulence, as well as of its possible abuses or mystifications, especially in pathos-charged, melodramatic renditions. In these respects, the theory of so-called realist, modernist, and postmodernist "stages" is of relatively little assistance in the attempt to elucidate situationally different torsions in a recurrent anxiety. One can, moreover, detect a sense of traumatic rupture—toward the past, possibly toward the future—within the repetitive temporalities in significant texts throughout the last two centuries. This sense is particularly urgent when the historical context rendered in the novel is the rise of the Nazis or, in a different register, the invasive spread of American consumer culture, but it is not absent even when the context is that of petty intrigues in Restoration France, the world of the intelligentsia in Czarist Russia, or life in the Midlands in "ante-Reform" England.

The notion of crisis is intimately associated with another topic of essential importance in reflections on the novel—that of time. The novel has conventionally been understood as a primary medium in converting chronology into significant story through plots that organize time into a beginning-middle-end structure. Recently, the key concepts with which to analyze the process of conversion have been those of diachrony and synchrony. Diachrony designates movement over time involving change; it is related to the trope of metonymy. Synchrony "stops" time at a given moment and displays its "sameness" or "nowness" (*Jetztzeit*, in Walter Benjamin's term) in a spatialized tableau; it is related to the trope of metaphor. (It is also crucial for the concept of "spatial form.") This format may facilitate the idea that ordinary reality or life is sheer, senseless chronology ("one damn thing after another"), while fiction transfigures or symbolically redeems chronology through the imposition of meaningful plots. I have questioned the cogency both of this model of understanding the relation between "reality" and "fiction" and the binaries that attend it. I have argued instead for a more intricate notion of the supplementary relation of seeming opposites, allowing one better to investigate the range of displacements (including possible contradictions) between and within them. I have, moreover, tried to link this notion to a historically informed understanding of the different sociocultural and political conditions or possibilities that inflect and help shape the specific nature of displacements and variable articulations. With special reference to the topic of time, I have attempted to examine the role of repetitive temporality as a process of recurrence with change—at times traumatically disruptive change—a process that has been explored with particular insistence in certain modern novels. The notion of repetitive temporality enables one better to see how novels not only convert chronology into meaningful structure through plot but also test the limits of meaning through complex interactions between chronology and plot, contingency and meaning, "ordinary reality" and "fiction."

One may also note (as should be readily apparent) that one thing undergoing crisis in the novels I discuss is the "monadic" or "bourgeois" individual whose rise was presumably coterminous with that of the novel itself. For in these texts the individual is very much on trial in ways indicating not only the role of newer collective (or at least impersonal) forces but also different possibilities in the relations of what may oxymoronically be called social individuals. The instability of the self in relation to itself and to partially internalized others is so recurrent and multifarious a concern that "decentering" seems too anodyne, almost too domesticating, a term to designate it. It is, however, more difficult to understand and evaluate this concern and the manner in which novels enact it. Simply to bemoan its aggravation of unreliability in relations or to celebrate its emancipatory power would be equally shortsighted.

The specific question raised with respect to each text treated is that of how precisely it (whether consciously or not) comes to terms with pertinent contexts and what political implications such a "coming to terms" may arguably have. The categories that guide the analysis in this regard have been those of the symptomatic, the critical, and the possibly transformative. I have not tried to offer a scoresheet that classifies and ranks each text according to how it tallies when judged in accordance with these categories; rather, the categories help shape without entirely predetermining the directions in which the analyses go. My contention is that these categories at least allow one better to investigate the intricate relations between "ordinary life" and its refiguration in literature than does the rigid, canonical binary opposition between ordinary (or "phenomenal") reality and fiction or the related idea that reality is suspended and bracketed in fiction. The idea that reality and fiction are two discrete "realms" is quite misleading, for it blinds one to the more subtle displacements and carry-over effects between the two as well as to the specific and mutable nature of the contradictions or modes of alienation that may arise between and within them. The binary is, moreover, a metaphysical residue that inhibits reflection about society, history, and politics, for even when it is a facet of a poetics that is manifestly critical of metaphysics, it functions to keep criticism within a metametaphysical orbit whose terms revolve around double binds and lead at most to reversals of established conceptual hierarchies (such as that between reality and fiction or between phenomenal experience and language).

The symptomatic refers to the largely unconscious assimilation and inscription of ideologies or assumptions prevalent in society and culture (including, of course, literary culture). Here, to echo Jacques Derrida, the "outside" of a text is already "inside" it, and there is no "outside-the-text." But a text may also render its contexts in critical and potentially transformative ways that close reading may disclose. The transformation in question may come in the form of uncanny play, but the subsequent question is the role of such play with respect to a larger sociocultural and political economy. Even when it radically disrupts that economy and marks its limits, the specific way in which it does so, and the implications of its sublime or strangely disconcerting *dérèglement*, change with the nature of the society and culture in which it operates. In this sense, there is something ideologically misleading in the "rewriting" or reprocessing of all texts in the same universalizing terms, even when those terms stress the impasses of universalization or theorize the aporias of theory. And instead of an invariable movement "from . . . to" (for example, the movement from a "restricted" economy in which "play" has useful functions to a "general" one in which it explodes utility and accentuates the ambivalent relation of life and death, creation and destruction), one has a variably iterated interaction between binding structures and challenges to them—an interaction that very much depends for its specific articulation on sociocultural and political conditions. (This is a point upon which Georges Bataille, confronted with the Nazi variant of sacrificial *dépense*, was anxious to insist.)

Two prominent textual modes of critical reinscription and carnivalesque stylization that have appeared repeatedly in this study are irony and parody. They are modes of doubling and repetition that offer at least the occasion for critical distance on phenomena rendered in a text, and they may play a role in the critique of ideologies. At the limit, they may seem to outwit themselves and intimate the possibility of a sociocultural and political framework in which they would not disappear but might conceivably assume more many-sided, indeed ambivalent forms as modes of praise-abuse and as contestations of commitments (even—perhaps especially—when the latter are affirmed as legitimate). But one point of this study has been to indicate the limitations of general theories of irony and parody, whether as forces in the critique of ideology, as formalistic techniques of narcissistic, negative transcendence, or as unruly modalities of what Baudelaire termed *le vertige de l'hyperbole*. What should emerge from the preceding chapters is the need for careful, differential investigations of the inflections and cross-hatchings involving irony and parody in different texts, including the complex relations between the ironic-parodic and the "straight" or serious.

If there is one general notion if not "theory" of the novel that is especially active in my analyses, it is Mikhail Bakhtin's understanding of the novel as a self-contestatory, carnivalizing genre that tests the limits of generic classification and enacts a dialogical interplay of often dissonant "voices" and ideological currents. This is a "theory" which, despite its difficulties, provides a measure of orientation in research while resisting full closure or "monologism" in one's understanding of novelistic discourse. My own insistence upon the intricate and variable interaction of symptomatic, critical, and possibly transformative elements in the novel's relation to its pertinent contexts may itself be read as an attempt to inflect this "theory" in more insistently political and historical directions. In the process, I stress the dimension of "dialogism" that bears upon the interchange of voices that may not be neatly separated into discrete entities in a literal dialogue: that is, the interchange whereby the self is altered by the other and a hermeneutic of transparent consensual understanding is challenged and perhaps disoriented by contestatory "others" not subject to full conscious mastery. Modes of "internal alterity," such as those brought into relief by the very interplay of (ironic) distance and (empathetic) proximity, are, I think, the most provocative dimensions of the notion of dialogism. They pose the problem of "working through" relations in a manner that helps control compulsive repetition but that also situates the desire for total mastery as an impossible and possibly destructive ideal. They affect, moreover, the relations not only of text and context, author and narrator, or narrator and characters in the past but also that between contemporary readers and their "objects" of investigation. It is in this sense that historical inquiry into texts and their political resonances comes, in displaced or "transferred" ways, to implicate us as readers.[1]

The approach I take is dialogical in at least three senses: it addresses itself to other readers as it addresses texts or discursive problems, and—without feigning to provide full speculative mastery or, in Nietzsche's phrase, to seeing around its

---

[1]For a more extensive discussion of this question, see my "History and Psychoanalysis," *Critical Inquiry* 13 (1987), 222–51.

own corner—it attempts to be self-critical (that is, it thematizes the problem of its own limits). This approach requires the inclusion and interrogation in the principal text of material that more orthodox methods might relegate to footnotes. The interchange with other critics is essential to a "dialogical" approach as I understand it, and the polemical turn my argument at times takes should not conceal my indebtedness to other critics—not least to those I in part criticize.

The texts I have chosen for attention are in some sense "canonical." They would probably appear on lists of "great novels," although the specific series I discuss (or any analogous to it) would probably be read only in departments of comparative literature or in relatively rare programs in intellectual history. I do not believe in destroying canons ("canon-busting") if this means no longer reading texts that have traditionally been included in them. Indeed, I think that texts included in canons have critical potentials often occulted in canonical readings of them and that it would be foolish to neutralize these potentials through a quasi-ritualistic condemnation of canons. My approach questions the canonical uses to which certain texts have been put, and one of the incentives of its "noncanonical" readings is precisely to destabilize and contest such uses. As in the case of such modes as irony and parody, however, one should not underestimate the power of "recuperation" or the possible adaptation of one's approach to legitimate or solidify precisely those conditions one intends to criticize. Here one can only be explicit and insistent in what one is trying to do, do it as well as one can, and guard against tendencies in one's work that lend themselves to uses that one questions. I would add that the readings in this study not only bring "canonical" texts into contact with issues that are often avoided in canonical uses of them but also raise questions about certain markedly noncanonical readings and their ideological implications.

Specifically, the readings I propose depart from two seemingly opposed but perhaps complementary and mutually reinforcing tendencies in recent criticism: overcontextualization, historicization, and documentary reductionism, on the one hand,

and formalistic hypostatization—including the universalizing fixation (or compulsive "fetishization") of deconstructive techniques—on the other.

In the former case, reductionism need not be manifest (it may even be explicitly rejected), but the methods of analysis may involve either a type of documentary overdetermination (in accordance with the dictum "the thicker the description, the better") or a conception of historicist comprehension (for example, by construing texts as symptoms or instantiations of predetermined categories, codes, stages, or "modes of production"). Such methods radically downplay critical and transformative dimensions in the text's work and play. My own strategy is to resist the temptation to provide a seemingly exhaustive, intellectually satisfying sense of contexts (particularly immediate contexts) and instead to motivate my selection of pertinent contexts by what I see as significant questions in reading and criticism. More precisely, I would maintain that the grounds on which to motivate contextual choices—while of course always open to counterargument—are both intellectual and sociopolitical and that they depend in good part on the interpretations one is trying to counteract or to reinforce and the sociopolitical possibilities one is attempting to disclose. Hence, for example, a stress on the mutations of the carnivalesque is motivated by a critical concern for the actual and desirable interaction of work and play in culture. It is also motivated by a judgment about the relative underemphasis of this issue in theories of modern society and culture, including certain variants of Marxism. The general incentive of this non-contemplative strategy is to facilitate an exchange between past and present that recognizes and intensifies our implication in processes of reading in ways that may have import for the future. At best such an approach may avoid the illusory explanatory effect held out by an uncritical amalgamation of relatively conventional accounts of contexts and equally conventional if not banal readings of texts.

I have intimated that historicism may both stimulate and have a relation of mutual reinforcement to a tendency that is often deceptively taken as its alternative: formalism. In its most familiar guise, formalism relegates contexts to a background if not a coffee-table status, and its focus is upon the internal functioning of a text. But formalism may also come in an intertextual and multileveled format, whereby contexts from popular, commodified, and high culture are reduced to set pieces, and their relations to texts are "negotiated" through facile associationism, juxtaposition, or pastiche. Whatever the success of my efforts, I have tried to keep a distance from both historicism and related formalisms by attempting to articulate ways in which a critical concern with history implies an interest in form that need not eventuate in formalism.

I have also intimated that the use of certain reading techniques—particularly when they are oriented toward the evacuation of signification or the disclosure of discursive impasses—may be manifestly ahistorical or remain on the level of vague allegorical indirection. I do not claim to have "solved" the problem of the relation between the use of politically motivated categories (such as ideology and critique) and analyses sensitive to the workings of aporia and undecidability which at times brilliantly illuminate the more uncommonly "playful"—or indeed the disorientingly mad—movements of texts. In fact, I do not think that such a problem can be "solved." At best it may be posed and explored; it may also become transformed in more or less unpredictable fashion with larger sociocultural transformations. But I am convinced that historical and political inquiry must be conjoined with a sensitivity to matters of form, including their limiting and anything but formalistic modalities that are explored by "deconstructive" criticism at its most compelling. In the latter respect I can pretend little more than to have tried to set the stage for a more extensive, intensive, and internally self-questioning mode of criticism. The one elementary point on which I would insist, however, is that radical ambivalence, "play," and undecidability apply on very "fundamental" levels (such as the relation of inscription and world, life and death, seriousness and laughter); decision and choice pertain to local matters of interpretation as well as to specific policies and institutional arrangements. These two levels cannot be neatly separated, but one level should neither obliterate nor be confounded with the other. Indeed, the specific nature of their mutual articulation is a crucial issue in any mode of critical thought that addresses historical and political issues.

One tendency of both modern literature and modern criticism is to draw upon such older, "playful" popular forms as the carnivalesque and to use them as a protest against more dominant or hegemonic forces that affect popular culture itself (for example, in the integration of popular culture into the dominant system and the commodity form). But "high-cultural" activities are themselves threatened by co-optation by dominant forms such as commodification as well as by a hermetic use of the carnivalesque—hermetic in the modern sense of making something inaccessible to a larger public and even inserting it into a narrowly elitist framework. The hermetic appropriation or displacement of the carnivalesque is a crucial but often ignored problem in modern literature and criticism. And a hermetic, "difficult" style is itself a problematic political gesture in the way it involves an attempt to turn one's back on society and throw what might be called an aesthetic moon at it. Indeed, hermetic-carnivalesque devices may become one-sidedly technical and negative—not ambivalent in combining criticism or negation with preparation for renewal. One problem, already posed in the nineteenth century and intensified in the twentieth, is how to translate older popular and carnivalesque forms into an elite or high culture that resists commodified or mass culture but must come to terms with its own sociopolitical implications, including a tendency toward hermeticism and elitism as well as toward overly technical and narrowly negative reductions. This problem is transferred into intellectual history and other disciplines that study high culture—a problem that is in no sense easy to negotiate but that should be recognized and worked through. A challenge faced by a hybridized genre is to offer critical accounts of difficult objects of study that make them as accessible as possible without suggesting that it can do what only major sociocultural and political transformation might allow.

I noted in the Introduction that a recurrent motif of this

study is the way significant novels themselves resist providing satisfying symbolic resolutions to the problems they disclose (for example in the form of fully concordant plot structures) and at most suggest transformative possibilities that the novel alone cannot realize. I also indicated that this is a way of making challenging contact with history by throwing readers back on their own need to come to terms with these problems. One may see this point as a revisionary reading of negative capability or as a more positive valorization of Lukács's idea that novels pose questions they cannot answer in their own restricted terms. In any event, I confess both to emulating these novels in my own discursive strategies and to the conviction that historiography in general has in this respect something to learn from modes of discourse it has often used as mere documentary evidence in conventional reconstructions of the past. To make these points is not to dismiss all forms of unity and closure, but it is to insist upon their contestable nature. It is also to intimate the desirability of a context (or a "general text") in which one has a viable interaction between unifying forms (prominently including widely accepted, binding norms) and contestatory forces, among which one must list "carnivalesque" renditions (and undoings) of affirmed legitimate structures themselves. One sign of a legitimation crisis is the unavailability of this kind of interaction. (Its place is taken in modern society by labor, defined in accordance with technically rational and instrumental efficiency, and privatized "leisure time," which is split off from production but recycled into a commodity system on the level of consumption and serviced by so-called culture industries.) One requirement of any attempt to foster the emergence of such an interaction is not to avoid disclosing problems in conditions in which it is unavailable, in attempts (including one's own) to achieve it, and in its functioning in the event that it does come to pass.

Index

Adams, Robert M., 19n
Adorno, Theodor, 1, 152, 163
Agulhon, Maurice, 83–85
Anaxagoras, 188
Andrewes, Lancelot, 65
Ashton, Rosemary, 81n
Auerbach, Erich, 16–17, 129–31,
  133–37, 143
Augustine, Saint, 157, 199

Bach, Johann Sebastian, 186
Bakhtin, Mikhail, 9, 13n, 37, 178,
  208
Baldick, Robert, 90n
Barnes, Djuna, 129
Baronius, Cesare, 63–65, 67
Barthes, Roland, 87n
Bataille, Georges, 207
Baudelaire, Charles, 207
Baudrillard, Jean, 109n
Beckett, Samuel, 18, 102
Beethoven, Ludwig van, 160, 168
Benjamin, Walter, 137, 204
Benny, Jack, 190
Blanqui, Louis-Auguste, 91
Bonaparte, Charles Louis Napoleon,
  84, 90
Bonaparte, Napoleon, 23, 89
Bosch, Hieronymus, 187
Bouts, Dirk, 193, 196

Brabant, R. H., 57
Brooks, Peter, 110n
Brunetière, Ferdinand, 87n
Bruno, Giordano, 66
Bürger, Peter, 137
Burke, Kenneth, 112, 115

Campanella, Tommaso, 66
Camus, Albert, 22
Carnegie, Dale, 188–89
Casaubon, Isaac, 56, 62–69, 80n
Chernyshevsky, Nikolai, 37, 46, 51
Clement of Rome, 178–79
Compagnon, Antoine, 87–89
Conroy, Mark, 110n
Corelli, Arcangelo, 187
Culler, Jonathan, 109n

de Man, Paul, 61
Denis the Carthusian, 196
Derrida, Jacques, 206
Dostoevsky, Fyodor, 4–5
  The Brothers Karamozov, 52
  Notes from Underground, 35–55
  The Possessed, 36
  Winter Notes on Summer Impres-
    sions, 37
Dürer, Albrecht, 194

El Greco, 197
Eliade, Mircea, 132

Index

Eliot, George, 4–5
  Middlemarch, 56–82
  The Mill on the Floss, 80n
  Scenes of Clerical Life, 56
Eliot, T. S., 56, 131–32
Ellmann, Richard, 56–59, 80n–81n
Emerson, Caryl, 37n
Erasmus, Desiderius, 63
Erlich, Paul, 182
Evans, Isaac, 80n–81n

Faguet, Emile, 87n
Flaubert, Gustave, 18
  Bouvard and Pécuchet, 87–88,
    102, 106
  Madame Bovary, 57, 88, 101, 104
  The Sentimental Education, 83–
    110
Fourier, Charles, 36
Frank, Joseph, 36n, 129–34, 137
Frederick the Great, 116
Freud, Sigmund, 25, 113, 115

Gabrieli, Andrea, 187
Gabrieli, Giovanni, 187
Gaddis, William:
  J R, 177, 192
  The Recognitions, 154, 175–202
Goldmann, Lucien, 87
Graves, Robert, 190–91
Green, Jack, 175, 176n

Hardy, Barbara, 69n
Harvey, William John, 69n
Heidegger, Martin, 113
Heller, Erich, 111–12, 115–17, 152
Hemmings, Frederick William John,
  26
Hertz, Neil, 57–62
Hitler, Adolf, 167, 170, 173
Homer, 84
Huizinga, Johan, 195–96

Ibsen, Henrik, 177

Jameson, Fredric, 137n
Joyce, James, 102, 131, 132, 177, 181
Jung, Carl, 179, 181

Kapila, 188
Kitchel, Anna Theresa, 70n
Koenig, Peter William, 180n
Kracauer, Siegfried, 129
Kuehl, John, 176n

LaCapra, Dominick, 8, 13n, 208n
Lanson, Gustave, 87n
Lenin, Vladimir Ilyich, 38
Lermontov, Mikhail, 40
Lewes, George Henry, 70, 80n
Locke, John, 61
Louis XVIII, 89
Lowe-Porter, Helen Tracy, 115, 151n
Lukács, Georg, 20, 116, 135, 213
Luther, Martin, 169

Mackay, Robert William, 57
Mahler, Gustav, 116
Mann, Thomas, 4–5, 18
  Death in Venice, 111–28
  Doctor Faustus, 116, 123, 127,
    135, 150–74, 177
  The Magic Mountain, 152
  *Reflections of a Nonpolitical
    Man*, 127, 159
Marcuse, Herbert, 189
Markham, David, 175
Martineau, Henri, 26
Matlaw, Ralph, 40n, 52n, 54
Memling, Hans, 193
Miller, J. Hillis, 58, 59, 61
Mitchell, Stanley, 116n
Monteverdi, Claudio, 168
Moore, Steven, 175–76, 180n

Nekrasov, Nicolai, 43, 51
Neufeldt, Victor, 67n
Nietzsche, Friedrich, 18, 113, 119,
  140, 153, 156, 158, 162, 169,
  170, 191, 208

Palestrina, Giovanni Pierluigi da,
  186
Paracelsus, 186
Pascal, Blaise, 87
Pattison, Mark 56, 62–66
Plato, 121, 131, 179

Pound, Ezra, 131, 132
Pratt, John Clark, 67n
Proust, Marcel, 102, 131

Renan, Ernest, 87
Ricoeur, Paul, 13
Robespierre, Maximilien de, 91
Rousseau, Jean-Jacques, 32, 46

Saint-Réal, César Vichard de, 31
Saint-Simon, Claude-Henri, comte
    de, 36
Sand, George, 88
Sartre, Jean-Paul, 86
Scaliger, Joseph, 63, 67
Schiller, Friedrich, 114
Schoenberg, Arnold, 152, 156
Schulte-Sasse, Jochen, 137n
Shakespeare, William, 56, 67, 69
Shaw, Michael, 137n
Simmons, Ernest Joseph, 36n
Socrates, 48, 117, 121, 124, 191
Sorel, Georges, 165
Spencer, Herbert, 57
Stallybrass, Peter, 13n
Stendhal, 2
    Red and Black, 15–34

Taine, Hippolyte, 87
Terdiman, Richard, 13n
Theresa, Saint, 70
Titian, 197
Tocqueville, Alexis de, 21, 89, 91

van der Weyden, Rogier, 193, 196
van Eyck, Jan, 193, 195, 196
Vergil, 188
Vincent de Paul, Saint, 88

Wagner, Richard, 161
Weber, Max, 122
White, Allon, 13n
White, Hayden, 8
Wittgenstein, Ludwig, 156
Woolf, Virginia:
    To the Lighthouse, 129–49
    Mrs. Dalloway, 140
Worringer, Wilhelm, 130

Yates, Frances, 65–67

Zoroaster, 157

Library of Congress Cataloging-In-Publication Data

LaCapra, Dominick, 1939-
  History, politics, and the novel.

  Includes index.
    1. Fiction—History and criticism. 2. Literature and history.
  3. Politics and literature. I. Title.
  PN3343.L33 1987   809.3'9358   87-6686
  ISBN 0-8014-2033-4 (alk. paper)